DUE

Cat. No. 23-221

Theory
Building

THEORY BUILDING

Revised Edition

Robert Dubin

THE FREE PRESS
A Division of Macmillan Publishing Co., Inc.
NEW YORK

Collier Macmillan Publishers
LONDON

Copyright © 1969, 1978, by The Free Press
                    A Division of Macmillan Publishing Co., Inc.

The Free Press
A Division of Macmillan Publishing Co., Inc.
866 Third Avenue, New York, N.Y. 10022

Collier Macmillan Canada, Ltd.

Library of Congress Catalog Card Number: 77–90010

Printed in the United States of America

printing number

2 3 4 5 6 7 8 9 10

Library of Congress Cataloging in Publication Data

Dubin, Robert.
  Theory building.

  Bibliography: p.
  Includes index.
  1. Social sciences--Methodology. 2. Social
science research. I. Title.
H61.D82 1978   300'.1'8   77-90010
ISBN 0-02-907620-X

For John, Lucy, Amy, and George

Contents

Preface to the Revised Edition

The Path of life is to abide by discipline, and he who ignores correction goes astray.

—THE JERUSALEM BIBLE, *Proverbs*, 10:17

THE FIRST EDITION of this book has been useful to teachers and working researchers—theorists. It has been even more useful to students preparing to undertake these roles. The continual utility of the volume in the nine years since publication has led me to undertake improvements.

The changes were of three kinds. Naturally, I wanted to improve the clarity of exposition, so that the entire book was re-examined in fine detail to improve writing style and remove ambiguities. Equally important were revisions to insert new material. To repair the most notable of the omissions, I have added two entirely new chapters. The new first chapter is designed to provide an overview of theory building so that the reader always has a "big picture" point of reference to which to return as the details of theoretical models and their test are unfolded. The new final chapter is an explicit discussion of systems theory and systems analysis showing the linkages between this mode of thinking analytically and the exposition of theory building as set forth in this volume. This new chapter demonstrates both the utility of my approach to theory building and the applications of systems analysis, with which it has a natural affinity. The third change was a reconsideration of some of the ideas as originally presented. Changes have been made that I hope tighten up some of the arguments.

I have been aided in this task by feedback from a number of users of the first edition. Especially important to me has been the detailed and always thoughtful responses of my colleague Rein Taagepera, whose doctorate in physics and professorship in political science make for a breadth of background that proved invaluable in providing me with sympathetic criticism.

R. D.

University of California
Irvine
January 1978

Preface
to the First Edition

Man proposes a system of hypotheses: Nature disposes of its truth or falsity.
Man invents a scientific system, and then discovers whether or not it accords
with observed fact.
—R.B. BRAITHWAITE *Scientific Explanation*

THIS VOLUME is the product of a long-time need to scratch an intellectual
itch. I was educated in the social sciences at the University of Chicago in
an atmosphere permeated by constant clashes between self-conscious empiricists and rather defensive theorists. The empiricsts were clearly on the
attack, and their parade caught me up in the vanguard. But I was not a
wholehearted marcher under the banner because of a nagging need to find
purposes for my own research in the products of the archenemy, the
theorists.

This constant shuffling back and forth between theory and the empirical world became the subject of a seminar in theory building that I
initiated ten years ago [in 1955] and that drew students from all the
behavioral sciences. Here attention was centered on trying to bring together theory and empirical research at a level where there were immediate, practical, and needed reuults for the working social scientist.
For my own empirical work, the philosophers of science and the logicians
had always been inspiring and suggestive, but I felt the need for more
specific operational linkages between theory and research that could be
put to everyday use by a practicing researcher.

The vantage point of this volume is the position of the scientist doing
research who is concerned with why he is testing predictions and what
their consequences are. This leads one constantly to ask the philosopher
of science, "What are you saying that is useful and meaningful for me?"

The utility test is designed to maximize comprehension of the philosopher's position, not to question it on the assumption that it may be wrong. A major result of raising the utility question is that some of the philosopher's conclusions will be put in different relationships from those traditionally considered. At the same time, a parallel reordering of some of the procedures of scientists will be analyzed.

I have confidence that this volume achieves its aim of providing a practical and useful tool for theorists-researchers. The ideas have been tested in use by successive generations of students in the behavioral sciences who took them and analyzed published studies. We concluded that the analytical tools set forth here could be used profitably to diagram the theories being tested and their linkages with empirical results. Even more revealing, we found out readily how inept many social scientists were in formulating models and/or subjecting them to empirical tests. This, of course, became an additional reason for writing this volume. Finally, we found out that students could construct their own theoretical models and carry out the research operations for testing them with facility, guided by the ideas of this book. Thus, in keeping with the spirit of this volume—that the scientist always tests the theory he creates—it can be asserted that such tests have been made with positive results.

I am also mindful of the fundamental orientation of Karl Popper that the proper expectation of scientific research is to disconfirm a theory so that it may be replaced by a better one. To this orientation I wholly subscribe. Indeed, it was for this reason that the book was so long in preparation, for I wished to test, retest, and revise the ideas to make sure they had some correspondence with the reality of "doing science." I am fully prepared for the continual revision and even overthrow of the structure of ideas here presented. If in some way this volume pushes a colleague to "do it better," then that alone may be its justification for publication.

To the early generations of students in the theory building seminar the search for a rapprochement between science and philosophy of science could hardly have provided definitive answers. The point has now been reached where some practical and sensible ideas may be stated about how theory and research articulate. Partly to repay the patience of the early students in the seminar, and mainly because I have found real applications for the conclusions (and hope similarly situated scholars also will), the ideas have been assembled in this volume. No portion of the ten chapters has been previously published.

It is a pleasure to acknowledge indebtedness, with profound thanks, to those who have made contributions to this work. In addition to the successive groups of students in the theory building seminar, whose perplexities forced real tests of these ideas, thanks are due Professor Hubert M. Blalock, University of North Carolina, who commented on the prepublication edition of the book and who had his students in a course on theory construction do the same. Their reactions have been valuable. A number of my individual students, working with the prepublication edition, improved its contents and style by their perceptive comments. My colleagues in the behavioral sciences at the University of Oregon have been generous in contributing by discussing various points as I needed their help. I think they would prefer to be designated a collectivity, for it is one of the few, but important, virtues of a relatively small university that periods of time may be found for intellectual leisure in which faculty members from several disciplines engage each other's minds.

R. D.

Theory Building

... philosophical disquisitions about the nature of the social sciences are not likely to be fruitful without an incisive analysis as to how empirical social research does actually proceed.

—PAUL F. LAZARSFELD, "Latent Structure Analysis," in S. Koch (ed.), *Psychology: A Study of a Science*, vol. 3

Furthermore, the doctrine put forth in this work is not a logical system resulting solely from the contemplation of general ideas; it has not been constructed through the sort of meditation that is hostile to concrete detail. It was born and matured in the daily practice of the science.

—PIERRE DUHEM, *The Aim and Structure of Physical Theory*

Introduction

The observational-theoretical dichotomy ... *My contention here is simply: (1) The* problem *for which this dichotomy was invented ... does not exist. (2) A basic reason ... given for introducing the dichotomy is false: namely, justification in science does not proceed "down" in the direction of observation terms. In fact, justification in science proceeds in any direction that may be handy.... (3) ... whether the reasons for introducing the dichotomy were good ones or bad ones the double distinction (observation terms-theoretical terms, observation statements-theoretical statements) ... is ... completely "broken-backed"....*

—H. Putnam, "What Theories Are Not," in E. Nagel, P. Suppes, and A. Tarski (eds.), *Logic, Methodology and Philosophy of Science*

MOST BOOKS on research methods and statistical technology contain approximately the following statement: "If you want to test an hypothesis, then ..." There follows extensive elaboration of many ways of making the empirical tests. If, in innocence, you ask, "But where do I get the hypothesis to test?" you may search fruitlessly for adequate explanation in these books. Ordinarily your attention is directed for answers to treatises on logic, scientific method, epistemology, and the philosophy of science.

It is the intent of *Theory Building* to address this situation. This book is centrally concerned with answering these queries: (1) What is the source of an hypothesis to test? (As we shall see, the source is a theoretical model.) (2) What are the necessary and sufficient characteristics of a theoretical model that will generate empirically testable hypotheses? (3) What is the nature of the test of an hypothesis? (4) What are the feedbacks from the empirical test of an hypothesis to the theoretical model generating it?

The purpose of this volume, then, is to provide for working researchers a handbook of practical usefulness that may become a frequently consulted source along with reference books on research

1

technologies. It is the intent to bridge the gap between theoretical models and empirical research in a way that proves intensely practical for daily application to the tasks of research. The bridge here proposed is viewed as a functioning rather than a static bridge—it is concerned with the *interaction* between theory and research. Emphasis is put upon the traffic between theory and research and the essential links that maintain their constant interaction.

In order to build this connecting bridge in terms of linking functions, most of the analysis is given over to examination of the content of theoretical models, accompanied by a briefer discussion of research operations. In the usual training of behavioral scientists dominant attention is placed on learning research operations. There is justification, therefore, in favoring the analysis of theory in this volume on the assumption that most social scientists already know a good deal about research technologies.

This volume, then, is addressed to the tasks of scientists. It is an attempt to provide a handbook for the daily work of scientists (theorists and empirical investigators), indicating one way to link theory with research. The particular focus of attention is on the needs of working researchers, who, it may be assumed, have general familiarity with the fundamental contributions of the philosophers of science. This book is an attempt to put together some of these contributions in a manner to permit their ready employment whenever a study is designed and executed.

The steps in scientific activity are put in an ordered sequence indicated by the chapter titles. It is believed that these steps represent a comprehensive coverage of the manner in which scientific theories are developed as part of empirical investigation. It is also assumed that this order of presentation is logically coherent.

It would be presumptuous of the author, a behavioral scientist, to use illustrations in the exposition drawn from the physical and biological sciences. The bulk of the examples come from realms familiar to the writer, the social sciences. It is hopefully believed that the ideas contained in the volume will be useful to any scientist. This will have to be judged by natural scientists without the benefit of illustrations that might draw their attention to applications in their own endeavors.

The title *Theory Building* was chosen because it symbolizes the always present goal of scientists' activities. Their task is to build viable models of the empirical world that can be comprehended by the human mind. These theoretical models are intensely practical, for the predictions derived from them are the grounds on which modern man is increasingly ordering his relationships with the environing universe.

The purpose of this study is to maximize the congruence between the scientist's science and the philosopher's science. Insofar as this goal is achieved, we can see the additivity of knowledge in two areas of thought that have been singularly independent of each other, although focused on a common problem.[1] The end result of our enterprise from the working scientist's viewpoint will, I hope, be his ability to do better what, in any event, will continue to be the scientific occupation. Whether there will be any consequences for the philosophers of science is to be determined by those specialists.

I want to emphasize strongly that the first eight chapters, and especially Chapters 2 through 8, are concerned almost exclusively with models or theories. All the assertions made in these chapters are concerned with theory building. It is not until Chapter 9 is reached that attention turns to a continuous examination of the real world that theories model. This is specifically called to your attention to insure that you will keep in mind through the first eight chapters that the components of a theory are being analyzed. The bridge to the empirical world to *test a theory* is not reached until Chapter 9. However, in the first eight chapters, reference is made repeatedly to the world of experience, as facts drawn from it are employed in building a theory.

---

[1]This failure to bridge between the scientists' and the philosophers' view of science is bitterly bemoaned by a notable behavioral scientist. "Philosophers of science are not interested in, and do not know what the work-a-day empirical research man does. This has two consequences: we have to become our own methodologists, or we have to muddle along without benefit of the explicating clergy." Paul F. Lazarsfeld in E. Nagel, P. Suppes, and A. Tarski (eds.), *Logic, Methodology and Philosophy of Science* (Stanford, Calif.: Stanford University Press, 1962), p. 470.

CHAPTER ONE

To Begin With

... the most difficult thing in science, as in other fields, is to shake off accepted views, to observe with one's own eyes, and think with one's own brains...

—GEORGE SARTON, *The Civilization of the Renaissance*

IN THIS VOLUME the elements of a theoretical model are analyzed one by one. It is necessary to take something apart in order analytically to know what it is made of and how. One potentially unfortunate consequence of this procedure is that we will see the trees while failing to apprehend the forest. It is, therefore, best to start our analysis with an overview of what this book is all about.

I will proceed in four steps: (1) setting forth the relationship between the theorist and his theory; (2) illustrating a theoretical model with an example; (3) demonstrating the structure of a theory by describing the parts (and their relationships) that compose the theory of our example; and (4) indicating how we come to prefer one theoretical model over another.

As the main body of the analysis unfolds in succeeding chapters, you may have occasion to come back to this starting point to re-establish how the parts of a theoretical model fit into the whole model.

Theorist and Theory

A theorist is someone who observes a portion of the world around him and seeks to find order in the booming, bustling confusion that is the realm of experience. The idea of order, and the tools utilized to create the sense of order, are in the mind of the theorist.

This is an important point, for it means that the locus of theory is the human mind. The mind is where the "need" for theory (order) exists.

The mind is also where the logical operations take place on the basis of which a theory is constructed.

What I mean by the "need" for a theory is very simple. This "need" arises from the fact that order in human experiences is not directly derivable from the orderliness of the experiences themselves. This need is often characterized as the "curiosity" of the observer, or scientist-theorist, whose curiosity is satisfied when order is imposed on experience. Thus, idly to observe two young children at play will not tell the observer very much about the play activity. The observer's curiosity must be focused on the play activity rather than on the attending mothers or the playground setting. This attention focusing is itself a mental activity.

Once attention is focused so that the object of attention comes to the foreground and other experiences become background, the "need" for a theory may be generated. The observer begins to ask questions about the content of that which he has put in the foreground of his attention and thus begins to sort parts of his experience into classes of objects or events. Other questions arise about how these parts or events are related to one another. Finally, a point of confidence may be reached where the observer (now called a theorist) concludes that he understands these experiences because he has been able to label and describe the things in his attention and how they relate to each other. The observer may even proceed to the next stage in satisfying his "need" for theory by projecting into a future time period what will happen in the system of things upon which his attention is focused. Thus, a prediction is made from the theory about what will happen in the real world that the theory is modeling. This "need" may finally push the observer (at this point called a researcher) to the point of testing whether evidence can be found that the prediction was accurate.

To summarize: The "need" for theories lies in the human behavior of wanting to impose order on unordered experiences. Experiences are not ordered by Nature. There is no "harmony of the spheres" except as the human mind conceptualizes "spheres" and their harmonious interactions. The human mind has a "need" to see order in Nature, or, more broadly, in all experience. It goes without saying that the same set of experiences may be ordered, or theorized about, in very different ways. For example, the human body was once modeled by the Greek scientist Hippocrates as containing the four humors of blood, phlegm, yellow bile, and black bile—a far cry from contemporary models of biology.

What are the instruments used to create theories? Again we come back to the observer and the sensory and mental operations utilized by the observer. Experiences pass through the senses and are registered in the mind. Such sorting and ordering of inputs of experiences as occur are done according to the logic inside the head of the observer.

The senses are selective in what is perceived, and the mind is discriminating with respect to the logic by which the perceived experiences are ordered.

When we admit that the human pursuit of theory is not intended to second-guess God and His ordering of the universe nor to penetrate the orderliness of Nature by discovering her "natural laws," we have one basis for understanding the acts of theory building. With human observers in the center of the stage, the world is viewed from the human vantage point. We make sense out of God's universe at an un-Godlike level of comprehension. We have come to admit that "natural laws" are less than universal and eternal. In short, theories serve human purposes; their creation is motivated and their logic organized by the skills and limitations of human capabilities.

I hasten to assert that theory building is not antithetical to theology. Indeed, theorizing may be wholly compatible with theology when the theorist gives up the preposterous assumption that he is in a game of trying to understand the universe from God's standpoint. Such a stance is the height of insolence, serving only to reduce the competence of God to the level of a mortal—a blasphemy in Western religions.

Theories, then, serve to satisfy a very human "need" to order the experienced world. The only instrument employed in the ordering process is the human mind and the "magic" of human perception and thought. Whatever fads and fashions characterize the logic by which thought is carried on necessarily will be incorporated into the theoretical models developed.

Example of a Theoretical Model

We can briefly outline the features of a theoretical model before looking at an example of one that is widely recognized among industrial psychologists.[1] A theoretical model starts with things or variables, or (1) *units* whose interactions constitute the subject matter of attention. The model then specifies the manner in which these units interact with each

[1]This section is adapted from Robert Dubin, "Theory Building in Applied Areas," Chapter 1, pp. 17–39, in Marvin D. Dunnette (ed.), *Handbook of Industrial and Organizational Psychology* (Chicago: Rand McNally, 1976). Used by permission.

other, or (2) the *laws of interaction* among the units of the model. Since theoretical models are generally of limited portions of the world, the limits or (3) *boundaries* must be set forth within which the theory is expected to hold. Most theoretical models are presumed to represent a complex portion of the real world, part of whose complexity is revealed by the fact that there are various (4) *system states* in each of which the units interact differently with each other. Once these four basic features of a theoretical model are set forth, the theorist is in a position to derive conclusions that represent logical and true deductions about the model in operation, or the (5) *propositions* of the model.

So far, we see only the theoretical side of the theory-research cycle. Should there be any desire to determine whether the model does, in fact, represent the real world, then each term in each proposition whose test is sought needs to be converted into (6) *an empirical indicator* of the term. The next operation is to substitute the appropriate empirical indicators in the propositional statement to generate a testable (7) *hypothesis*. The research operation consists of measuring the values on the empirical indicators of the hypothesis to determine whether the theoretically predicted values are achieved or approximated in the research test.

It is useful to analyze an example to illustrate the elements of a theoretical model. We choose the Herzberg two-factor theory of job satisfaction since it is widely known among industrial psychologists and is readily explicated.[2]

Herzberg suggests that a situation of behavior is divided into two fundamental components from the standpoint of the actor: (1) extrinsic factors and (2) intrinsic factors. He also suggests that the reaction of the actor to a situation of behavior can be described as "satisfaction" or "dissatisfaction." The elements or "units" comprising the model are therefore: intrinsic factors, extrinsic factors, satisfaction, and dissatisfaction. It is the relations among these that constitute the Herzberg theory.

The system modeled by the theory is that of individuals interacting with their perceived situation of behavior. More particularly, the theory focuses on the situations of behavior that are routinely recurrent.

There are two fundamental laws of interaction among the variables, or units of the model. (1) There is an inverse relationship between the level of an individual's dissatisfaction and the perceived adequacy of the extrinsic factors of his situation of behavior. (2) There is a positive relation-

---

[2]See Frederick Herzberg, *Work and Nature of Man* (Cleveland: World Publishing, 1966), and also Frederick Herzberg et al., *The Motivation to Work,* 2nd ed. (New York: Wiley, 1959).

ship between the level of an individual's satisfaction and his perception of the adequacy of the intrinsic factors of a behavioral situation.

Herzberg focuses his two-factor theory on the situations of employment in an organization. There is therefore an implicit of "benign" boundary of the model limiting its anticipated application to a social situation in which an individual is a member of, or employed by, an organization. (A "benign" boundary is one beyond which the model is alleged not to hold, but where the characteristics of the boundary are not themselves relevant to the manner in which the model operates.) In Herzberg's view, incidentally, this theory is not restricted as to kind of organization or kind of economic system within which the organization operates.

There is also another benign boundary of this model; namely, that it does not apply to collectivities of individuals. It is not, therefore, a model of morale of organization members (morale being viewed as a collective phenomenon). Furthermore, the model is not a model of behavior in organizations and therefore does not include within its scope the prediction of behavior.

The limiting values (and therefore, boundaries) of the law of interaction are also clearly built into the model. The dissatisfaction variable has a zero value and may increase to a level where the system is destroyed (the system being the attitudinal reaction of the individual toward his environment); namely, where the individual either leaves the organization or is removed from it on the initiative of organizational functionaries (i.e., is fired). These two boundaries are clearly limits on the law of relationship between the individual's perceived payoff from the extrinsic factors and his level of dissatisfaction. In a parallel way, the relation between intrinsic factors and satisfaction has comparable limits. The lower limit of satisfaction is zero, and the upper limit is presumably high but unspecified, since, for example, a personality evaluating intrinsic factors may have an untested limit of expectation with respect to the level of anticipated satisfaction.

Having set forth the units of the theory, the laws by which they interact, and the boundaries of the theory, we need one additional element before we put the model to use, that is, the system states within which the theoretical model is operative. We think of a system state as a condition of the system being modeled in which the units of that system take on characteristic values that have a persistence through time, regardless of the length of the time interval. The system state is defined by the values taken by all the variables or units in the system. For example, in the Herzberg system we might characterize the individual as being in a state of equal dissatisfaction and satisfaction. We might characterize another state of the system in which the satisfaction level is far higher than the dissatisfaction level. A third system state might be the one in which the balance of dissatisfaction and satisfaction is outweighed on the dissatis-faction side. Thus, we might think of three system states in the relations between satisfaction and dissatisfaction levels of the individual. On the assumption that these might be persistent states for the individual, we would then have a basis for predicting for the model (1) the consequences of persistence of the state and (2) the states to which the individual is likely to go if he moves from that state to another.

Having established what are the essential features of the Herzberg model or theory (I use the terms interchangeably), we are now in a position to examine the propositions derivable from the model. Propo-sitions are truth statements about the model. (These are not necessarily truth statements about the real world the model represents.)

Propositions of a theory must be true because they are logical state-ments about the theoretical system. These truth statements are the kinds of propositions that can be stated for any model that has its units, laws of interaction among the units, boundaries, and system states specified.

We can make a large number of truth statements about Herzberg's model, but we will focus on only several for illustrative purposes. Some propositions that follow from Herzberg's model are: (1) An individual's attitudinal orientation toward his work is the sum of a level of satisfaction and a level of dissatisfaction. (This is not unusual; for centuries poets have emphasized the possibility of both love *and* hate characterizing orientation toward others.) (2) An individual may feel no satisfaction and no dissatisfaction about his situation of work—that is, he may be genuinely indifferent. (This is a perfectly logical truth statement about the model and a very important one, for it may characterize a significant body of industrial workers. It is also a proposition that has been singularly ignored by the Herzberg theorists.) (3) The level of satisfaction and the level of dissatisfaction felt by an individual toward his work situation are independent of each other.

We now come to the problem of matching the model with the real world which it is intended to characterize. At this point it becomes neces-sary to convert the propositional statements into hypotheses. An hypothesis is a statement of prediction of what will be true in the real world if the evidence from the real world is marshaled. For example, among the extrinsic factors of the work situation, or what Herzberg has called the hygiene factors, he has specified pay, technical supervision, the human relations quality of supervision, the company policies and administration, working conditions, and job security. Any one of these factors is itself an empirical indicator of extrinsic factors or can be converted into one. Obviously, pay is in itself a metric and can be measured directly. Working conditions, on the other hand, have to be further specified in terms of such elements as physical surroundings, facilities (e.g., toilets and washrooms available), or physiological conditions (e.g., rest periods). In the same way, the intrinsic factors of the work situation, which Herzberg defines as achievement, recognition, responsibility, and advancement, also have the potential for being made operational.

What is necessary now is to substitute operational terms into the statement of the propositions so that a parallel statement, called an hypothesis, becomes empirically testable. In the Herzberg model, we not only have to specify the extrinsic and intrinsic factors but in each case we have to further specify that it is the individual's perception of these factors which is being measured. Thus, we would not simply take pay level as the measure of extrinsic factors, but we would have to go to the individual to get from him his attitude about his pay level, which presumably would be expressed in terms of his comparison of what he gets with what he thinks he ought to get or expects to get in the way of pay. The operationalizing of the terms of a proposition in order to make an hypothesis is a very critical stage in the theory-research cycle.

An illustrative hypothesis derived from the Herzberg model would be: The level of a worker's dissatisfaction with his work situation, when measured by a Likert-type work-satisfaction question, is inversely proportional to his perception of the equity of his pay, as measured by his comparison with pay levels in other companies. The basic terms of the underlying proposition (dissatisfaction is inversely proportional to perceived equity of pay as an extrinsic job feature of work)—namely, *level of dissatisfaction* and *perception of pay* as an extrinsic work feature—have been operationalized in the hypothesis. Clearly, the hypothesis is now testable by making an actual inquiry of workers as to their measure of dissatisfaction and their perception of their pay.

If the given piece of research produces data that conform to the hypothetical outcome, we would conclude that the model is unchallenged at that state. Either the tested proposition should be subject to a replicative test in order to be certain that it is accurate, or, assuming that it is accurate, we may go on and test other propositions of the model. Where the hypothesis is disconfirmed by the data, the theorist-researcher is then required to examine immediately the possibility of revising the model so that it will generate propositional statements, or truth statements about itself, which will conform *post hoc* to the empirical findings that have disconfirmed a previous proposition. This, in turn, will result in new empirical tests of the model, and so on in further tests of the theory.

I have conducted this very brief examination of an illustration simply because it is desirable to keep in mind several very critical things about theory building and the theory-research linkage:

1. A theoretical model is limited in no way except by the imagination of the theorist in what he may use as elements in building the model, or laws of interaction among the elements, or boundaries that he chooses to set on the model. Thus, it is perfectly legitimate to build a theory of ESP, or "primal scream," or psychic healing that conforms to all the canons of theory building.

2. A theoretical model is not simply a statement of hypothesis; nor is it a catalog of the units or variables employed and their definitions; nor is it a descriptive statement of a world of the scientific imagination.

3. The argument about the *adequacy* of the theoretical model is always and only an argument about the logic employed in constructing it.

4. The argument about the *reality* of a theoretical model—that is, whether or not it indeed models the empirical world—is a scientific issue that is resolved by making research tests of the model.

5. A theoretical model is a scientific model if, and only if, its creator is willing to subject it to an empirical test. Otherwise it falls in the realm of philosophy or theology, which, incidentally, not only give us the logic by which to test the adequacy of scientific models but subject their own creations to the same logical test.

It is perfectly clear that theorists and researchers may be distinguished from each other by the point at which they enter into the theory-research cycle. However, it is improbable that theorists, if they are scientists, will be disinterested in or unable to carry out research to test theories, or that researchers will be so insensitive to what they are doing that they are not aware of the theories that they subject to tests.

Preferred Theory

By what means and according to what standards does one theory come to be preferred over another? This is a complex issue for which, at this stage, a partial and simple answer will have to suffice. The question, of course, is another way of asking, "What is truth?" Clearly this is not a question to be handled lightly. Yet there is a useful sense in which the answer can be simple without being simpleminded.

We make the step to the simple view by modifying the question, "What is truth?" into the query, "What is believed to be true?" By so doing we clearly make the head of the believer the location of "truth." This has immediate advantages, for I have already put the theory or model in the same location. Thus, the belief in truth and the thing being believed are joined at the same source.

Broadly speaking, the preference for one theoretical model over another is a matter of consensus. Usually experts are the people who share the consensus. If laymen are involved in a consensus, they often are persuaded to the choice by the endorsement of experts.

What is meant by consensus is that a group of people sharing an interest in some set of observations come to agree that one theoretical model best provides understanding or permits accurate predictions about the observational set. For such agreement to exist it is necessary that there be some common agreement on the observations to be included in the set (and obviously what is also excluded from the set). Thus, there is agreement on the boundary containing the observations whose features are to be modeled in the theory.

A second basis for the consensus is that the logic employed in building the theory be shared. Without this commonality the theory would have varying meanings to those who understand it according to different frameworks of logic.

A third basis for the consensus among experts is the "proof" of a theory through empirical tests. The most satisfying ground for giving certainty to a theoretical model is that the predictions made from it turn out to be accurate when data are marshaled in testing the model. The model is said to "fit" the data, even if the data have in fact been gathered to see if they fit the model's predictions.

Given the agreement to look at the same "things," to do so in the same way, and to have a level of confidence certified by an empirical test, then the preferred theory turns out to be the one on which most experts (and their lay disciples) agree. Does this mean that "truth" is so fragile that it depends on a mere consensus among experts? Truth, insofar as a theoretical model is "true," rests exactly on that slender base of expert consensus.

But can the consensus be wrong? The answer is "yes." One need look only at some of the gigantic struggles over theoretical models in science to realize this. Pasteur was castigated by his contemporary scientific peers whose consensus about the etiology of disease was focused on a model different from his.

In the end, theories will be put to use to provide understanding and to make predictions about future states of affairs. Whenever people agree among themselves that understanding has been more or less satisfactorily achieved or that predictions have proved accurate within agreed-to limits of error, then the theoretical models will continue to be favored. Thus, the continuing viability of a theory rests on human consensus.

The Tasks Ahead

From this point on we will deal with the parts of theoretical models and their interrelationships. It should always be kept in mind that the parts are intended to be fitted together into a whole model. The illustrative theory used in this chapter provides an example of how you can retain a grasp of the whole theoretical model even while dissecting it into its component parts.

CHAPTER TWO

Theory

Theories are nets cast to catch what we call "the world": to rationalize, to explain, and to master it. We endeavour to make the mesh ever finer and finer.

—KARL R. POPPER, *The Logic of Scientific Discovery*

IT IS APPROPRIATE to include in a book called *Theory Building* a chapter titled "Theory." Lest there be disappointment that the usual "fundamental" and sometimes turgid treatment of this topic is not found here, let me hasten to assert that only two simple purposes will be served by this chapter. My first purpose is to make clear the distinction between asking a question and doing research. This distinction is not always kept in mind by behavioral scientists. The second purpose is to present two contrasting goals of science and to show that these are coordinate, but not dependent, goals of scientific activity.

This entire volume is concerned with theory and theory building. I will take a series of ordered steps to put the whole of it together. This chapter sets the stage for what follows in the remaining ten. If the subjects of this chapter hold no interest for you, or if you have immediate need to build a theory, then you may wish to turn at once to Chapter 3, where the analysis of theory building proper begins.

Theory and Questions

It is notable in all sciences, but particularly in the behavioral sciences, that a scientist's reputation may be based upon his sole possession of a body of data. The man who first examines, describes, and reports some facts of the observable world is honored for this accomplishment.[1] It is

---

[1]There are many examples. For instance, the classic works of Lorenz in ethology, Burgess on the structure of the city, Sheldon in describing soma-types, and Booth in describing life and labor in London.

right and proper that he be so honored for he is contributing information or data to the body of knowledge.

Without gainsaying the contribution made by the addition of information to the body of knowledge, it is important to ask whether the ability to make such a contribution depends upon being a scientist (i.e., using that much abused procedure called *scientific method*) or is the product of being a good reporter. I think the answer is very clear. Good reporters can contribute new and sometimes important information to the body of knowledge. Good (or even bad) scientists can do the same thing, doing so not because they are scientists but because they are good reporters.

What, then, is the distinction between reporting and "doing science"? The distinction lies in whether the information is gathered for its own sake, or whether it is used to measure the values associated with "things" (called *units* of a theory, as elaborated in Chapter 4, and loosely called *variables* when talking about theories), the relationships among two or more of which is the focus of attention. The first procedure we call *description;* the second we call *research.*

Description and research are both part of scientific activity but contribute to it in distinctive ways. In Chapters 4, 6, 7, and 9, we will see how description contributes to the selection of units of a scientific model, to the location of its boundaries, to the determination of the system states in which it is to be found, and to the development of empirical indicators for measuring the values of the theoretical units employed.

I assume as a starting point that research is more than question asking. A piece of research tests an hypothetical prediction. The prediction, in turn, has antecedents in an explicit or implicit theoretical model. The research test of the prediction always provides a feedback to the model from which it is derived, either to substantiate the model's continued viability or to require its modification.

The general form of an hypothesis is a conditional prediction about the relationship between two or more things, followed by a figurative question mark. The question mark is the shorthand way of saying, "This prediction must be tested by marshaling measurements of these things in the observable world to see if their values predicted by the theoretical relationship can be empirically duplicated." The test of an hypothesis always relates back to the theory from which it derived. The rejected hypothesis requires the modification of the generating theoretical model or the reference of the results to an alternate model. The confirmed hypothesis requires a renewed search for further tests of the theory.

By way of contrast with an hypothesis, a question can stand alone, having neither antecedent questions from which derived nor succeeding questions to which it gives rise. When I ask, "How will you vote tomorrow?'' or "Do you approve of the policies of the Administration?'' and you answer, the information is in. An observer or reporter answers questions; a researcher tests predictions.

It is symbolic that the activities of scientists are called *research*. Separated into parts, the activities of research are a re-search—activities undertaken to repeat a search. The dictionary defines research as "a critical and exhaustive investigation or experimentation having as its aim the revision of accepted conclusions, in the light of newly discovered facts.'' The scientist is constantly concerned with re-searching the accepted conclusions of his field—the theoretical models he uses. He does this re-searching by probing for facts of the empirical world that falsify one or more predictions generated by his accepted conclusions, or theoretical models. Then the re-searching turns to the construction of new theoretical models to take the place of those no longer able to make sense out of the empirical world.

If we agree that research is more than answering questions, in the sense just indicated, an obvious conclusion follows. Theorizing as an integral part of empirical investigation, just as empirical analysis has meaning only by reference to a theory from which it is generated.

It is customary to view the relationship between theory and research from the vantage point of the former. This leads to asking, "What does research do for theory in the way of testing its utility, or correspondence with reality?'' If we turn it around and assume that scientists will do research as a normal activity in their subculture, we may then ask, "What is there about theory that has usefulness for the working researcher?''

These two questions meet at some point of the scientific enterprise. But the answers are significantly determined by the direction from which one approaches the meeting point. Coming from theory to research, attention is focused on truth, the nature of reality, the processes of knowing, and the logic of meaning statements. Starting from research and moving toward theory, attention turns to such issues as measurement in all its phases, translation of propositions into operational terms, and the reliability of empirical indicators.

There has been some tendency in the literature dealing with the connections between theory and research for the travelers to move toward each other from their respective starting points in either theory or research but to fail ever to meet head-on at any point of their journeys. Insofar as it seems to make sense to do so, this book is dedicated to producing a smashing collision on the highway connecting theory and research. The purpose is to generate a genuinely useful result (just as atom smashing produces new knowledge) rather than a pile of debris.

There has come increasingly into current usage the term *model* as a synonym of *theory*. One currently constructs models of social behavior rather than develops a theory. Also of contemporary interest is system theory, where *system* is substituted for *model*. I wish to avoid any argument over terms by asserting that in my view *theory* and *model* and *system* are identical for the purposes of this volume. This view is not necessarily shared by other writers in this field, who tend to view theory as fundamental explanation and model as representation of reality.[2] I will use the terms *theory, theoretical model, model,* and *system* interchangeably. All these terms will stand for a closed system from which are generated predictions about the nature of man's world—predictions that, when made, the theorist agrees must be open to some kind of empirical test. It is only on the grounds of empirical test that the theorist–model builder may be distinguished from the theologian. More will be said about this point in Chapter 11.

We may also distinguish an empirical system from a theoretical one. The former is what we apprehend, through human senses, in the environment of man. The latter is what we construct in our mind's eye to model the empirical system. The scientist focuses on making these two systems as nearly congruent as possible.

The excitement of scientific discovery has two dimensions important at this point. There is first the thrill of taking an outcome and constructing a model from which this outcome is predictable. The process is usually described as an inductive approach to science. Distinguishable from induction is the analysis of a scientific model that reveals an outcome not previously apparent either from an examination of the empirical world or from the obvious consequences of an existing theory. This is usually described as a deductive approach to science.

I will argue in this volume that the words *inductive* and *deductive* describe only a direction of movement. Focusing on induction and deduction separately leaves out of the picture that which is most important: the nature of the model to which both deduction and induction refer, and the linkages between the model and the empirical world to which it applies.

Goals of Science

Theories of social and human behavior address themselves to two distinct goals of science: (1) prediction and (2) understanding. It will be

---

[2]For a more extended description of the various usages of the term model see A. Kaplan, *The Conduct of Inquiry* (San Francisco: Chandler Publishing Company, 1964),

argued that these are separate goals and that the structure of theories employed to achieve each is unique. I will not, however, conclude that they are either inconsistent or incompatible. In the usual case of theory building in behavioral sciences, understanding and prediction are not often achieved together, and it therefore becomes important to ask why. It will be concluded that each goal may be attained without reference to the other.

I mean one of two things by prediction: (1) that we can foretell the value of one or more units making up a system; or (2) that we can anticipate the condition or state of a system as a whole. In both instances the focus of attention is upon an *outcome*.

As I employ the term *understanding,* it has the following essential meaning: it is knowledge about the interaction of units in a system.[3] Here attention is focused on processes of *interaction* among variables in a system.

The relationships between the goals of science and the analytical foci of attention in achieving these goals can be shown in a fourfold table like Table 2-1.

At first glance one would normally be constrained to argue that the four boxes of the table are simultaneously populated. That is, to achieve understanding of a social system, we need to know the interaction processes in it *and* the outcomes generated by these processes. Similarly, if we are to make accurate predictions about social phenomena, we have to know the processes built into these phenomena *and* the characteristics of all possible outcomes toward which the processes move.[4] This initial reaction is simply the assertion of a pious value position that bears little relation to the practices of social scientists. They actually operate in theory building and in doing research by working primarily in two of the four boxes, as indicated by the *X* entries in Table 2-1. What seems, in a

---

Chapter VII, in which five types are disinguished. See also H. Freudenthal (ed.), *The Concept and the Role of the Model in Mathematics and Natural and Social Sciences* (Dordrecht, Holland: D. Reidel Publishing Co., 1961).

[3]It will be recognized that this is not the same as *verstehen* sociology whose essential feature is the claim that the observer, being identical with his subjects, is able to "take the role of the other" (think, act, and feel like) when analyzing social phenomena, and hence can understand from the standpoint of the subjects being studied. My emphasis on interaction is identical with that of G. Bergmann who speaks of "process knowledge" and its interaction feature, which is the complete knowledge of the interaction among the variables of a system. See his "Purpose, Function, Scientific Explanation," *Acta Sociologica,* 5:225–238 (1962), and also his *Philosophy of Science* (Madison, Wisc.: University of Wisconsin Press, 1957).

[4]An excellent discussion of the distinction between understanding and prediction will be found in Kaplan, *op. cit.,* pp. 346ff.

Table 2-1.

ANALYTICAL FOCUS	GOALS	
	UNDERSTANDING	PREDICTION
INTERACTION	X	
OUTCOMES		X

logical sense, to represent the closure of the theory building–research cycle turns out to be largely ignored in the actual practices of theory building or researching.

This general point may be illustrated in several ways.

Merton's theory of deviant behavior is a good example of a model focused on outcomes, with the intent of predicting the types and relative frequencies of deviant behaviors in society. My own extension of his typology does exactly the same thing.[5] In both our papers the focus was on outcomes in trying to exhaust the complete range of possible outcomes and in trying to make the types generated mutually exclusive and internally homogeneous. As I pointed out, neither of us used a sophisticated model of social processes to generate the outcome categories of social deviation, and neither of us was disturbed by this failure.[6]

An obvious kind of prediction problem devoid of process knowledge is the forecast of fixed population characteristics from knowledge of characteristics of a sample drawn from that population. In voting forecasts, for example, a sample of the voting cohort is queried as to voting intention and the results projected onto the cohort as a whole to predict the election outcome. An examination of the typical prediction study in the behavioral sciences will reveal this same characteristic structure of the analysis. Parole success, outcomes of marriages, productivity and/or morale of industrial workers, election results, business-cycle fluctuations (especially in the study of consumer intentions), consumer behavior in the marketplace, population shifts, to mention but a few areas where we have made empirically grounded sociological predictions, are all studied in

[5]Robert K. Merton's famous paper is "Social Structure and Anomie," first published in the *American Sociological Review,* 3:672–682 (1938). For an extension of his typology of deviant adaptations see Robert Dubin, "Deviant Behavior and Social Structure: Continuities in Social Theory," *American Sociological Review,* 24:147–164 (1959), and Merton's response in the same issue of this journal.

[6]Dubin, *ibid.,* pp. 162–163.

terms of seeking indicators that will forecast outcomes. We are not concerned about the relationships that produced these outcomes.[7]

Let us turn to a comparable look at process analysis when it is used to increase understanding. Homans, for example, has stated and popularized the proposition that the liking of two people for each other is directly related to the frequency of their interaction because frequent interaction permits knowing about individual idiosyncrasies and therefore makes possible mutual adjustments to them.[8] This proposition not only has face validity but seems also to possess great power in permitting broad understanding of a wide range of social phenomena. Yet, if we examine specific social interactions, we are likely to discover that the predictive precision of this law of social interaction is surprisingly low. Examples: The UN-Chinese Armistice Commission has held 500 to 1000 meetings since its inception in 1953, with evidence that the individual negotiators on each side did not, in fact, increase their liking for their counterparts (does this suggest that if the initial contact is hostile, there may be a totally different kind of law of interaction that characterizes subsequent relations [e.g., under the circumstance of hostile contact, increased frequency of contact increases hostility]?). Sherif's important "Robbers Cave Experiment" demonstrated that two groups of boys in a camp situation maintained intergroup hostility in spite of daily contacts *until* the two groups were confronted simultaneously and jointly with a problem that could only be solved through their cooperation.[9] It was only after solving the group-relevant problem that measurable increases in friendliness between individual group members occurred. This suggests that in

[7]Indeed, the basic *unconcern* with process analysis has led, in the past, to some very imaginative speculation, *post hoc,* about the interrelationships among particular variables producing given outcomes. For example, it has been asserted that the American male bought a convertible model of an automobile as a mistress surrogate; that the Russian character was formed by swaddling in infancy; that successful marriage mates tended to be like each other; and that the preference for children in the American populace has shifted downward so markedly as to forecast a stationary population by 1970. All of these process speculations were either wrong or questionable. On the other hand, the forecast of the distribution of votes in an election typically increases in accuracy the closer the sample of voting intention is to the date of the election. Here the increase in precision of prediction depends on the patience of the forecaster in waiting until the very last minute to gather data and make his election prediction. He does not need any process knowledge of how the time gap between stated intention and actual behavior affects the latter.

[8]George C. Homans, *The Human Group* (New York: Harcourt, Brace & World, 1950), pp. 112 and 115. It is notable that the *because* phrase, the process statement, is separated by three pages from the prediction statement.

[9]Muzafer Sherif et al., *Intergroup Conflict and Cooperation: The Robbers Cave Experiment* (Norman, Okla.: University of Oklahoma Institute of Group Relations, 1961).

intergroup relations the frequency of interaction may have little or nothing to do with friendliness of the relations between individual members of the two groups. Here the frequency-friendliness proposition breaks down completely in its ability to predict the outcome of the interaction. Finally, we have only to consider the problem of divorce as it relates to frequency of interaction of mates to realize that the frequency-friendliness proposition would produce only mildly successful predictions of marital longevity.

In similar ways, the invasion-succession processes provide a broad base for understanding aspects of urban ecology;[10] the conflict processes for understanding war, union-management relations, and race and ethnic relations;[11] the empathic processes for aiding comprehension of face-to-face social interaction;[12] and the decision-making processes for better grasping the bases of purposive social action.[13] Yet in each of these process analyses there is a remarkable gap between the power of understanding they provide and the precision of the predictions of specific actions to which they give rise.

To summarize up to this point: (1) The prediction problem of behavioral sciences has been focused on reducing the differences between actual outcomes of social behaviors and predicted outcomes. This point of view places little reliance on the analysis of the processes that produce the outcomes being studied. (2) The process problem of social science has generated concern with the analysis of processes of social interaction that contribute to the understanding of why particular kinds of social events take place. The result has been that the level of understanding is broad but relatively imprecise in specifying the probable outcomes in concrete social situations.

This gives rise to two paradoxes. The first is the *precision paradox:* Why can we achieve precision in prediction without any knowledge of how the predicted outcome was produced? The second is the *power paradox:* Why can we achieve powerful understanding of social behavior without being able to predict its character in specific situations?

[10]*Cf.* A. H. Hawley, *Human Ecology* (New York: Ronald, 1950).

[11]*Cf.* Lewis Coser, *The Functions of Social Conflict* (New York: Free Press, 1956).

[12]*Cf.* L. S. Cottrell, Jr., "The Empathic Responses: A Neglected Field of Research," *Psychiatry,* 12 (1949).

[13]*Cf.* C. West Churchman, *Prediction and Optimal Decision* (Englewood Cliffs, N.J.: Prentice-Hall, 1961).

Precision Paradox

The precision paradox is fascinating. How is it possible to predict an outcome in the form of social behavior without knowing how this outcome was produced? In other words, how can we predict anything without knowing something about the phenomenon being predicted?

Much social science prediction is concerned with predicting the state of a system, usually a social system. It is to this prediction of system states that attention is first turned. By *system state* I mean a condition of the system in which there are persistent values of the variables (units) of the system. Each system state is distinguished from all others by the unique configuration of values for the variables in that state. (See Chapter 7, "System States," for a detailed analysis.)

In dealing with system states, the prediction problem is twofold. We either predict the length of time a given state of a system persists, or we predict the order in which system states succeed each other. We may, of course, also combine these predictions.

In *predicting the persistence of a given system state* we usually employ some broad classificatory scheme that specifies a range of values for system variables as the criteria of a given system state.[14] Thus, in business-cycle analysis, the direction of the curves measuring business behavior is the criterion of the prosperity or depression state of the cycle. Similarly, we distinguish between the states of normalcy and deviancy by using gross indices when examining individual behavior. Or we measure collective attitudes by giving distinctive state designations to those attitudes that cluster around the positive and negative poles of our attitude scales.

This means that very often we can predict the persistence of a system state, or its imminent change, by the degree to which the values of the system variables do or do not approach the boundary conditions of the system's states. For example, we would be constrained to predict a downward shift in the business cycle as being imminent if the summary value of stock market prices approaches its historic high level. Note the characteristics of this prediction: (1) We have some historic knowledge of the boundary conditions of the system states, and (2) we have some current measures of the variables whose values define the system state.

---

[14]The term "value" will be used repeatedly in this book to denote the quantity of a given variable. Thus it is to be distinguished from value as a moral concept as in "American values" or "the Protestant Ethic."

We then literally extrapolate from one to another state of our system.[15] Or, given values of the variables that do not approach the boundary conditions of a given state, we would predict the persistence of that state.

It should be clear that in predicting the persistence of a single state of a system we are not bound by any knowledge of *how* the system operates. All we need to know is enough history of all system states to define their boundary conditions and some current indicators of the variables that define these states. We can then often achieve very precise predictions about the length of time that a given state will persist. Such precision is not based on understanding the dynamics of the system. This kind of precise prediction rests only on accurate description of system states and on the availability of empirical indicators of these states. Indeed, in business-cycle prediction, knowledge that has obvious significance for future economic activity, the basic search has been for empirical indicators whose values lead in time and therefore foreshadow the movement of the entire cycle.

A special case distinct from the prediction of system states is the prediction of the values of one variable from the known values of another variable. Here, instead of predicting system-state persistence or change, we predict the value of one variable. Whether we use some form of direct bivariate analysis or experimental controls or multivariate analyses that hold constant individual variables, we use the same operational format as the one just described. For example, for every least square curve describing the relationship between two variables, we predict unknown values of the dependent variable either *between* known values of the independent variable (by interpolating) or *beyond* these known values (by extrapolating). The same class of information we need for predicting persistence of system states is also needed for predicting values of individual variables. Furthermore, this is the only class of information needed.

The second analytical problem in dealing with states of a system is to *predict the order of succession of system states.* Here a logical trick is typically used to give absolute precision in prediction. Consider a system to have only two states. Then, knowing the present state of the system,

---

[15]Implicit in this act of predicting is a law of systems that the late Professor Wirth was wont to characterize in the following aphorism: "If things continue in the future as they have been in the past, then things will be in the future as they were in the past." This is the classic assumption implicit in all extrapolation. It is, of course, a true assumption in many real situations, and consequently can provide the basis for precise prediction without having any knowledge of the internal characteristics of the system, the persistence of whose states is being predicted.

we can predict precisely that *if* it changes state, it must go into the other state.

Some of the great and respected ideas of sociology are grounded in this logical simplification: mechanical and organic solidarity, gemeinschaft and gesellschaft, folk-urban, sacred-secular, primary and secondary group, in-group and out-group, functional-dysfunctional. If we find a social system in one of these states and it changes state, then we predict with utter confidence the system will go to the second state—e.g., a sacred society that changes will become a secular society.

Obviously, we achieve absolute prediction about the succession of system states if we assume a system has only two states. For example, the inevitability of socialism in the Western world is clear-cut *if* we see developed socioeconomic systems as having only two states, capitalistic and socialistic, and find them presently in their capitalistic state. The prediction of the inevitability and permanence of socialism is made even more certain if we add the assumption that the oscillation between the states of an economic system is asymmetrical. Thus, the capitalistic state may be succeeded by the socialistic state, but never the other way around (the Chinese critique of Soviet socialism to the contrary notwithstanding). We can then add the second perfect prediction: that if the economic system is in its socialistic state, it can never return to a capitalist state. But this is like asserting that organic matter has but two states, life and death. Even the folk have the saying, "There is nothing as certain as death and taxes." Their prediction is absolute and certain, at least for the first portion of the saying.

It should again be obvious that precision in prediction, this time of the succession of system states, need not depend upon understanding how the system works. Even if three possible states of a system are postulated and each has equal probability of succeeding the others, we still have a fifty-fifty chance of being right in predicting the succession of states on the basis of *guessing* alone.

The precision paradox may be summarized as follows: It is possible to achieve high precision in predicting *when* changes in system states will occur and *what* states will succeed each other, without possessing knowledge of how the system operates. Furthermore, we can predict individual values of variables without knowing the connection between the forecasting indices and the outcome predicted.

It is the ability to predict accurately, from only incomplete knowledge of a system's functioning, that makes paradoxical our precision in predicting social behavior. Let it be at once clear that I am not decrying this state of affairs. I find it very comforting and encouraging for the enterprise of social science that we can make precise predictions out of ignorance!

I also see in the precision paradox one of the important reasons why there is both a distinctive technology of applied social science and a distinctive contribution of it to the corpus of the behavioral sciences. Applied social science focuses upon prediction, and insofar as it can get along without understanding, its contribution must be limited, although real and important.[16]

Power Paradox

The power paradox in social analysis is equally fascinating. Why is it that we can create models[17] of social behavior that are powerful in contributing to understanding, without providing, at the same time, precision in prediction?

It will be recalled that I defined *understanding* as knowledge about the interaction of units (variables) in a system. This understanding may be powerful. For example, we know for the American society that amount of education and lifetime earnings are positively related—the more education, the more total earnings. It is not hard to comprehend why the relationship is positive in a highly technical society. In short, we can understand why education and total earnings are positively associated. If we then made the specific prediction that the lifetime earnings of the graduates of Vassar College will be greater than the total earnings of female high school graduates of Poughkeepsie, N.Y. (site of Vassar), we might make a very imprecise prediction. (Many Vassar girls marry and earn little in their lifetimes, whereas a very high proportion of girls completing high school, but no more, will enter and remain in the labor force with substantial lifetime earnings.)

The disjunction between power of understanding and precision in prediction rests essentially on three factors. (1) The development of a model as a system for comprehending a limited realm of knowledge is

---

[16]See, for example, Alvin W. Gouldner and S. M. Miller (eds.), *Applied Sociology: Opportunities and Problems* (New York: Free Press, 1965), and an older volume illustrating the nature of applied theory, Ronald Lippitt, *Training in Community Relations* (New York: Harper & Row, 1949).

[17]The formal analysis of scientific models is presently reaching a climax in an exciting set of developments. An excellent symposium dealing with this issue is H. Freudenthal (ed.), *op. cit.*

necessarily bounded, and hence excludes realms of phenomena. This may have the effect of excluding crucial variables that contribute significantly to an outcome but not to an understanding of the operation of the particular system being analyzed. (2) A model may be a deliberate oversimplification of a range of phenomena that makes for better understanding of the simplified realm but cannot directly generate precise predictions. (3) The model for understanding may focus on broad relationships among the variables composing it and consequently emphasize such a feature as directionality of relationship, which is not itself sufficient to determine precision in prediction.

Each of these three points will be examined in turn.

Limited Domain

An essential characteristic of a powerful model is that it distinguishes a limited phenomenon and focuses analytical attention only upon that realm. The consequence is that for that domain the analytical model makes sense and provides understanding of specific empirical facts that are defined as falling within its scope. In addition, an illuminating insight is contributed to social analysis when we can employ the description of a class of social behavior to tell us what *not* to expect in that domain. It is no accident, for example, that Cooley named his primary group in focusing analytical attention upon it and left for successors the problem of calling all those group structures not included within his domain *secondary groups*. The understanding derived from Cooley's analysis is at least as much an understanding of what is *not* a characteristic of primary relations as it is an affirmative theory of primary-group behavior.[18]

Simmel's famous analysis of the stranger is a powerful model for understanding interpersonal relations. Yet attempts to apply his rules for interaction between strangers to specific situations may generate imprecise predictions about the content or mode of interaction that may ensue. This becomes apparent when the model is applied to interacting strangers who are of different ages, sexes, races, or who do not share a common language, values, or institutional practices. Indeed, even with no such differences separating the strangers, the mere initial failure to assign status to each other would modify the first phases of interaction from what

---

[18]Cooley's model was not even very good as a theory of primary-group behavior, for he appears to have been wrong in considering the childhood peer group as the social microcosm that is the principal carrier of adult-like behavior systems.

they would have been had such status assignments been initially possible.[19] Differences between strangers and the failure to make status assignments may be variables excluded from consideration in a theory of stranger relations that make a significant difference in predicting the outcome of stranger interactions.

In some of the areas where process models have been developed it is clear that deliberate exclusions of realms of phenomena are intended. In game theory, for example, the models of two-person nonzero sum games add a cardinal bit of knowledge to understanding by making clear that there may be n-person games, zero-sum games, or both. These domains are not included in the coverage of the models of two-person, nonzero sum games and require distinctive models of their own.

Simplification

My second point is that models of process may be deliberately oversimplified in order to clarify understanding. Here the well-established scientist's trick of holding constant, or controlling, is employed in building the model in order that the resulting simplification may improve understanding. This is a highly essential feature of scientific model building but one most bitterly rejected by social-science naturalists with the claim that social phenomena are inherently complex and beyond being understood through simplistic models. There are a number of examples of why this conclusion is at least problematic. Karlsson's model of information spread is based on the analysis of ''a piece of information that is so simple that it is either communicated without change, or not communicated at all.'' Admittedly, there may be a few bits of real information that meet this rigorous criterion, but given this simplification, Karlsson was able to develop a model of information diffusion in social groups that contributes to understanding.[20]

Oversimplification may increase understanding without improving predictive precision. Indeed, there may even be an increase in understanding with a corresponding decrease in predictive precision. Simplification in the model may actually reduce precision of prediction, especially under

---

[19]An amusing illustration of the consequence of failure to assign status is the true story of Bing Crosby, the singer, who, returning from a camping trip unshaven and ill-kempt, was refused lodging in a hotel until he was able to identify himself unequivocally, upon which the red carpet treatment was accorded him.

[20]See G. Karlsson, ''A Model of Information Diffusion,'' in *An Influence Model* (Umeå, Sweden: Dept. of Sociology, U. of Umeå, 1968, Research Report No. 1).

the circumstance where variables excluded from the model are the ones whose values are good forecasters of outcomes even though the relationships of such variables to the processes producing the outcomes are not understood.

Broad Relationships

My third point about process models is that they may focus on broad relationships and in consequence may provide imprecise guides for prediction of outcomes. Insofar as we are interested in such broad characteristics of a relationship as directionality or rates of change and critical values of individual variables (e.g., values at the moment when other related variables reach zero or limiting values), we may contribute to understanding without attending to or improving precision of prediction.

Let me illustrate the difference between these two points of view with a simpleminded example. When the productivity of industrial workers is studied *in situ,* we reach conclusions about the relationship between output and such group characteristics as morale. The studies seem to indicate some positive relationship such that an increase in morale is related to an increase in output. But *in situ* we have tested this relationship only within very narrow limits. Excluded, for example, is a wide range of low levels of output because, should they be reached in reality, the work organization would take corrective measures. So we really know nothing about how morale and output relate at the low extreme of output. It could very well be that the relationship disappears or becomes negative or curvilinear. Yet should we develop a theory to express this relationship and actually test the process model empirically, we would be contributing to understanding without necessarily improving prediction. There would never be an opportunity to make a prediction at the extreme low values because the organization would have taken corrective action before that point was reached (e.g., fired low-producing workers). This is an instance of how the theoretical model may be very fundamental to understanding without having any practical direct consequences that can become the object of predictions of outcomes.

In a directly analogous fashion the contemporary research on sensory deprivation[21] is providing an exciting contribution to understanding the nature of self-identification. We really have nothing to predict about the

[21]Summarized in Philip Solomon et al. (eds.), *Sensory Deprivation* (Cambridge, Mass.: Harvard University Press, 1961).

state of sensory deprivation because this is neither a customary nor readily encountered real state of the individual. But by studying experimental subjects in a state of sensory deprivation we contribute importantly to an understanding of the stability of their self-images, of some mechanisms for maintaining them, and of the processes of mental life when these images become lost or distorted. Here we have an example of the study of a realm of behavior in which the understanding has surprising consequences not anticipated and not readily employed in predictive statements.

The power paradox may be summarized as follows: A theoretical model that focuses on the analysis of processes of interaction may contribute significantly to understanding. This understanding may be achieved by limiting the system being analyzed, by simplifying its variables and/or the laws of interaction among them, and by focusing on broad relationships among variables. Understanding of process, when achieved, does not *necessarily* provide the basis for accuracy of prediction about the reality being modeled by the theoretical system.

Prediction and Process

These introductory remarks may be considered a footnote to the usual discussions of theory building in social science. I find such a footnote necessary as an additive to incisive analyses like those contained in an important paper by Zetterberg.[22] Professor Zetterberg attacks two central problems: the ordering of propositions and their verification. In setting forth the classifying characteristics of propositions, he makes no distinction between propositions dealing with outcomes and those dealing with process. Consider the following example from Zetterberg, ordering four propositions in a chain.

1. Persons who occupy *central* positions, that is, interact with other group members, tend to obtain a better *knowledge* of their needs and attitudes;
2. Persons who have better *knowledge* of the needs and attitudes of others can more easily issue directives acceptable to others and thus tend to obtain higher *authority;*
3. Persons of higher *authority* tend to receive more *prestige;*

[22]Hans L. Zetterberg, "Notes on Theory Construction and Verification in Sociology," paper delivered at the Fifth World Congress of Sociology, Washington, D.C., 1962.

4. Persons with *prestige* become sought-after interaction partners, and thus tend to obtain *central* positions in the group.[23]

Propositions No. 1 and No. 3 are clearly ones dealing with *outcomes*. Proposition No. 1 declares that persons who have central positions have better knowledge, and No. 3 asserts that persons with high authority have high prestige. We test both propositions by measuring values on the four outcomes: centrality, knowledge, authority, and prestige, and then relating the values on each pair of outcomes to see if their predicted association holds. (I am not concerned here with the empirical indicators of any of these outcomes, simply assuming that we can secure operational measures of each.)

But now consider propositions No. 2 and No. 4. Both are *process* propositions. Let me illustrate with proposition No. 2, which claims that possession of better knowledge permits easier issuance of directives, which then results in higher authority. Note the process statement that links the two outcomes (knowledge and authority): "more easily issue directives."[24] This is a process statement because it says what goes on, a process taking place, inside the knowledgeable person. We can never measure the ease of issuing directives by using any indices based upon the directives issued (e.g., their number or length or salience for the group). If we really mean "ease of issuing" as the process statement, then we have to go to the issuer and determine from him his "ease while issuing," and the comparative rank of this ease among all those who ever issue directives (at least in the group under study).

I am sure that in the chain of propositions used by Zetterberg as an illustration, the two process propositions were never intended to be tested empirically. In principle they are testable. But their function, as displayed by Zetterberg, was to link two propositions dealing solely with outcomes. This is an enlightening example to illustrate the twin paradoxes. The outcome propositions used by Zetterberg may have high precision in prediction. His two process propositions may contribute to our power of understanding.

High precision in prediction may be independent of any understanding of the process producing the forecasted outcome. Powerful understanding

---

[23]*Ibid.*, quoted from the manuscript.

[24]You will also note that there is a second process statement contained in the proposition, namely, "acceptable to others." Thus, the proposition has two process statements, the one dealing with the knowledgeable person ("more easily issue directives") and the other with his audience ("acceptable to others"). For purposes of analysis we will ignore the second process statement, although it too could be analyzed in a fashion identical with our treatment of the first process statement.

of the process of interaction does not, by itself, guarantee precision in prediction.

Theories give the scientist opportunity to develop *understanding* of the relations among units upon which he focuses. An elaboration of the understanding aspect of theory building is to be found in Chapter 5, "Laws of Interaction." The theories that catch " 'the world' to rationalize, to explain, and to master it," in Popper's words, permit prediction of values of the units of the model or states in which it is to be found. The specification of the uses of theory for prediction will be found in Chapter 8, "Propositions." These two chapters taken together suggest the ways in which the goals of science are realized.

INTERLUDE ONE

So early in the game, let us play it joyously.

—ANON., *Welsh Song*

Often it seems that there is a fine line separating serious theory from nonsense. That is, of course, if the theory is viewed from the outside without the puckered-brow concentration of the humorless. This brief interlude is designed to encourage the enjoyment of theorizing without its occasional pretentiousness.

NEURO-SOCIOLOGY: THE SCIENCE OF EUMEROGENESIS*

Neuro-sociology is the study of eumeromorphic behavior unmediated by cognitive or conscious processes. It may seem strange, but only to those, perhaps, who lack a positivist understanding of science, that one should include nonteleological elements within the purview of sociology. But if one begins with exordium variables, then the roots of behavior must be sought in the somatic realms.

Theology begins, quite rightly, with the question of *creatio ex nihilo*. Sociology must begin with the question of *cognito ex nihilo*:[1] does knowledge come out of nowhere, or out of somewhere? And if the latter, where? Common sense, as it so often does, seeks to provide an answer. The man in the street will say, "I feel it in my bones." And he thinks, therefore, that he has reached the seat of knowledge. But the hardheaded

---

*From "Socinus Grelot," *Sociologomachy: A Guide to Modern Usage* (New York: Free Press, 1961), pp. 3–5. Copyright © 1961 by The Free Press, A Corporation; used by permission.

[1]One can recognize here a possible modification of the Cartesian formula. Our seventeenth-century philosopher had said, *cogito, ergo sum*. Our twentieth-century existentialist could say, *cognito, ergo sum*.

33

osteopath can ask, rightly, "Do these bones live?" And without the nerve tendrils, clearly they do not. It is not in the bones, but in the synapses that the fundamental reflexes and behavioral syndromes are born. This is not to say that Man is a neurospast. That would be a specious form of reductionism. But all twitching does begin in the nerves, and it is to the neuroses that we must turn for knowledge.

As a new science, neuro-sociology has only begun to trace the very fibres of being. As yet, one can only report on a group of ongoing research projects. We hope that these five projects may serve to illustrate the range, versatility—and dare we say, promise—of neuro-sociology.

(a) *Group sleep-walking.* What may at first seem a tendentious undertaking—the study of group sleep-walking—gains relevance when we understand the relation of this research—to the degree that we can declassify the security material—to military sociology. For in this project (Defense Contract NS-2516XF), neuro-sociology studies the energy exchanges of a battalion of recruits, routed out at night, for a twenty-mile forced march with full pack. Clearly, while walking, energy is "spent"; but equally, while sleeping, energy is "stored."[2] A battalion of men on a long march will often fall asleep while walking. Through socio-voltameters, we can measure the energy exchange. Neuro-sociometrics allows us to measure both straight line and wobbly line patterns while sleep-walking.

(b) *Group sleep-talking.* A contribution to family sociology. The project, using a mixed sample, is studying the verbal interaction of husband and wife in sleep, using an Interaction Process recorder, with a motion-picture adapter for non-verbal gesture patterns.

(c) *The Japanese literacy rate.* Many observers have commented on the fact that the consumption of reading material in Japan is higher than in any other country in the world. Sociologists, seeking to explain this phenomenon, have sought to identify ecological variables (the long commuting between home and workplace); aesthetic variables (the calligraphy of Japanese ideographs); or cultural variables (neither the chrysanthemum nor the sword), as the key determinants. Neuro-sociology, believing in the law of parsimony, offers a simpler hypothesis, at least for its heuristic value. It is to be observed, from neuro-introspection, at least, that it is simpler for the head (in response, perhaps, to the laws of gravity, or because of the tendon attachment to the torso), to move more easily in vertical rather than horizontal fashion, to shuttle,

---

[2]A startling illustration, too, of *synergism,* and a proof, on the physiological and theological levels, of the powers of regeneration.

that is, up and down, rather than to shake it to and fro.[3] When one recalls that Japanese is written from top to bottom, rather than from left to right . . .

(d) *Phase movement in small groups.* An apodictic study of Joule's cycle as it operates in small group discussion.

(e) *Empathy in the Dyad.* Those acquainted with the recent work of Bruner, Goodnow, Austin, Osgood, Suci, Tannenbaum and Newcomb (see supra, p. 16) and the recent emendations by Triandis, will know that "cognitive similarity affects the process of interpersonal communication." In other words, people who think alike will talk to each other more readily than people who do not. (To be technical, syndetic pairs are more likely to have a higher correlational ratio and lower analysis of variance on the semantic differential than asydetic pairs.) Struck by this finding, neuro-sociologists have reasoned that people who feel alike will more likely attract each other than people who do not. Our theory, therefore, suggests that people who see eye-to-eye form syndetic categories: they achieve, in short, perceptual conjuctivitus.

[3]This immediately suggests, as one can see, a four-fold table:

	TO	FRO
UP		
DOWN		

CHAPTER THREE

Units of a Theory: Initial Distinctions

The locus problem may be described as that of selecting the ultimate subject-matter for inquiry in behavioral science, the attribute space for its description, and the conceptual structure within which hypotheses about it are to be formulated. Quite a number of alternatives present themselves, and have been selected in various inquiries: states of conscious acts, actions (segments of meaningful behavior), roles, persons, personalities, interpersonal relations, groups, classes, institutions, social traits or patterns, societies, and cultures. With respect to each of these there is the associated problem of the unit, *that is, of what constitutes the identity of the element selected. Are legal institutions, for example, quite distinct from the institution of the state or part of it, and if so, in what sense of "part"? Are Dr. Jekyll and Mr. Hyde one person or two? Does the Mason-Dixon line divide two societies or only localize certain social patterns?*

—ABRAHAM KAPLAN, *The Conduct of Inquiry*

IT IS MOST USEFUL to start our analysis of the building blocks of theory with the notion of concept. The idea of a concept has a ring of familiarity about it to almost everyone who has ever professed interest in theory and science. A concept also has many meanings. For that reason alone we all feel comfortable with concepts, however differently we may conceive of their nature.

The purpose of this chapter is to translate the notion of concept to the more colorless and neutral term *unit*. A concrete meaning will be given to the term *unit*. We will then examine some important distinctions between paired characteristics of units in order to draw out their consequences for the manner in which we build theories. This chapter is in preparation for Chapter 4 in which are set forth the specific classes of units employed in social theory.

Concept and Unit

Let us start with the relationship between concept and unit. It is necessary in every science to have a way of designating its subject matter. Sciences deal with things. Sciences are focused on aspects of the world perceived by man. For those aspects of this world that constitute the subject matter of a given discipline, the science must have some terms.

The terms designating the things about which a science tries to make sense are its concepts. Kaplan has put the matter succinctly.

> The important terms of any science are significant because of their semantics, not their syntax; they are not notational, but reach out to the world which gives the science its subject-matter. The meaning of such terms results from a process of conceptualization of the subject-matter. In this process the things studied are *classified* and *analyzed:* several things are grouped together and particular things assigned to the several groups to which they belong. . . . The concept of "paranoid," for example, puts into a single class a certain set of persons, and is itself analyzed into such patterns as delusions of persecution, auditory hallucinations, impairment of ego-functions, or the like. Each of these patterns in turn is a classification, grouping together a set of actions, verbal or otherwise as the case may be, and without regard to the actors performing them.[1]

In this view, acting as a scientist depends on conceptualizing those things to which attention is given in the scientific inquiry. If the term *concept* were used only in this sense, we would employ it to mean the things out of which we build theories. But concepts may also mean whole theories or laws of science or even "conceptual frameworks," so dear to the heart of behavioral scientists. This confusion as to meaning of *concept* has led me to employ the more neutral term *unit* to designate the things out of which theories are built. This follows Kaplan's usage, as stated in the quotation at the head of this chapter.

Units are not theories. A collection of units that are called the subject matter of a scientific discipline does not constitute the theory of that discipline. It is only when the units are put together into models of the perceived world that theories emerge. This putting together of the units (or concepts) of a discipline into models is what Bergmann suggests gives significance to the particular collection of units with which a scientist chooses to deal. Significance in Bergmann's sense is to be distinguished from truth. Thus,

---

[1] Abraham Kaplan, *The Conduct of Inquiry* (San Francisco: Chandler, 1964), p. 50.

A concept is neither true nor false, only propositions are. A concept is neither valid nor invalid, only arguments are. Yet there is a distinction of ''good'' and ''bad'' among defined descriptive concepts. To have a name for it I shall say that a concept either is or is not *significant*. A concept is significant if and only if it occurs, together with others, in statements of lawfulness which we have reason to believe are true. It follows that some concepts are, in an inherently vague sense that cannot and need not be made more precise, ''more'' significant than others. For instance, a concept that occurs only in one or two tentative and isolated laws is ''less'' significant than one that occurs in a well-established theory of considerable scope. It follows, furthermore, that what is not significant today may become so tomorrow.[2]

Bergmann's statement foreshadows our analysis of laws of interaction in Chapter 5. It is sufficient at this point that we understand that units are not by themselves the sufficient components of a theory.

Regarding the units of theory, there is another issue directed at the question of the physical existence of the units employed by theoreticians. Do the units employed in behavioral science ''really'' exist? Or, indeed, is it necessary that the ''reality'' of units be the criterion for acceptance or rejection of units employed in a discipline? The so-called ''instrumentalist'' position on this point has never been fully resolved, as Nagel suggests.

One final comment on the instrumentalist view must be made. It has already been briefly noted that proponents of this view supply no uniform account of the various ''scientific objects'' (such as electrons or light waves) which are ostensibly postulated by microscopic theories. But the further point can also be made that it is far from clear how, on this view, such ''scientific objects'' can be said to be physically existing things. For if a theory is just a leading principle—a technique for drawing inferences based upon a method of representing phenomena—terms like ''electron'' and ''light wave'' presumably function only as conceptual links in rules of representation and inference. On the face of it, therefore, the meaning of such terms is exhausted by the roles they play in guiding inquiries and ordering the material of observation; and in this perspective the supposition that such terms might refer to physically existing things and processes that are not phenomena in the strict sense seems to be excluded. Proponents of the instrumentalist view have indeed flatly contradicted themselves on this issue.[3]

[2]Gustav Bergmann, *Philosophy of Science* (Madison, Wisc.: University of Wisconsin Press, 1957), p. 50.

[3]Ernest Nagel, *The Structure of Science* (New York: Harcourt, Brace & World, 1961), p. 140.

Nagel follows this conclusion with an analysis of the realist view of theories and an extended discussion of the criteria of physical reality.[4] He initiates the discussion with the statement that "it is a matter of historical record that, while many distinguished figures in both science and philosophy have adopted as uniquely adequate the characterization of theories as true or false statements [realists], a no less distinguished group of other scientists and philosophers have made a similar claim for the description of theories as instruments of inquiry [instrumentalists]."[5] The last sentence of the discussion concludes, "In brief, the opposition between these views is a conflict over preferred modes of speech."[6] We will return to this problem with a very simple resolution of the issue in the section of this chapter entitled "Real and Nominal."

In normal scientific discourse we use phrases like _____ is the antecedent of _____, or _____ varies with _____, or _____ is a function of _____, or if _____, then _____ with a probability of X. In each instance we fill in the pair of blanks with clearly specified things. These things are the units of a theory that are the focus of attention in this and the following chapters.

Thing Versus Property of Thing

As we shall see in Chapter 4 when we consider classifying units of a theory in the behavioral sciences, and probably in all sciences, we build our theories about the properties of things rather than about the things themselves. We focus our theories upon selected characteristics of objects rather than upon the objects.

This may at first appear curious because intuitively we may feel that objects are more visible and more readily apprehended than characteristics of them. We can see individual persons, but we have to struggle to invent methods for apprehending their morale. We can walk around and map the boundaries of a city, yet we intrude something we conceptualize as "ecological structure" when examining the relationships between a central city and its suburbs. Why do we go to morale or ecological structure as the analytical focus of attention? These are properties of people and cities, not the things themselves.

[4]*Ibid.*, pp. 141–152.
[5]*Ibid.*, p. 141.
[6]*Ibid.*, p. 152.

It seems to me that the answer is a simple one having entirely to do with man's limited capacities as an observer and his equally limited capacities for recording and retaining many simultaneous observations. We simply are not capable of seeing things whole. Nor is man capable of retaining and recording complex phenomena coming within the range of his sensory fields. It is necessary to acknowledge that man, who builds theories to model his world of observation, has genuine limits on his capacities to grasp complex observations.

Granted such limitations as part of the biology of man, it seems reasonable to conclude that man, the scientist, will solve the problem of his limited capacities by modeling only that which can sensibly fall within his ranges of observation and comprehension. This means he will be selective in what he picks out of his fields of observation to deal with analytically. This in turn means that he will deal with selected concrete or abstract characteristics of things rather than with things as wholes.

We are alleging, then, that the characteristic concern with properties of things rather than with things themselves as the units of theories is a consequence of man's biology rather than the nature of things. Once we accept this simple assumption, we are freed of the hoary issue of dealing with the essence of things. We simply admit that we do not know what things "really" are or are "in essence." Nor are we any longer interested in this issue. The more viable assertion, at least for the scientist, is to declare that it is a mere inventory problem to add up all the properties of things at any given time, for both man's imagination and his skills in extending observations must inevitably add to the inventory in the future. We have only to note what has happened in the subatomic jungle to realize that with more than thirty fundamental particles of matter already experimentally demonstrated, and with more undoubtedly still to come, it seems scarcely meaningful to say that matter "in essence" is the sum of its known parts today or its even more numerous parts in the year 2000.

Probably the most important consequence of dealing with properties of things as the units of theory is the release of imagination that it affords. The moment we can divide up a thing into two or more of its properties, it then becomes possible, at least imaginatively, to ascribe to it still other properties. This release of imagination is enhanced when we look upon the properties of a unit as providing opportunities to test relationships with other properties, and not merely as a new tally in the inventory of the unit's totality.

You will note that I have not made any assertion about the reality of any ascribed properties of a thing. It is not necessary. Indeed, this is one of the fundamental starting points for any scientist. He starts by wonder-

ing about the properties of things and may be quite imaginative in ascrib-
ing particular properties to particular things. This is one of the sources of
creative theory. Pasteur, after all, was ridiculed by his scientific peers
almost universally because he imagined that a then unknown thing called
a *microbe* could cause a specific disease. Chen Ning Yang and Tsung-Dao
Lee won their Nobel Prize in 1957 because they were imaginative enough
to think of electrons as being left-handed rather than right-handed in the
direction of their orbits.

It should also be clear that I have not asserted anything about the
operational character of the properties of things that are the units of a
scientific theory. The issue of operationalism comes in much later in the
theory building-testing cycle. Specifically, much will be made of operationalism in Chapter 9, "Empirical Indicators." There we will give full
credit for all that is usefully claimed for operationalism, and simply
ignore those claims that are irrelevant.

Unit Versus Event

For purposes of any scientific theory we need to distinguish between a
unit and an event. The distinction rests on the question of number. An
event happens only once; any particular event has a population of exactly
one. Any time we encounter a situation where the possible population is
exactly one, we are dealing with an event.

It follows then, that a unit of a theory must ultimately be able to count
two or more entries in any tabular cell for which the unit provides one
column or row designation. In a specific situation under investigation the
population may in fact be zero, but over many samples of such situations
the investigator must postulate that the population exceeds one.

The reason for distinguishing between a unit and an event is twofold:
(1) We want to distinguish certain types of historical explanation from
theory, and (2) we want to dispose of the nagging problem of the uniqueness of all things at each point in time.

An historical explanation of a unique event that seeks out the antecedent causes of this event is not a theory. Such an explanation may be quite
accurate and fully supported by available facts. The explanation may even
have long-term currency among experts, being accepted as correct for
many years. It is, nevertheless, an explanation of something that occurred
only once. Its antecedents and their modes of combinations can only
explain that one event, no more. Confronted with another singular event,

the historian must marshal new explanations, doing this endlessly for each new event. What he has learned about the antecedents of one event are not applicable in explaining another event.

Theory, on the other hand, is concerned with modeling the processes and outcomes of particular units interacting in systems, whenever these systems exist and under all conditions of their existence. For example, should our historian shift his problem from explaining the origins of the American Civil War to a search for the origins of war, then he becomes a theorist and his theory will contain as one of its units, war as a social relationship. War becomes a unit of this theory precisely because attention is now focused on a property of groups for which there is a population of more than one (all the wars of human societies or all the wars of the Western world or all the wars of the United States). Any predictions about the group property "war" must hold for all members of groups characterized by this property.[7]

It should be clear, then, that much of the time social scientists and historians are theorists, actively testing their theories in the empirical world. But many historians and social scientists who work with events are not theorists testing theoretical models, even though they offer as their products cogent and valid explanations of the events with which they deal.

The contrast between *unit* of a theory and *event* is crucial in distinguishing two empirical positions that oppose each other on philosophical grounds. Briefly stated, the conflict may be summarized in the following terms: One school holds that all points in time are events. At the moment you read this you are one person, but by the time you get to the end of this chapter or even of this paragraph, you are another person. Obviously, you have aged, tired, become hungrier, and so on, all of which are measurable properties of you and which therefore are empirically available. From this point of view, the scientist is constrained to claim that he is describing chains of events. At best, scientific generalization is limited to describing those chains of events that seem to be like each other. But the dilemma is that the events that make up the chains are, by definition, unique, which then raises serious questions about the identity among sequential chains that link such events.

[7]The following conclusion by Brodbeck agrees with this analysis. "There is no such thing as 'historical' explanation, only the explanation of historical events." May Brodbeck, "Explanation, Prediction, and 'Imperfect' Knowledge," in H. Feigl and G. Maxwell (eds.), *Scientific Explanation, Space, and Time,* Minnesota Studies in the Philosophy of Science, vol. 3 (Minneapolis, Minn.: University of Minnesota Press, 1962), p. 254. See also Kaplan, *op cit.,* pp. 367ff.

Among its more moderate proponents, the opposing school concedes the event character of many properties of things. But the argument goes on to conclude that there are also properties of things that are independent of events. It is to this second class of properties that scientific attention is turned, and they become the units of scientific theories. This book is written from the standpoint of this second position.

It should be clear that I am not here identifying event with the property "time." We can, for example, employ time as a unit in a theory. Such an assertion as "The longer two groups are in contact, the greater will be the amount of cultural exchange between them" employs time as a unit in a theory of intergroup relations. A simple empirical test of the assertion (I will later call this a *prediction*) is to plot on one axis of a coordinate system the amount of time pairs of social groups have been in contact with each other, and on the second axis the sum of the cultural items originating in each member of the pair that are now found in the other. If the assertion is accurate, then there ought to be a correlation significantly greater than zero, and the slope of the line describing the relationship should be positive.

Attribute and Variable

Units of a theory may be either attributes or variables. This distinction turns out to be exceedingly important for the structure of tests used when a theory is confronted with empirical data. It is for this reason that the notions of *attribute* and *variable* will be elaborated in some detail.

An attribute is a property of a thing distinguished by the quality of being present. The thing always has this quality if the attribute is a property of the thing. All things having a given attribute property constitute a set of identities on that attribute property. All other things are in a set identified by the lack of the given attribute property. For example, social groups are defined as possessing the property of membership interaction; failure to possess this property will lead to a given collectivity being classified as a nongroup (e.g., an aggregate such as an occupational class).

A variable is a property of a thing that may be present in degree. There may be some of the property present or a lot of it. We may express the degree of presence of the variable property of a thing by either a cardinal or an ordinal scale. What is significant when we employ a vari-

Table 3-1

	ATTRIBUTE *A*	ALL *Not-A*s
ATTRIBUTE *B*	cell #1	cell #2
ALL *Not-B*s	cell #3	cell #4

able unit in a theory is that our attention becomes focused upon the amount or degree to which this property is present in the thing.

Let us now turn to the problem of the structure of a theory as it relates to the employment of attribute and variable units or combinations of both.

When a theory employs only attribute units, the minimum formulation of a relationship between two units in order to constitute a theoretical model is a 2 × 2 table of the form shown in Table 3-1. The importance of recognizing the 2 × 2 table as the complete formulation of a relationship between two attribute units is the following: Cell #1 has values on both attributes. This, obviously, is an important cell expressing the relationship between *A* and *B*. In social research we are often so optimistic that we are inclined to build models that imply, if not state, predictions like "All *A*s are *B*s" (e.g., delinquent children come from broken homes, working-class members vote Democratic). Our optimism is, of course, never realized, for there are always some *A*s that are not also *B*s, some *B*s that are not also *A*s, and if we look hard enough at the empirical domain we are modeling, we may even find some *not-A*s that are *not-B*s.[8]

If we really mean "All *A*s are *B*s," we may also mean "All *not-A*s are *not-B*s" (cell #4), and we may choose among several alternatives for expressing the relationships in cells #2 and #3. We may even specify the proportions with which *A*s and *B*s are associated in the four cells as follows: "90 percent of all *A*s are *B*s; 10 percent of *A*s are *not-B*s," and so on. Even in such instances, however, it is clear that the total set of any theoretical predictions made about the relationship between two attribute units must be made for all four cells of the table of relationships.

Let us now focus our attention on cell #1 of Table 3-1. This cell tells

---

[8]If optimism is not enough to encourage us to neglect cells #2, #3, and #4, we may employ research tricks to secure the same result, e.g., because we look for cases where there are values on both *A* and *B*, we would not include in our samples instances where both are absent and, if we find such instances, we are likely to "purify" the sample by casting them out. Thus, a person who refuses to respond to any questions in a survey research study may be a cell #4 case, although we do not know this for certain. We usually ignore such instances, after piously reporting their total number.

us that attribute *A* and *B* are simultaneously present. Suppose now that *A* and *B* are both variable units. This means that each may be measured on either an ordinal or an interval scale. If both are measured on an ordinal scale, then the standard research design is for the purpose of testing some theoretical prediction about the relationship between the rankings of both variables. If both variables are measured on an interval scale, then we make a test of some predicted relationship between the quantities of each. Finally, if one is measured on an ordinal scale and the other on an interval scale, we test the relationship between the ranking on one variable and the quantity on the other.

Note carefully that when we employ only variable units in a theory *we are focusing attention on only a single cell* of the basic 2 × 2 table, as represented in Figure 3-1. There is nothing in the theory that says anything about the other three cells of the table. Nor is it then appropriate to examine empirical data that would fall into the other three cells, for such data would have no relevance for our theory.

The point just made should not be confused with the situation portrayed in Figure 3-2. Here we have data displayed in a cell #1 situation where the variables can be each measured on an ordinal or an interval scale. You will note that there are some cases that fall at the zero value of *A,* some at the zero value of *B,* and one that has a zero value on both scales. These three classes are *not* instances of cell #2, #3, #4 entries. For example, the three cases of zero values on *A* where there are values on *B* are *not* cell #2 entries, which would be a *B, not-A* cell. The zero values on *A* are real values of *A* and should not be confused with the *not-A* category.

Another limitation to analysis is revealed when we employ a combination of attribute and variable units in a theory. This usually occurs when

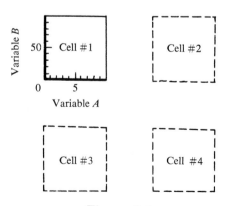

Figure 3-1

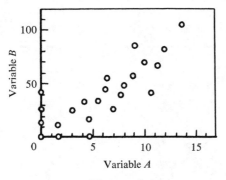

Figure 3-2

we draw some sort of broad attribute distinction and then ask, "How does the distribution of a given variable unit differ between these two attribute units?" The classical illustration of this theoretical problem is the controlled experiment in which one attribute unit is labeled *experimental group* and the other *control group*. These two groups are distinguished by the fact that one has the property "subject to some sort of experimental treatment" whereas the other has the property "excluded from the experimental treatment." We then seek to measure some variable characteristic of both groups in order to determine whether or not the experimental treatment makes a difference. This, of course, is just one illustration of theory employing attribute and variable units. In social science, contrasting sexes, social classes, urban-rural background, authoritarian-democratic atmosphere, and so on, have an identical structural format.

In terms now of our 2 × 2 table, this combination of attribute and variable units involves comparing the internal distribution of the population in cell #1 with the internal distribution of the population in cell #4. The situation is illustrated in Figure 3-3. You will note immediately that the structure of the comparison we are making is to contrast the distribution of the measured variable in cell #1 with the distribution of the variable in cell #4. The more customary way of presenting the comparison is to place the distributions (or statistics like means and standard deviations representing the distributions) in the same column, as shown in Figure 3-4. This, of course, obscures the fact that we are really comparing results in cell #1 with those in cell #4.

The logic of this design is impeccable. It insures that the special combination of "experimental-treatment" (*A—B*) is contrasted with "control—no treatment" (*Not-A—Not-B*). The design is intended to insure that there is complete independence of each combination of attributes from the other combination.

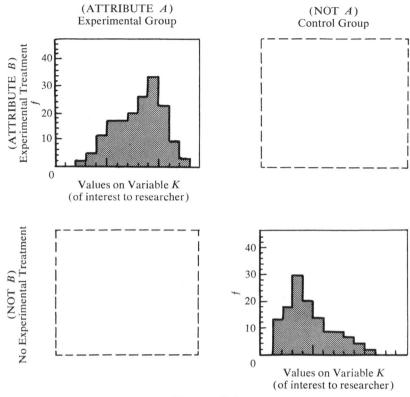

Figure 3-3

We may now summarize the consequences of employing attribute and variable units in building a theory. (1) When two attribute units are employed, the structure of the theory expressing their relationship leads to predictions about the empirical distribution of a sample population among all four cells of a 2 × 2 table. (2) When two variable units are employed in a theory, the structure of the theory expressing their relationship leads to predictions about the direction and degree of relationship between the variables only in cell #1 of a 2 × 2 table. (3) Where units employed in a theory are a mixture of attribute and variable units, the structure of the theory expressing their relationship leads to comparisons between cells #1 and #4 of a 2 × 2 table regarding the dissimilarity of the distribution of the variable in those two cells.

The point needs to be given strong emphasis. The kinds of units employed in building a theory, whether attribute or variable, make a difference in the structure of the theory, the kinds of predictions it generates, and the extensiveness of the tests that can be made of it.

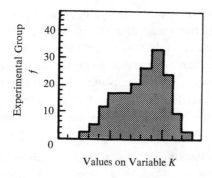

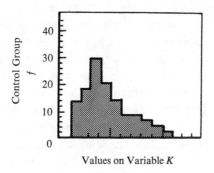

Figure 3-4

This distinction between attribute and variable units as they are related to the *structure* of a theory being tested departs radically from the usual treatment of the difference. It is common to consider attribute units as more primitive than variable units. Whenever available, variables are, therefore, preferred as being more exact and being more nearly attuned to a rigorous scientific discipline. In short, variable units are considered to have greater precision than attribute units. I am asserting that the problems of rigor and exactness are issues of measurement that *apply equally* to both attribute and variable units.[9] What distinguishes the two is their *function* in a theory and its testing, not their relative susceptibility to satisfying the criteria of measurement.

It should be recognized that a variable measure can always be converted to an attribute measure by turning the metric into class intervals. This is commonly done by using a mean or median to dichotomize a

---

[9]*Cf.* C. West Churchman and Philburn Ratoosh (eds.), *Measurement: Definition and Theories* (New York: John Wiley & Sons, 1959).

distribution of scores, or by employing other criteria to convert a continuous distribution into contiguous classes. However, attributes are seldom readily converted into variable measures. This, of course, argues for the practical utility of variable measures since they may be employed with greater versatility than attribute measures of the properties of units.

Lord Kelvin's statement made toward the close of the nineteenth century reminds us of the older view expressing preference for variable units.

> When you can measure what you are speaking about and express it in numbers, you know something about it; when you cannot express it in numbers, your knowledge is of a meager and unsatisfactory kind.[10]

Let it be clearly understood that I am not asserting a preference for either variable or attribute units in theory building. I do not join with Lord Kelvin and his many followers down to the present day who claim dial readings to be the goal of empirical description. Nor do I prefer more the humanistic position that the logic of human thinking is grounded in attribute distinctions that must perforce become the methodological cornerstone of theories in the social sciences.[11] My position is clearly that both attribute and variable units have their place in theory building. They are different places, however, and the working scientist is well advised to know what they are.

Real and Nominal

Philosophers distinguish between real and nominal definitions, and this contrast carries through much of the discussion in the philosophy of science. The contrast is expressed in contemporary literature on the philosophy of science as the distinction between a realist and an instrumentalist position. Logically, it would appear that units of a theory could also be placed into the real and nominal classes. This conclusion seems well taken and will be accepted as a starting point here.

We will agree that units of a theory, as properties of things, can be

---

[10] As quoted but not endorsed in G. Udny Yule and M. G. Kendall, *An Introduction to the Theory of Statistics,* 11th ed. (London: Charles Griffin and Co., 1937), p. 1. The Churchman-Ratoosh volume, cited in the previous footnote, contains many correctives to this Kelvinistic enthusiasm for variable units as the only respectable ones in science.

[11] The humanistic position is particularly well revealed in Max Weber, *The Methodology of Social Science* (New York: Free Press, 1949), where it is given a formal expression in what is identified as the ideal-type method.

called real units or nominal units. This distinction, however, rests only on the ability of the scientist ultimately to secure empirical indicators of the units he employs in his theories at the points where tests are made of the theories.[12]

Where there is some confidence that such empirical indicators are available or can be invented (i.e., instruments can be developed to produce empirically ascertainable traces), the unit of a theory for which the empirical indicator stands will be called a *real* unit. Where empirical indicators are not considered to be available to stand for a unit, it will be designated a *nominal* unit.

The distinction between a real and a nominal unit rests solely upon the probability of finding an empirical indicator for the unit. This means that every nominal unit has the potentiality of being converted into a real unit with progress in the technologies of developing empirical indicators. This point is a crucial one for the working scientist and probably is one of the important features of his outlook that distinguishes him from the philosopher of science. The working scientist is quite willing to gamble on finding or inventing empirical indicators for any units that he finds interesting enough to build into his theories. The philosopher of science may feel constrained by his beliefs about the essential and limited reality of things to hold that there is an immutable category of nominal units. The philosopher of science would probably never give a second thought to ink blots, but Dr. Rorschach did, much to the enrichment of the technologies of projective testing and to the increase of knowledge about the human psyche.

It has been one of the contentions of the extreme operationalists that only real units are properly employed in theory building. The reasoning is that unless one can ultimately produce a measurement operation to stand for each unit of a theory, the theory is untestable and therefore only entitled, at best, to the status of a theology.

This argument may be countered in a very simple way. The working scientist says that at some point, when confronting the empirical world, he needs indicators for the things he finds "out there." But, and this is critical, if he cranks up his curiosity only with those things for which he already has empirical indicators, then (1) he probably will never attempt to discover new empirical indicators (as he cannot think of looking for new things if his only tools of imagining are the representations of what he knows already), and (2) he probably will devote a majority of his research to wholly trivial problems. Consequently, when he builds the theories he will want to test, he will be perfectly willing to include in the

---

[12]Empirical indicators are discussed in Chapter 9.

theories nominal units, if they prove to be useful. The test of *useful* is simply whether or not the new theories give him something new or different to look for in the empirical world.

Now in order to crank up the scientific imagination in this way we have to pay a price. The price is that we will not be able to measure some parts of our theories because there are nominal units involved in them. This is not the only reason why a whole theoretical model is never completely tested by empirical research; it is an important one, however. This cost is a genuine one, for it means that portions of many theories cannot be tested.

I think, however, that the profits that derive from investment in nominal units to build theories far outweigh this cost. The profit lies in the imaginative extension of the domains of scientific curiosity, in ultimately adding to knowledge by increasing the realms of the known and the knowable, and in pointing out more accurately the realms of the unknown.

Such units of social science theories as id, ego, anomie, tele, syntality, conflict, power, charisma, subjective probability, maximization, culture, and society have played important roles in the development of scientific theories in psychology, sociology, political science, economics, and anthropology. Each of these is a nominal unit denoting either a presumed thing or a presumed process characterizing social life. The unit *mass* is a nominal unit of physics that is central to theories in that science, and I am certain that each scientific discipline has its comparable nominal units. The point is that working scientists could not do without nominal units.

The issue for the working researcher is not to insist that theories contain only real units. The issue is rather to insist that the structure of theories be clearly understood so that the functions of nominal units in them will be readily recognized. It is true that empirical tests are made only of real units and their interactions. It is equally true that whole theories often contain nominal units that, although presently beyond empirical reach, are nevertheless essential to the theory. Their essentiality rests on the fact that understanding of the real units and their behaviors is increased when the nominal units are included in the theory.

The problem of nominal and real units will arise again when we examine the propositions and hypotheses of a theory in Chapters 8 and 10 and when we turn to empirical indicators in Chapter 9. For the purposes of the present discussion it is sufficient to assert that we will make a place for both nominal and real units in building theories.[13]

---

[13]It should be noted that a theory built solely of nominal units can be accorded only the status of a theology, not that of a scientific theory. The two differ, however, only in the kinds of units each contains and not in logic of construction or coherence of structure.

Primitive and Sophisticated

When the philosopher of science deals with logical structures he is constrained to point out that a starting point upon which defined categories rest is one or more undefined or primitive terms. This is the familiar process of following a line of regression back to a starting point, which starting point is an assertion of faith rather than something definable in still other terms. For if this starting point can be defined in still other terms, then they and not it are the primitive starting points.

In an analogous way we may think of units of a theory as being primitive in the sense of undefined starting points. What I will mean by a *primitive* unit is that it is undefined. This distinguishes any such unit from another category I will call *sophisticated* units, by which I mean that they are defined units.

A first reaction to this distinction is that we need not give any place to primitive units in theory building because we can always *arbitrarily* define any unit and therefore put it in the category of the sophisticated. This, of course, is true if we follow the usual procedure of the philosopher of science. We could then build any theory on a foundation of primitive *terms,* using only sophisticated *units* that are defined in such terms. If we turn to the working researcher, however, we find that he does not quite do this. What he very often does instead (but not always because not all his analytical problems are the same) is put an unknown X into his theory and then spend his time trying to discover this X. The scientist is perfectly willing to use a primitive unit precisely because it then presents him with an important research problem to turn X into a sophisticated unit of his theory.

What are the circumstances under which the scientist will employ primitive units in his theories? These circumstances are several. The first is when there is some empirical finding that is not attached to a theory. The second occurs when a new theory is emerging. Let us briefly examine these two circumstances.

Many of the empirical findings of scientific researchers are extensions beyond predicted findings demanded by tests of a starting theory. The scientist then is faced with the need for making some sense out of his observations. A typical way to do this is to say, "There is something, X, that must be introduced into my theory to account for this finding." When this X is introduced, the scientist may treat it as a primitive unit or he may attempt to make it into a sophisticated unit. In either event, however, he starts with X as a primitive unit. When Dr. Fleming was confronted with some odd stuff under his microscope, he was first inclined to consider it an accident of the research process. He then said, in effect, there is some *X* here that is somehow connected with what appears in the field of the microscope. When his attention turned to explicating this *X,* we were given the gift of penicillin. The point is, of course, that the admission of a unit as a primitive unit into a theory immediately cries out for translation into a sophisticated unit. But this is done only by starting with a primitive unit.

The employment of primitive units in building a new theory occurs in one of the generalizing stages of the scientific enterprise. This happens as follows. Suppose the scientist is confronted with several findings that operationally cannot be quite the same things. That is, the operations by which the empirical indicators were measured were not identical. The scientist then looks at these findings and in effect asks, "Is there anything in common among these findings? Do these findings somehow or other have a common core because they are really empirical indicators of the same thing or unit?" The answer to this question may simply be a name applied to this thing, an identifying label that serves to tag it but not to define it. Once this tagging is done, the scientist is then in a position to focus attention on the tagged thing and bring it into a new theory as a nominal or a real unit.

A beautiful example of using primitive units in theory building is revealed any time factor analysis is employed in research. The fundamental characteristic of factor analysis as a statistical technique is that it can take an assortment of empirical indicators (like tests, for example) and objectively demonstrate which indicators sort together with which others, and what is the minimum number of distinctive groups into which all used indicators can be sorted. The outcome of this objective sorting process is to produce factors that are simply numbered or lettered or tagged with a name. Either number or letter will serve just as well, but the scientist immediately begins to examine those empirical indicators that load heavily on a given factor and tries to generalize a descriptive term that will denote his guess as to what those empirical indicators have in common. This generalized descriptive term then becomes a primitive unit of a new theory and undergoes whatever transformations are necessary to convert it into a sophisticated unit in order that the new theory may be built.[14]

We may now summarize what appears to be an essential difference between a philosopher of science and a working scientist in their treat-

[14]A good example is Raymond B. Cattell, H. Breul, and H. Parker Hartman, "An Attempt at More Refined Definition of the Cultural Dimensions of Syntality in Modern Nations," *American Sociological Review,* 17:408–421 (Aug. 1952).

ment of the primitive unit. The scientist often starts with empirical observations from which he generalizes a primitive unit. The philosopher of science starts in his mind with a primitive unit. Both proceed beyond this point in identical manners to build a theory by incorporating the primitive unit or converting it into a sophisticated one. The difference, then, is whether one starts with the empirical world to generate a primitive unit or within the mind with an imagined primitive unit. I think it makes a real difference in what kind of theory emerges, even though the processes of theory building beyond the state of designating a primitive unit is the same for both philosopher and scientist.

Collective and Member

One final general distinction needs to be kept in mind. It is the difference between a class considered as a unit and the individual members of that class being treated as units. In mathematical terms this is the distinction we draw between a set and elements composing the set. The purpose of making this distinction is simple. We need some way to designate many things sharing at least one common characteristic and to be able to treat them as a unit in a theory. Under other circumstances we may want to treat one or more of the individual things as a unit by itself, independently by the fact that it shares membership in some collective unit by virtue of having at least one characteristic in common with all other members.

For this distinction between set and element we will employ the somewhat more graphic labels popularized by Professor Paul F. Lazarsfeld. He calls the set a *collective* and the element a *member*.[15]

There is an exceedingly practical consequence of making the distinction between collective and member. It calls the theorist-researcher's attention to the fact that there may be serious logical dangers in building theories that deal simultaneously with collective and member units. This danger is not true of all theories, but it does exist for some, and where the logical impasse is possible, the difference between collective and member will aid in showing it up. For example, Robinson has pointed out the logical dangers of using ecological correlations based on collective units

[15]See Paul F. Lazarsfeld and Herbert Menzel, "On the Relation Between Individual and Collective Properties," in A. Etzioni (ed.), *Complex Organizations: A Sociological Reader* (New York: Holt, Rinehart & Winston, 1961), pp. 422–440.

to predict the behaviors of members of these same collective units. He demonstrated that correlations based upon measures of a collective that give rise to what he calls ecological correlations have different values than the correlations based upon measures of the members composing the collectives. He concluded,

> The relation between ecological and individual correlations . . . provides a definite answer to whether ecological correlations can validly be used as substitutes for individual correlations. They cannot.[16]

The collective-member distinction really underlies the intellectual issue called *reductionism,* which seems such a hardy perennial in the social sciences. Largely for imperialistic reasons each social-science discipline seeks to keep its theory from being "debased" to a different level of explanation. It is especially notable that the disciplines seem to have a fear that they can ultimately be shown to be mere branches of psychology and that all social-science theory rests upon psychological theory. Durkheim, for example, raised this battle cry for sociology and made it an article of faith that a sociologist must swear to use only "social facts" in doing sociology.[17]

Whatever intellectual imperialistic purposes such admonitions may serve (and they are useful as tools of academic imperialism), the ranting against reductionism contributes nothing to the issue of whether or not there is some linkage among the various levels of analysis. We can see the possibility that each member of a collective may itself be a collective for its interior member units. Thus, one can analytically go from society to group to person to organs to cells to atoms. What becomes a critical question is how these levels of analysis link with each other between adjacent levels and how they link up between levels separated by one or more intervening ones. I will attempt a straightforward answer to this question at the end of Chapter 5, "Laws of Interaction" and in Chapter 6, "Boundaries." The distinction between collective and member turns out to be useful in sorting out the levels of units that enter into a theory.

---

[16]W. S. Robinson, "Ecological Correlations and the Behavior of Individuals," *American Sociological Review,* 15:351–357 (June 1950), p. 357. This paper stimulated a number of others that addressed the identical problem with good effect. See, for example, L. A. Goodman, "Ecological Regression and Behavior of Individuals," *American Sociological Review,* 18:663–664 (Dec. 1953); L. A. Goodman, "Some Alternatives to Ecological Correlation," *American Journal of Sociology,* 64:610–625 (May 1959); and O. D. Duncan and B. Davis, "An Alternative to Ecological Correlation," *American Sociological Review,* 18:665–666 (Dec. 1953).

[17]Emile Durkheim, *The Rules of Sociological Method* (New York: Free Press, 1950).

CHAPTER FOUR

Units of a Theory

Because any real "machine" has an infinity of variables, from which different observers (with different aims) may reasonably make an infinity of different selections, there must first be given an observer. . . ; a system is then defined as any set of variables that he selects from those available on the real "machine." It is thus a list nominated by the observer . . .

—W. ROSS ASHBY, *Design for a Brain*

My next step is to allow my notion of thing to range from dated sense-data, to physical events, to material objects, and to arbitrary classes of things and organized classes of things, so that my thing can be any thing. Envisaging thing in this way will make room for models being concrete or abstract to various degrees and in various manners.

—Y. R. CHAO, "Models in Linguistics and Models in General," in E. Nagel, P. Suppes, and A. Tarski (eds.), *Logic, Methodology and Philosophy of Science*

IT HAS BEEN my long-held conviction that a significant block to understanding theory building has been the attempt to make the units employed fit the requirements of the logics involved in developing and testing a model. This had led philosophers of science to be preoccupied with those formal characteristics of units that conform with logical operations. For example, as we saw in the preceding chapter, philosophers have been concerned with the realist-instrumentalist issue. This is a natural matter of concern if attention if focused solely on the uses of a theoretical model. But we have been able to relegate the issue to the realm of "some initial considerations," important only as a starting point, after which we can turn to consider units of a theory in their own right.

A scientist looks at things in the world of observation and then attempts to model their interactions. The issue for the scientist is whether or not at the starting point of building a model there are any constraints on the units he may employ. The scientist is less interested than the philosopher in how the units chosen to build a theory will conform with logical operations. To the scientist the issue is rather how the units employed relate to the things he observes. Chao is most accurate in the heading quotation when he concludes that for the scientist, "my thing can be any thing." This unconstrained willingness to admit all possible units into a scientific model provides the widest range of opportunities for theory building.

There would be utter chaos if no order existed among the possible units available for developing a model. The probability of replication of research would be materially lowered as well. Fortunately, it is possible to classify the units employed in behavioral theory into a limited set of types and to then examine the manner in which mixed types may be incorporated into the same model.

Initially in this chapter a typology of units of theories is developed that has as one of its main purposes to reach conclusions about the kinds of units that can and cannot go together in the same theoretical model. Attention turns next to a consideration of descriptive research and the logical and statistical technologies available for the discovery of new units to be employed in theories. The discussion then takes up the question of parsimony in the number of units to be employed in a given model and how to apply statistical tests of parsimony. Finally a few loose ends are tucked into the end of the chapter to bring us back to the big problem highlighted in the opening quotation from Ashby, that the units of a theoretical model constitute "a list nominated by the observer."

Types of Units (EARSS)

The previous chapter started with the assertion that the units of a theory are properties of things rather than the things themselves. We are now in a position to undertake a classification of such properties. This is a classification of all sophisticated units, with only those further limitations as noted that apply to summative kinds of units.

I will label and describe five types of units for which the mis-spelling of *ears* (EARSS) provides a useful mnemonic device: enumerative unit (E), associative unit (A), relational unit (R), statistical unit (S), and summative unit (S).

Enumerative Unit (E)

An enumerative unit is a property characteristic of a thing in all its conditions. That is, regardless of the condition of the thing that can be observed or imagined, it will always have that property. We mean by the notion of "condition" all the states under which the thing will be found. In Chapter 7 specific consideration will be given to system states as a feature of theories. At this point we can work with the equivalence of *condition* and *system state* without further specification.

The universality with which all members of the set of an enumerative unit possess the property holds for either attribute or variable enumerative units. Where this property is an attribute, then it is always present. Indeed, by its very presence, it can become the shorthand identifying tag for the entire thing. Where the enumerative unit is a variable, then a count among all the sample members of the thing determines *how much* of the enumerative unit each possesses. It is this counting process associated with an enumerative unit that gives rise to its name. Examples of enumerative units are shown in Table 4-1.

For attribute enumerative units the unit designation may become the basic criterion for sorting out the sample composed of such units. Thus, we may seek a sample of social groups with closed boundaries or with limited purposes or with both. We may choose a sample of males or a sample of persons with strong motivation to conform to social expectations. In each instance, all things accepted into the sample must possess the attribute or attributes being counted. In a similar way, when we use variable enumerative units it will be noticed that we count how much of the unit is a property of the thing. We determine how much cohesion the group exhibits (and if the answer is none, then it is not a group) or how many members compose it. We measure how old a person is or the number of acts in which he has engaged during a given unit of time.

The enumerative unit is universal—the characteristic property is always present in the thing and is counted in any sample of the things under

Table 4-1

	THINGS	ENUMERATIVE UNITS (PROPERTY OF THING)
ATTRIBUTES	Social Group	Boundary Purpose
	Person	Sex Motivation
VARIABLES	Social Group	Cohesion Size
	Person	Age Social Act

investigation. This universality is a significant feature of enumerative units for it serves to distinguish this type of unit from an associative (A) unit. There can never be a zero value for or a sample member who does not exhibit the characteristic of an enumerative unit. There can be for associative units. Thus, education is an associative unit for a thing labeled *person* because when measured by formal education, some persons may have none.

There are two complementary features, then, of enumerative units. (1) The property is universally present in all states of the thing. (2) This means that any unit for which there is a zero value or an absent condition is not an enumerative unit.

Associative Unit (A)

An associative unit is a property characteristic of a thing in only some of its conditions. In all respects save one it is identical to an enumerative unit. The one difference is that there is a real zero or absent value for associative units.

The existence of a zero value for a unit is a critical feature of that unit. There are consequences, for example, for measurements that relate to the possibility of a zero value existing for a unit. There are other kinds of consequences in which we have both positive and negative values of the unit. Does the value of the unit pass through zero in going from positive to negative values, or vice versa? Or looked at another way, if there is the possibility of a zero value of the unit, then do we also entertain the possibility that there are negative values as well? None of these issues are germane to enumerative units. These issues are very important, however, to associative units and the kinds of models in which they are employed.

The convention of calling these units *associative* units has been adopted because it seems to describe adequately the fact that such units are characteristic properties of some but not all states of the thing. They are associated, in other words, with the thing partially and under limited conditions.

Table 4-2 illustrates associative units. It should be understood that the illustrations used here and with the discussion of the other types of units are by no means exhaustive.

For each of the illustrative associative units shown in the table, there is a possibility that the value of the unit may be zero or negative, or both, in one or more states of the thing. There is the possibility, for example, that a social group operates at least some of the time without reference to

Table 4-2

	THINGS	ASSOCIATIVE UNITS
ATTRIBUTES	Social Group	Leadership Myths
ATTRIBUTES	Person	Affective Response Productive Skill
VARIABLES	Social Group	Bonded Indebtedness Degree of Stability
VARIABLES	Person	Formal Education Income

myths characteristic of it. A person may exhibit positive, negative, or no affect in a given situation or action, or we may count the individual's skill in doing productive work as ranging from high skill to no skill (the zero value in this instance). We might even find a metric for measuring affective response, in which case we could consider this a variable associative unit, ranging in values from strong positive through zero (neutral) to strong negative. When we examine the variable associative units of Table 4-2, we can see that a group defined as a governmental unit may either have or have not a bonded indebtedness, the exact amount of which may be measured on a dollar scale. We may also measure a group's stability on an interval or ordinal scale (by counting membership turnover, for example) to find whether it is at all stable and, if so, to what degree. Finally, we may use years of formal schooling to measure an individual's education, with none being the zero point on the scale, and do the same thing for a person's income, passing through a zero point to negative values if we refine the associative unit to call it *net income*.

All these illustrative associative units have zero values, and some have negative values. This point will become especially pertinent when we consider any whole theory. Whenever we employ associative units in a theory, we may expect that there will be some states of the system being modeled in which these associative units will have zero values or even go to negative values.

The zero value becomes important for two reasons. (1) It first of all means that any predictions we make about the system must cover those states of the system in which the incorporated associative units go to zero or become negative. Thus, when we employ associative units, we automatically force our predictions about the theoretical system to include states in which these units really go to zero or take on negative values.

This becomes one test of the completeness of the predictions generated by the theory. (2) The empirical-description side of the coin is also important here. Suppose we describe an empirical situation in which a property of a thing has a zero value for that situation (e.g., the property is denoted by an associative unit). Then we would probably build a theory completely excluding this property, unless we had one or more additional empirical situations to describe in which the property had a nonzero value. Thus, associative units may be excluded from a theory simply because we have poor description of the empirical world, and happened, by chance, to pick situations to describe in which the excluded associative unit had a zero value. Indeed, one of the ways in which we formally admit this kind of error is to assign the title *intervening variable* to such an associative unit when we discover some positive or negative values for it later on. A more extended treatment of intervening variable appears later in this chapter, in the discussion of parsimony in the number of units employed in a theory.

To summarize, there is one outstanding feature of an associative unit: it must be able to have a zero, or nonpresent, value. Enumerative and associative units have been distinguished on the basis of the zero value assignable to the latter. Attention now turns to consider three additional types of units whose definition moves into entirely new dimensions.

Relational Unit (R)

A relational unit is a property characteristic of a thing that can be determined only by the relation among properties. These relations may be of two general sorts. The first is the relation based on *interaction* among properties, as when we might consider subordination to be a property of a person *when* he is in interaction with a superior. The second form of relation is based on the *combination* of properties, as when we examine the sex ratio (ratio of males to females) of a population group.

A relational unit, then, identifies a property of a thing by calling attention to the fact that the property is derivable from at least two other properties. For example, a subordinate and a superior, when they interact, have as an outcome one property called *subordination*. The properties of being a superior and of being a subordinate, when taken together, produce the property of a relationship called *subordination*. Similarly, the property "male," and the property "female" (when they combine, *not* interact!) produce the property "sex ratio."

It is apparent that a relational unit is more complex than an enumerative or an associative one. Its very complexity is a distinct advantage in building theories about social phenomena, which tend to be complex. Employment of a relational unit really permits us to make one term stand for two properties of a thing. At the same time we sometimes are prone to lose sight of this and reify the relational unit, obscuring the fact that it is not itself a property of a thing but a property of two or more properties of things. For example, in sociology we may speak of an anomic individual and assume that the person has the property of anomie. Actually, of course, we mean that the attitudes held by the person toward norms of a social group combine or interact in a way that is characterized as anomic—the interaction of personal attitudes and social norms produces the attitude of normlessness held by the person.

Since several examples have been used to describe relational units, no illustrative table will be employed. Instead, I will underscore the fact that such units are commonly employed in the behavioral sciences without recognition of their characteristic form. We will employ a unit like *ethnocentrism* as though it were a property of a group when what we mean is that it is the consequence of the ratio of group members' preference for fellow members over other-group members. We analyze sibling rivalry and tend to forget that the term designates a condition of relations between siblings as a consequence of the relations of each to his parents. We use the term *status* without recognizing that it arises only in the comparison among two or more individuals and that its achievement or ascription involves an interaction between an evaluator, a standard, and the subject of evaluation. We discourse about elites or power elites and sometimes lose sight of the fact that a nonelite, and relations with it, are necessary to make sense out of the property "elite."

Relational units are defined as a property of two or more properties of things. Note that both properties and things can be plural. In the example of sibling rivalry, the property of the sibling relationship and the relation of each child to each parent are all summed up in the term, giving us plural properties (child-child relationship, parent-child relationship) and plural things, children and parents. The price we pay for having available single relational units to sum up two or more properties of things is that we are likely to ignore the summing-up feature of the unit. This may be a heavy cost to the theorist-researcher, as his theory may be incomplete and his empirical indicators inaccurate. This, of course, does not argue against the use of relational units in building theories. Indeed, I am claiming they are exceptionally useful. It should be recognized, however, that they may be misused.

In the behavioral sciences we are particularly addicted to the use of relational units in building theory because such units cover so much with so little effort. It is well to be clear in understanding the complex character of such units when they are employed. If we are not clear, we can often pass off tautologies for conclusions, viz., if we assert that a frontier society typically has a very high sex ratio (ratio of males to females) and is a characteristically male society, we have said the same thing twice under the guise of generalizing.[1]

Statistical Unit (S)

A statistical unit is a property of a thing that summarizes the distribution of that property in the thing. A statistical unit derives its name from the fact that we have adopted statistical terminology dealing with measures of central tendency or of dispersion as the nomenclature for statistical units. For example, the mean or median income of a population group may be employed as the unit of study, and this measure may be taken to stand for income distribution in the group as a whole. Or we might designate a group being studied as *heterogeneous* on some property and proceed to contrast it with a *homogeneous* group on the same property, thus taking into account the differential dispersion of the property in the two groups.

In general we can distinguish three classes of statistical units: (1) units summarizing a *central tendency* in the distribution of a property; (2) units summarizing the *dispersion* of a property; and (3) units locating things by their *relative position* in a distribution of a property. Median income, as noted, may be taken to stand for the income distribution of an entire group and used as an analytical unit in theories about income, its distribution, and its relations to other social phenomena. Dispersion of a property may be summarized in a statistical unit that stands for the property in the group as a whole, as when a population group is designated as culturally unitary or culturally diverse, or an individual as moody or stable. Finally, we often use statistical units to designate relative position, employing terms

[1]Examples abound, even in good textbooks. "Some communities are organized around a few occupations which engage chiefly one sex. For example, mining, cattle raising, or lumbering will attract a disproportionate number of males. Such areas have extremely high sex ratios." George A. Lundberg, Clarence C. Schrag, and Otto N. Larsen, *Sociology* (New York: Harper & Row, 1954), p. 83. Or consider the following conclusions about the adaptation and integration of several groups (both being relational units): "In the long run, maladaptation will lead to malintegration." Harry C. Bredemeir and Richard M. Stephensen, *The Analysis of Social Systems* (New York: Holt, Rinehart & Winston, 1962), p. 57.

like *high status* or *underachiever* to denote a property of an individual or *middle class* and *underdeveloped* to denote a property of a group.

In employing statistical units for analytical purposes, we have to recognize and be familiar with the underlying statistical reasoning that gives particular meaning to each of the three classes of statistical units. When we employ any notion of central tendency, we assume that a property can be best summarized by its most common value (mode) or its middle value (median) or its average value (mean). When we use a central-tendency measure as a unit for describing a property, we become very conscious of its limitations in describing the dispersion feature of the property.

When dispersion-type statistical units are used, we give up the opportunity to express the central tendency in the population being measured. For example, if we were to take income range to measure the homogeneity or heterogeneity of residents of suburbs, with no further specification of statistical unit, we would be uncertain regarding the most representative incomes in the suburbs being studied.

When ranking or relative-position statistical units are used, they imply but do not necessarily designate the structure within which the position is to be found. Thus a group designated *middle class* may suggest a pretty good notion of the class structure within which this unit lies. Suppose, however, we converted measures of intelligence to standard scores and then designated percentile rank for individuals in standard scores. In the second instance we know the structure of percentile ranks to sum from zero to 100, but because we have used standard scores, we do not know from our percentile rankings what the actual scores were. The standard scores would facilitate comparisons between Navajo and white American children, for example, by contrasting the proportions of each to be found in each percentile rank, but we would not know from this information what relationships the actual scores of the two groups bore to each other.

In general, statistical units are very convenient units to employ in research and theory building. Indeed, we habitually use this kind of unit largely because we have become sophisticated in putting much of the data of the empirical world into statistical form and it seems but natural that we retain this form in our analytical units.

It should be clear that statistical units have their special usefulness as well as their unique limitations. Within their own province such units yield excellent results when employed in theory building. But again, as with all the types of units we are describing, there is no logical reason for preferring statistical units over other types.

Summative Unit (S)

The final class of units of a theory are designated *summative* units. I mean by a summative unit that it is a global unit that stands for an entire complex thing. Such global units are common in the behavioral sciences. It has become a fixture in recent American sociology to speak of the "mass society"; in economics we employ the designation "underdeveloped economy" to denote a wide set of properties that characterize such an economy; in psychology a summative unit is represented by the "other-directed" personality; and in anthropology such an analytical unit as "extended-kinship system" is a summative unit.

The central feature of a summative unit is that it seems to draw together a number of different properties of a thing and gives them a label that highlights one of the more important. A mass society is massive, but it also is heterogeneous, pluralistic, diffuse in goals, and so on. The unit *mass society* comes to stand for all of these properties and many more. We even feel that we can characterize an entire society as a mass society and then proceed to compare it with a class society or a caste society, using two additional summative units to form the comparison.

Analytically a summative unit is one having the property that derives from the interaction among a number of other properties. Without specifying what these other properties are, or without indicating how and under what circumstances they interact, we add them all up in a summative unit. Thus, a summative unit has the characteristic of meaning a great deal, much of which is ill-defined or unspecified. A considerable body of social-science literature is filled with such units. We feel no hesitancy in designating societies as gemeinschaft or gesellschaft types, as folk or urban, as sacred or secular. These units convey a great deal of meaning in communication, although they sometimes vary in content. In any event, a summative unit is always diffuse rather than precise, and implies much more than it states in its definition.

What, if anything, can be done with summative units when they are employed in theory building? It will be recalled that summative units are global and serve to characterize a bundle of properties at one time. Summative units are thus the most complex of all, as there is really no limit to the number of properties being characterized or to the ways in which these properties are related to each other. May we then employ such units in our theories with any profit or utility?

My answer is no. Such units are useless in theories and theoretical models that are designed for the purpose of testing propositions. Summative units have their function in a scientific discipline but not in relation to theoretical models.

Let us start with a quotation from Paul Lazarsfeld.

All the social sciences deal with concepts that seem somewhat vague. Who can, in practice, recognize an extrovert personality? Who has not read many discussions as to the real meaning of public opinion? Who can say precisely what a folk society is? There are various reasons why the social scientists' language has so many of these terms. . . . In some cases we can, by the nature of the concept, only observe symptoms, behind which we assume a more permanent reality. This would be true, for example, in the case of personality notions. In other matters the object of investigation is so vast that we can analyze only certain aspects of it: notions like patterns of culture of *Zeitgeist* belong here. For still other purposes the problem itself seems to require a looser kind of formulation: whenever we study adjustments—e.g., in marriage, in job performance, or in standard of living—we find that large numbers of actual solutions may serve the same functional purpose.

This peculiarity of the social scientists' intellectual tools has been deplored by some, considered as unavoidable by others. Most of all, however, it has been covered with nomenclature. Syndromes, genotypes, underlying concepts, hypothetical constructs, and many other terms have been used. It is hard to say to what extent we have today a clear formulation of the problem behind all these terms, let alone clear directions on how to deal with them in the pursuit of empirical research. And yet it is in the course of actual investigations that some clarification is most needed. For if we have to decide whether there is increased bureaucratization in government, or whether city life makes people progressively neurotic, we must get some measures of these tendencies. And whatever index we use, we make implicit assumptions about the meaning of the kinds of terms we have just exemplified.[2]

This quotation calls our attention to some of the shortcomings of summative units, at the same time alerting us to the fact that such units are commonplace in the social sciences.

The special usefulness of summative units is revealed by examining the structure of education in any behavioral-science discipline and probably in others as well. The beginning student is given a grasp of a field through contact with the summative units employed herein. From this he

[2]Paul F. Lazarsfeld, "Latent Structure Analysis," in *Formulations of the Person and the Social Context,* vol. 3 of Sigmund Koch (ed.), *Psychology: A Study of a Science* (New York: McGraw-Hill, 1959), p. 477. Used by permission of McGraw-Hill.

gets a global view of what his discipline is all about and may even begin
to feel that he understands the content of the theories with which he deals.
In advanced instruction, attention typically shifts to more restricted types
of units and the global grasp of the subject matter of the discipline becomes splintered into bits of intensive knowledge that deal with only parts
of the familiar summative units. There is thus a pedagogical purpose
served by the use of summative units that is useful and efficient. At the
same time, developed sophistication in an intellectual discipline leads to
the substitution of the first four types of units of analysis for summative
ones.

Complex Units

It is possible that a unit employed in a theory may satisfy the definition of two or more classes of units at the same time. For example, the
unit *sex ratio* (ratio of males to females in a group) clearly belongs to the
relational class of units. This same unit may be a member of the enumerative class if we take sex ratio to stand for a characteristic of a group, or it
may be classified as an associative unit if it is a property of a group that
includes the possibility of being an all-female group (i.e., where the sex
ratio = 0). Finally, the sex ratio may be a statistical unit if comparisons
are made among groups according to the value of the sex ratio of each.
There is no essential problem in keeping clear the distinctive ways in
which the same unit may be classified into the four classes of units. What
is not always kept in view is the fact that the same named unit may have a
different meaning if it moves from one class to another. This, of course,
alerts the theorist to the need for distinguishing between the name used for
a unit and the context in which it is employed. Take again the unit *sex
ratio*. In a comparative study of birth rates, the sex ratio could be a
relational unit and, in this context, would denote the exposure opportunities that relate to intercourse probabilities and hence conception. In a
study determining the ecological structure of a city, on the other hand, the
sex ratio could be used as a statistical unit whose value for census tracts,
for example, would aid in locating distinctive types of neighborhoods.
The essential caution to keep in mind is that the same unit built into
one theory may have a different usage in another theory, even though an
identical name is used in each case. A significant aid in sorting out these
differences is the EARSS classification of units of a theoretical model.
When a named unit falls into more than one class, this fact may be taken

as a signal to test whether it is then being used differently in the respective models in which it is employed.

The Fit of Units with Each Other

Quite aside from the usefulness in research and theory building that comes from classifying units of analysis, there is another consequence to consider. Is it possible that we can mix and match different types of units in our theoretical models, or must we be restricted in some way because of the nature of the units themselves? This is a pertinent question, for if any restrictions exist, this means that we have to find the rules governing them in order to build permissible theories and avoid the logically inadmissible.

There is no difficulty in perceiving that theories built up of identical types of units present no analytical problems. We would feel logically comfortable if a theory had only enumerative or only associative units employed in it, for example. Similarly we would not blanch if we were presented with a theory employing only relational units or statistical units but *not* summative units. Essentially the notion of logical consistency seems to be the criterion employed when we accept a theory composed of a single type of unit.

The effect of employing only enumerative units results in the use of just the first quadrant of a Cartesian coordinate system, in a two-unit theory. In this quadrant all possible values of the two units can be plotted, and because they are enumerative units, neither has a zero value or negative values. Figure 4-1 illustrates where our analytical attention is

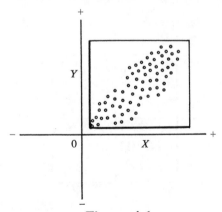

Figure 4-1

focused. In principle, this can be extended to *n*-dimensional coordinate systems with the analogous quadrant being populated, although only the two-dimensional situation has been illustrated in Figure 4-1.

In a similar fashion the effect of building a theory of only associative units may be visualized. With a two-unit theory all four quadrants of a Cartesian coordinate system would be utilized, as shown in Figure 4-2.

Similarly, combining enumerative with associative units in a single theory results in the spread of data through two of the four quadrants of a Cartesian system. This is portrayed in Figure 4-3.

In general, we may conclude that both enumerative and associative units may be employed without restriction in the same theory either together or exclusively.

Relational units, as we have seen, are in themselves complex, being the property derived from the interaction or combination of two or more other properties. How then may relational units be used in conjunction with other types of units? It seems clear that relational units may be employed exclusively in a theory with no difficulty. Indeed, a good deal of social-science theory is built out of relational units. For example, it is possible to build a theory about subordination and sibling rivalry, both units being themselves relational units. We could theorize that those who experience minimum sibling rivalry as children in other than single-child families will exhibit the most acceptant behaviors in situations demanding subordination as adults. The assumption is that learning and accepting a place in a birth-ordered social system is positively socializing with respect to behaving like a subordinate as an adult.

Relational units can also be combined with either enumerative or

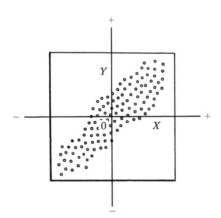

Figure 4-2

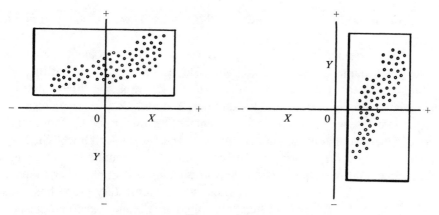

Figure 4-3

associative units in the same theory. Logic would suggest that if relational units are the product of two or more properties of things, and these properties are themselves either the elementary enumerative or associative properties, then there should be no difficulty in using relational units with either enumerative or associative units. This in fact is the case.

It is of particular interest to note the special research design used when relational units (made up of the combination or interaction of enumerative and associative units) are combined with other enumerative or associative units. This results in a trait-analysis format. That is, the relational unit is assigned the status of dependent unit in the design, and we then proceed to use enumerative or associative units as the units whose values predict the values of the relational unit. Thus, we may use the relational unit *leadership* as the dependent unit and attempt in the theory and its related research to account for the variance in the amount of leadership that may be associated with such units as birth order, education, and age. The purpose of such research is to find those traits that seem to account for the unit values of the relational unit, leadership.

One of the obvious logical impasses that is almost never recognized in research is the attempt to break down the dependent relational unit through a theory that relates it to the component properties of which it is constituted. For example, suppose we took intelligence as the dependent relational unit (it does, in any system, turn out to be a relational unit determined by the combination or interaction of primary mental abilities) and correlated it with number ability or verbal ability. When we do this, we are, in effect, guaranteeing a correlation because the enumerative units are, in their interaction with others, the components of the relational unit whose values we consider dependent upon the identical enumerative units. Put another way, it we relate a thing to itself, we are bound to find a correlation.[3]

Self-correlation should not be confused with the goal of parsing a complex relational unit into its parts. There is a very important theory-building research activity that is directed at finding the constituent units of a relational one. Some very seminal research and the developments of a first-rate research technology have centered on this problem. For example, when Thurstone sought out the "primary mental abilities" he was trying to find the minimum number of enumerative units that taken together would describe intelligence, an obvious and important relational unit. Thus, the research goal was to find the elementary properties, and their mode of combination, that constitute the relational unit *intelligence*. In attacking this problem Thurstone developed multiple-factor analysis as an exceptionally useful and important research technology addressed to this parsing problem. Particular attention to this issue occurs in a succeeding section of this chapter dealing with discovering new units of analysis.

[3]Following is an example of self-correlation involved in employing a relational unit based upon combination. You will note that the author reported the correlation between his composite measure and the four individual measures making up this composite. It is not surprising that these self-correlations are among the highest in the table.

Matrix of Intercorrelations of Variables Relating to Eminence for 566 Highly Visible APA Members Who Received Their Doctoral Degress in the Period 1930–44

	(1)	(2)	(3)	(4)	(5)	(6)	(7)	(8)
(1) APA Offices Held								
(2) Total *Psych. Abstracts* Counts	.32							
(3) 1950–53 *Psych. Abstracts* Counts	.20	.52						
(4) *Annual Review* Citations	.31	.42	.63					
(5) Journal Citation Counts	.39	.47	.36	.61				
(6) Composite of 1, 3, 4, 5	.80	.53	.52	.71	.82			
(7) No. of votes received	.64	.47	.43	.58	.68	.81		
(8) Current Ph.D. Students	.11	.19	.23	.18	.18	.20	.23	
(9) Total Ph.D. Students	.23	.25	.17	.29	.32	.35	.34	.63

From K. E. Clark, "Studies of Faculty Evaluation," in *Studies of College Faculty* (Boulder, Colo.: Western Interstate Commission for Higher Education, 1961), p. 43. Reprinted by permission of the publisher, Western Interstate Commission for Higher Education.

The first prohibition against the use of certain combinations of units in theory building is

A relational unit is not combined in the same theory with enumerative or associative units that are themselves properties of that relational unit.

To derive the second prohibition against certain combinations of units, let us continue the analysis with an examination of statistical units. The very nature of statistical units is that they describe properties of collectives. That is, the property of central tendency or of dispersion or of relative position can only be described for a collective unit. This now raises a problem. Can we employ units describing a member in the same theory with units describing a collective? We divide the problem into two parts.

Where a unit describing a property of a collective and a unit describing a property of a member deal with a member that is part of that collective, then we cannot employ these units in the same theory. Suppose, for example, we know from a study of school children that the relationship between intelligence and test scores in arithmetic may be expressed in the statement "On the average, test scores rise two points with every increase of five points in measured intelligence." We now use this knowledge based on the collective "school children" to predict that two children drawn from the same sample population will have arithmetic scores differing by 10 points if one measures 100 on IQ and the other measures 125. We are trying to predict, from a knowledge of two statistical properties of a collective, the values that will be associated with a member of that collective. Robinson has shown that this cannot be done.[4] The logic seems clear. Even though the value of the property on the member has gone into the determination of the property of the collective, we cannot locate from a knowledge of the collective property the value of the member property. It will be noted in Table 4-3 that the collective property "average numerical value" for the group composed of *A, B, C, D,* and *E* is 16. This empirical property of the collective does not permit us to draw any inference about the value of the member property for any individual member. There is an infinite number of sets composed of five members, constituting collectives that can have the collective property of an average numerical value of 16.

This gives rise to the second rule regarding the combination of different kinds of units in the same theory.

Where a statistical unit is employed, it is by definition a property of a collective. In the same theory do not combine such a statistical unit

[4]W. S. Robinson, "Ecological Correlations and the Behavior of Individuals," *American Sociological Review,* 15:351–357 (June 1950).

Table 4-3

MEMBER	MEMBERS' NUMERICAL VALUE
A	5
B	15
C	17
D	19
E	24

with any kind of unit (enumerative, associative, or relational) describing a property of members of the same collective.

There is one general exception of the rule just stated. This exception deals with the empirical location of a sample with respect to a universe and is not, properly speaking, a problem for theory building. Suppose we ask the question, ''Does a given sample set of values of a property for a group of members indicate that these are members of a given collective?'' Here the problem is to determine in which collective a sample of members belongs. For such a problem the property value of the members individually may be compared with the value in the collective to reach a decision. Suppose, for example, that the range of values for a collective is between 10 and 63 and members of a sample have property values ranging between 64 and 72. It would seem reasonable to conclude that this group of members does not belong to the specified collective. The theory of the statistical tests of significance rests on the solutions of this problem of the location of members with respect to the properties of collectives. The answer as to whether the sample belongs in the collective or not only answers that question and has no further theoretical significance. Why it does or does not belong in the collective is not revealed from a knowledge of the property characteristics that have established this membership or nonmembership.

A more complex problem has to do with whether or not we can employ statistical and other types of units in the same theory when the other types of units are properties of things not members of the statistical unit being employed.

When statistical and enumerative (or associative) units are joined together in the same model, the typical (but not logically necessary) format is to use a statistical unit expressing relative position. For example, in survey research the respondents in a sample may be divided into three subgroups, high, low, and average, in a statistical unit measuring one collective characteristic. These relative positions are then cross-tabulated with a characteristic measured by an enumerative or associative unit. Consider a table in which productivity is the statistical unit:

Relation of Group Belongingness to Productivity (Workers in a Tractor Factory)

EMPLOYEE QUESTION: "Do you feel you are really a part of your work group?" (*Significant between .05 and .10 level.*)

EMPLOYEES WITH PRODUCTIVITY OF:	REALLY A PART (1)	INCLUDED IN MOST WAYS (2)	INCLUDED IN SOME WAYS (3)	NOT ASCERTANED	TOTAL	N
100–119%	58%	24%	10%	8%	100%	327
90–99	56	29	10	5	100	762
80–89	51	31	13	5	100	452
70–79	52	28	10	10	100	269
40–69	46	31	15	8	100	275

The authors conclude from this table that "high-producing employees . . . reported that they felt that they were 'really a part of their group,' in contrast to the lower producers who were more likely to say that they were 'included in some ways but not in others,' or that they did not really feel that they were members of the group."[5]

This descriptive conclusion is wholly inadequate, as a glance at the table will reveal. Apparently the conclusion derives from an exclusive focus of the 58 percent of the first cell of column 1 and the 15 percent in the last cell of column 3. All the off-diagonal values are ignored, as are the relations among column percentages. For example, among the lowest-productivity workers there are 46 percent who feel they are "really a part" of their own work group, which hardly fits the conclusion of the authors. (Furthermore, the authors reached the conclusion that the lowest producers " . . . did not really feel they were members of the group," a result for which there are no data presented at all!)

Caution must be observed in employing statistical units in the same model with enumerative and associatie units. The caution is this: *Do not*

[5]The table is from p. 626 and the quote from pp. 624–625 of Robert L. Kahn and Daniel Katz, "Leadership Practices in Relation to Productivity and Morale," in Dorwin Cartwright and Alvin Zander (eds.), *Group Dynamics* (New York: Harper & Row, 1953). Reprinted by permission of the publisher.

draw conclusions from only one portion of the empirical relationships found.

When statistical units are employed in a model together with relational units, the caution just stated becomes even more imperative. Such a model employs the most complex units possible. Consider the following illustration.

Katz and Lazarsfeld devoted a full volume to the analysis of personal influence. At one point they were concerned with the leadership of women in public affairs. Their data first led to the conclusion that

> Women of the high status level are three times more likely to be public affairs leaders than women of low status. . . .
>
> We asked the women in our sample about several items which were then current in domestic and foreign affairs and from their responses constructed an index of public affairs information. . . . Table 33 indicates the relationship between status level and public affairs information and interest:

Table 33. *Information Level Increases with Each Step Up the Step Ladder*

SOCIAL STATUS LEVEL	PER CENT WITH HIGH INFORMATION	TOTAL (= 100%)
High	72%	(197)
Middle	52%	(253)
Low	28%	(246)

. . . Because the distribution of information among the three status levels parallels the distribution of opinion leadership, we were led to ask . . . whether it might not simply be that the more informed people are the opinion leaders and . . . that status is related to public affairs leadership only insofar as it brings with it differing concentrations of informed people. If this is so, we should find that equally interested people, regardless of their status level, should have roughly the same chances for opinion leadership. Table 34 shows . . . that this is not the case:

Table 34. *Public Affairs Leadership Still Varies According to Social Status Even When Information Level Is Controlled*

INFORMATION LEVEL	PER CENT WHO ARE PUBLIC AFFAIRS LEADERS		
	HIGH STATUS	MIDDLE STATUS	LOW STATUS
High	21% (141)	15% (127)	10% (69)
Medium	16% (45)	11% (79)	8% (77)
Low	— (11)	2% (40)	1% (97)

The highly informed woman of high social status is twice as likely to emerge as a public affairs leader as the equally informed woman of low status. . . . It is evident, therefore, that . . . advanced knowledge, in the arena of public affairs . . . cannot operate independently to generate opinion leadership. Along with information and interest there must be some objective "enabling" factor which makes it possible to translate subjective predispositions into the actual give-and-take of participation and leadership. In the case of public affairs, this enabling factor is social status. . . .[6]

It will be noted that the second relationship, as revealed in Table 33, is between a statistical unit, *percent with high information* (based upon a metric, *index of public affairs information*) and a relational unit, *social status level.* In order to establish how these units are related to leadership, the authors were constrained to subdivide the individuals in each social status level into three groups distinguished by their level of information. Then, within each cell, the proportion of women of that status level and level of information who were public affairs leaders was set forth. Thus, in Table 34, 21 percent of the 141 high-status—high-information-level women were leaders. From this subdivision of the sample by the addition of the associative unit *leadership in public affairs,* it is then possible to work out the relations between status (a relational unit) and informational level (a statistical unit) as they together are related to leadership.

The analytical steps, as far as units are concerned in this example, include (1) finding a relationship between a statistical and a relational unit, (2) introducing a new unit into the model, and thereby changing the starting model, in order to simplify the relations between the statistical and relational units, and (3) then concluding how the three units are interrelated.

The Katz-Lazarsfeld example may be generalized. A model employing statistical and relational units is one foredoomed to be subdivided into several theories. Such models, however, are quite useful in exploratory research, where the field being probed is little known and the models of it are imprecise. The guidance given to research by models composed of statistical and relational units permits a gross empirical attack on a domain from which future refinements may evolve.

Turning to summative units, it may first of all be asserted that such units are employed widely in two related contexts. (1) When the beginning student is being inducted into an intellectual domain, his introductory contacts are largely focused on summative units of analysis. (2) When the expert in a field of inquiry is addressing a lay audience, he will

[6]Elihu Katz and Paul F. Lazarsfeld, *Personal Influence* (New York: Free Press, 1955), pp. 274–275. Quoted by permission of the Free Press.

employ summative units. Both cases display a common feature: a field is being presented to a nonsophisticated audience.

Summative units, therefore, serve a very important purpose in sensitizing an audience to the boundaries of an intellectual domain and giving it some grasp of the main dimensions of that field.[7] In short, summative units are functional in education. This is not to be ignored as an important and useful function. Nor should an instructor in a beginning course of a discipline eschew summative units because they lack utility in theory building. An important skill of an educator is being able to sensitize a beginning student to a field by employing summative units, and then weaning the student from global units of analysis to the kinds of units employed in building scientific models. This is indeed the history of all courses beyond the introduction to a social-science discipline.

> *Summative units have utility in education of and communication with those who are naive in a field. Summative units are not employed in scientific models.*

This section started with the mnemonic device, EARSS, to identify units employed in theory building. The final conclusion is that the last S, standing for summative units, is inadmissible. Thus, we simplify to EARS to denote the following: E = enumerative units; A = associative units; R = relational units; S = statistical units. Theories in the behavioral sciences employ these four types of analytical units. Their employment in conjunction with each other is subject to the limitations suggested in this section.

Selecting Units

In principle there are no limitations on the selection of units to be employed in a theoretical model. The theorist has unlimited opportunities to employ units of his choice. Once he has made his selection, the constructed models must conform to the limitations set forth in the previous section for employment and combination of units.

It has not always been accepted that the theory builder has unrestricted choices among units. In the recent past, important social scientists have urged that only units capable of being operationalized were admissible in

---

[7]This is exactly what Herbert Blumer meant when he suggested that theory served to sensitize the expert who was exploring a realm of his own field new to him and his colleagues. See Herbert Blumer, "What Is Wrong with Social Theory?" *American Sociological Review*, 19:3–10 (Feb. 1954).

theory building.[8] In a contemporary period, Talcott Parsons has urged that the formulation of theories as mathematical models may be premature because, we may infer from his argument, the units required may be unduly restrictive.[9] Mathematical models do *not* require units that must be in some metric form, although some scholars may confuse precision of units with their analytical power. Our discussion should have made clear that attribute units can, in fact, be more powerful than variable units that are denoted by a metric.

At the other extreme have been social analysts who have employed summative units in what has long passed for theory in various social-science disciplines. Summative units do not have a place in theories. However, the phrase *frame of reference* describes an intellectual construct in which summative units play a central role. All frames of reference employ summative units, and some are made up exclusively of summative units. A frame of reference is an educational device used in orienting a layman (student or non-expert) to a field of inquiry, as already noted in the discussion of summative units. When summative units are employed in analytical thinking, they succeed admirably in functioning to delineate a frame of reference. A frame of reference is constructed by educators for pedagogical purposes, legitimate in their own right. Theories and models are *not* frames of reference.

Discovering New Units

The discovery of new units to be employed in theory building is basically achieved through a process of classification. Such classification has two general forms. We either take a broad unit and *subdivide* it, or we elaborate a residual unit into a substantive one and thus *extend* the existing classification scheme.

Invention by Extension

The invention of new units by extension of an existing classification scheme is probably the more familiar procedure. What is involved here is

[8]An important figure in sociology who exercised influence in this direction was George A. Lundberg. See his *Foundations of Sociology* (New York: Macmillan, 1939).

[9]See Talcott Parsons, "The Sibley Report on Training in Sociology," *American Sociological Review*, 29:747–748 (Oct. 1964).

the addition of new categories to an existing classification, or the specification of a previously recognized residual category. This can best be illustrated in the description of the origins of a classification of industrial work groups by Sayles.

> As the data were accumulated and reviewed it appeared that what was being described to us was not one but a variety of work groups. These groups differed from one another very substantially, particularly in the way in which they dealt with any problems they faced. For the sake of convenience we have attached names to the four types most clearly distinguishable: the *Apathetic,* the *Erratic,* the *Strategic,* and the *Conservative.*[10]

Extension of classification is vigorously employed in the discovery of new units in the behavioral sciences. Rostow, for example, did this when he invented the classification scheme delineating the levels of economic development; and Freud did this when he distinguished the ego from the id and both from the super-ego. In sociology Burgess extended the units for analysis of the ecology of the city with his concentric zones, and this in turn was modified by Hoyt, who further superimposed a sector structure upon the zone classification. Merton developed his fourfold classification of individual deviant adaptations to social systems, and Dubin later extended this to include group deviations and found that the scheme required fourteen classes of deviant adaptations instead of four. The examples come readily to hand, and you can easily draw upon your own experience to multiply the illustrations.

The salient feature of the extension of an existing classification scheme is that it is one process for discovering new units. Each time a classification scheme is extended by adding new categories or specification of a residual category, one or more units are added to the repertory. We ordinarily do not think of invention in these terms, and it is therefore worth underscoring this point.

Invention by Subdivision

When a class is subdivided, the operation is typically for the purpose of securing finer discriminations within the range of existing units. Most

---

[10]Leonard R. Sayles, *Behavior of Industrial Work Groups* (New York: John Wiley & Sons, 1958), p. 8. Note that Sayles "invented" new types of industrial work groups and implies a residual category that remains unnamed but out of which other students may well develop additional types of work groups.

often (if not always) this is accomplished by using other existing units as the basis for subdivision. For example, within the units *male* and *female* we may wish further to distinguish marital status and age. The resultant typology might be represented by units *males-married-young, males-single-young, males-married-old,* and *males-single-old.*

It is notable that in this subdividing process well-known units are typically employed. The inventiveness involved in producing a new unit is entirely tied up with the particular combination of familiar units. The subdivision process, then, involves emphasis on the inventiveness of the theorist in the manner in which he combines familiar units into unique combinations to produce a new unit.

There is no principle that demands only that familiar units be employed in the subdivision process, as in our previous example. In principle, we may use either customary or new units to achieve subdivision. The fact that one may produce new units out of the familiar is, of course, an extremely comforting circumstance for the theorist-researcher. It means that to be original demands only a focus on the recombination of the familiar rather than the sometimes more strenuous demand to be original by creating an entirely new unit from thin air.

There are available specific research technologies that are addressed to the problem of the discovery of new units of analysis through the twin processes of extension and subdivision. The use of the so-called ''null hypothesis'' is addressed to the problem of invention by extension. The technology of factor analysis produces an objective solution to the issue of invention by subdivision.

Invention and the Null Hypothesis

When the null hypothesis is employed the purpose is to inquire as to whether the designated *not-X* unit is really *X*. When we use the null hypothesis, our assumption is that there is no significant difference between measured values of the sample representing the *X* unit and those representing what is designated *not-X*. If no statistically significant difference is found, it is safe to assert that both samples may be counted as being examples of the *X* unit. If, however, there is a statistically significant difference, then we are impressed with the need for inventing a unit specification for what we had previously been satisfied to call the *not-X* unit. In short, the empirical reality of a population bearing a *not-X* unit designation leads us immediately to translate this residual definition into an affirmative one. Under these circumstances the null hypothesis plays an exceedingly important role in the process of discovery of new units of analysis.

Invention and Factor Analysis

Factor analysis is an especially powerful tool for inventing new units by subdivision. In much simplified form the procedure of factor analysis is to subdivide a unit into other units. Thus, intelligence as a property may be subdivided into primary mental abilities;[11] culture may be accurately described as the composite of specific national characteristics;[12] and personality may be mapped into its component parts.[13]

The essential feature of this process of discovery of new units through factor analysis is to subdivide a large unit and then establish the relationship of the new units to each other. The complement of new units taken together constitutes the factoring of a starting unit through factor analysis. The particular beauty of this technique is that it provides an objective way for determining how far one goes in the factoring process and when to stop. The technique has been employed primarily in psychology, where it was developed, and is only lately coming into use in sociology and anthropology. It could find much wider application in these disciplines but perhaps will not because of the more common tendency to invent new units by extension.

It might even be suggested that the stage of development of a discipline is revealed by the emphasis on the ways in which new units are advanced in the field. If extension is the method primarily employed, then the discipline is probably relatively new, and analytical attention is still directed at filling *out* the collection of analytical units employed. If the discipline is well established, then analytical attention may turn to filling

[11]*Cf.* L. L. Thurstone, *Primary Mental Abilities,* Psychometric Monographs No. 1 (Chicago: University of Chicago Press, 1938); and L. L. and T. G. Thurstone, *Factoral Studies of Intelligence,* Psychometric Monographs No. 2 (Chicago: University of Chicago Press, 1941).

[12]See the work of R. B. Cattell: "The Principal Culture Patterns Discoverable in the Syntality Dimensions of Existing Nations," *Journal of Social Psychology,* 32:215–253 (1950); "The Dimensions of Culture Patterns of Factorization of National Characters," *Journal of Abnormal and Social Psychology,* 44:443–469 (1949); and, with H. Breul and H. P. Hartman, "An Attempt at More Refined Definition of the Cultural Dimensions of Syntality in Modern Nations," *American Sociological Review,* 17:408–421 (Aug. 1952).

[13]See, for example, R. B. Cattell, *Personality: A Systematic and Factual Treatment* (New York: McGraw-Hill, 1950).

in the analytical units employed, in which case subdivision will be employed.

Invention and Scale Analysis

There is a special case in social science, inspired by factor analysis, in which the problem of discovery of new units is the focus of a research technology. Scale analysis is used in the general circumstance where the investigator is concerned with finding out whether certain things hang together. The technique was developed especially to deal with the responses of individuals to questions in order to find out whether the response to one question was directly linked to the response to another.[14] When these linkages occurred with a high degree of invariability, then the questions were said to scale and the response patterns to differentiate respondents into distinctive types of units of analysis.

From our standpoint, what is most interesting is that items that do not scale according to the technical criteria of scale analysis are discarded. The criterion of discard is that the items do not scale with those retained. There is no contention that the discarded questions do not measure something. Hence, scale analysis is an effective way of inventing new types in the scale developed or in the distinctive scale types that emerge from a study. We also have, and this is scarcely given recognition, an effective negative way of inventing new units from among the items discarded as being nonscalable in a given instance. Indeed, this discard heap of nonscalable items should be guarded jealously as an important source for the discovery of new units of analysis. Unfortunately, our habits of research report writing do not encourage this stockpiling of intellectual discards.

Invention and Intervening Variable

To employ the concept of intervening variable usually involves an implicit admission that the starting theoretical model is inadequate and

[14]An excellent discussion of the bases and techniques for scale analysis is to be found in S. A. Stouffer et al., *Measurement and Prediction: Studies in Social Psychology in World War II*, vol. 4 (Princeton, N.J.: Princeton University Press, 1950). The inventor of scale analysis, Professor Louis Guttman, has written Chapters 2 and 3 of this volume and included a bibliography on scale analysis at the end of Chapter 3. The first six chapters of the volume deal with scaling and scale theory. Most contemporary textbooks on social statistics contain standard treatment of scaling.

must be supplemented by addition of the intervening variable. When the relationship between two units of a model is the focus of attention, it is presumed that the values of the units co-vary. We have already indicated that the choice of particular units employed in a model is arbitrary. The model builder is wholly free to choose those units that to him make sense as the components of a theoretical model. Having made such initial choice, however, he is subsequently constrained, as we shall see in the next chapter, to determine laws by which these units interact in order to produce the outcome values for the units predictable from the model. Given this task as the task of model building, the researcher must make certain that every unit employed in the model interacts in a lawful way with at least one other unit of the model.

The arbitrary focus on particular units to be employed is often dictated by the current intellectual fashions and fads of a discipline. In order to retain disciplinary respectability, and at the same time deviate respectfully from the current fads and fashions, a researcher often employs traditional or highly reputable units. He moves toward innovation and deviancy by considering alternate units as intervening variables in the models he constructs. Thus, there tends to be introduced into theoretical model building a process of gradual revision by which intervening variables become the vehicles for modifying traditional units of analysis. Subsequently, the researchers may take the new intervening variables as the now established traditional units, discarding the older traditional units as being more remote from the outcome values of the units they are attempting to predict. The intervening variable in this context plays a role in the intellectual preferences for particular units of analysis. Intervening variables provide a mechanism for changing traditional units of analysis. The notion of intervening variable turns out, then, to be a convenient fiction by which the traditional units employed in a discipline come to be modified.

In the logic of intervening variable, there are three senses in which the concept has been employed. (1) The intervening variable, or, as I shall now designate it, the *intervening unit,* is seen as being literally closer to the outcome being predicted by the model than the unit being intervened upon. The theorist asserts that he can predict the outcome values of a unit from the values of the intervening unit because the connection with the unit whose values are being predicted is more immediate and direct than is the linkage between the outcome and the original unit employed. In this first logical sense, research tactics are directly initially at the analysis of models in which the units chosen are lawfully related to each other in the most direct possible fashion. If parsimony in model building is a desirable goal, then the model should employ a minimum number of units. The selection criterion for satisfying parsimony can be the immediacy of the relationships among the units in predicting the outcome values for any single one.

A second logical view of intervening units is this: (2) The values of a given unit are related to the values of another unit by two routes. The first route is a direct relationship between the two units. The other route is through a third unit.[15] Thus, the two original units included in the theory turn out to be related in a dual fashion, requiring the addition of a third unit to the model in order to describe the total relationship. In this sense of the intervening unit, the criterion of parsimony in model building (as examined in the case in the preceding paragraph) would no longer be appropriate. Consequently, it would be inaccurate to discard either unit being intervened upon in favor of the intervening unit as dictated in the first case. On the other hand, to include such an intervening unit in this second case also requires that the laws of interaction among the units of the model be modified. This is made necessary to take into account both direct interaction among the units and also indirect interaction through linking chains in which some units stand in an intermediate position between others. Thus, the consequence of using intervening units in this second case is to develop more complicated theoretical models by adding one or more units and laws of interaction to the model.[16]

There is a third case in which the idea of intervening unit plays a part. (3) A unit chosen for a model may be designated as an *ultimate antecedent* because it is temporally prior and lawfully connected to the outcome being predicted. An intervening unit may be viewed as being temporally closer to the outcome unit. In this case the researcher uses a chain type of model because he is interested in temporally linked chains in which the discovery of all possible links in the chain is of central concern. Thus, in a sequence, if A precedes B and B in turn precedes C, it may be argued that A is a more important antecedent of C than B because A occurs first in time in the linked chain of A to B to C. In such a situation, B would be called an intervening unit. It should be noted that this case can be distin-

---

[15]*Cf.* H. A. Simon, "Spurious Correlation: A Causal Interpretation," Chap. 2 in his *Models of Man* (New York: John Wiley & Sons, 1957).

[16]For an example of exactly this situation, see the discussion in L. W. Hoffman and R. Lippitt, "The Measurement of Family Life Variables," Chap. 22 in P. H. Mussen (ed.), *Handbook of Research Methods in Child Development* (New York: John Wiley & Sons, 1960), especially pp. 947–949.

guished from Case 2. In this third case the ultimate unit farthest removed from the dependent unit is linked to the latter only through one or more intervening units, and never directly. There is an obvious consequence of this linkage system among units of the model. If the values of unit A are predictive of the values of unit B and these in turn are predictive of the values of unit C, then we need two separate and distinct laws of interaction to link A with B and B with C. In this third case, it is impossible to establish a law of interaction between unit A and unit C. From this standpoint, the intermediate unit B can no longer properly be thought of as an intervening unit. It has just as much independence as any other unit.

Invention and Discarded Units

In general it should be pointed out that it is not uncommon to strain for consistency in or among units of analysis, with the result that important data may be cast out that could be the source of invention of new units. Put another way, the theory builder is often well advised to inquire about the data that researchers collect but subsequently exclude from their research analysis. These data may be mined for important insights about new units.

When it is possible to postulate *no* interaction between two units, we may exclude one or both from a model. In one sense the statement of no relationship between two units is a lawful one, but it is in the form of a null statement. The purpose of considering this possibility in building any theoretical model is that it leads directly to limiting the units among which choices will be made. Thus, to say that there is no relationship between two units is to say that there is no theoretical model for which these two units taken together can constitute components.

There is a caution to be observed here, however. Because previous studies have found no relationship is not necessarily a good reason for continuing to believe no relationship exists. One point at which scientific ingenuity is exercised is to reexamine such rejected pairs or n-tuples of units for the possibility that a lawful relationship between them and other units can be postulated. If, for example, you are not interested in bananas in the first place, then you will not look to see if the volume of bananas imported is lawfully related to the U.S. birth rate. Statistics texts have used their empirical relationship to demonstrate spurious correlation. I would argue that the empirical correlation may be subject to lawful formulation, and this possibility should never be ignored, even though it may have a face improbability.

Descriptive Research

There is no more devasting condemnation that the self-designated theorist makes of the researcher than to label his work *purely descriptive*. There is an implication that associates "purely descriptive" research with empty-headedness; the label also impiies that as a bare minimum every healthy researcher has at least an hypothesis to test, and preferably a whole model. This is nonsense.

In every discipline, but particularly in its early stages of development, purely descriptive research is indispensable. Descriptive research is the stuff out of which the mind of man, the theorist, develops the units that compose his theories. The very essence of description is to name the properties of things: you may do more, but you cannot do less and still have description. The more adequate the discription, the greater is the likelihood that the units derived from the description will be useful in subsequent theory building.

CHAPTER FIVE

Laws of Interaction

We are thus to understand by a law in science ... a résumé in mental short-hand, which replaces for us a lengthy description of the sequences among our sense-impressions. Law in the scientific sense is thus essentially a product of the human mind and has no meaning apart from man.

— KARL PEARSON, *The Grammar of Science*

Science never professes to present more than a working diagram of fact. She does not explain, *she states the relations and associations of facts as simply as possible.*

— H. G. WELLS, *The Work, Wealth and Happiness of Mankind*

What is needed in experimental psychology more than anything else is to formulate problems and investigations so as to reveal functional relations. ... It is by the discovery of functional relations and their rationalization that scientific laws are established.

— L. L. THURSTONE, *The Reliability and Validity of Tests*

THE GENERAL STRATEGY of this chapter is to examine ways in which units of scientific theories are linked with each other. The initial discussion covers definitions and a view of causality. The heart of the chapter is the analysis of three classes of laws of interaction. Attention will then turn to some operating problems in formulating these connections among units of models. Finally, a number of related issues involved in building laws of interaction into theoretical models will be considered.

Scientific Law

An indispensable step in developing a scientific model is to specify the interactions among the units employed in it. Beyond description of units, science is centrally concerned with relationships among things. The preceding chapter specified things as *units*. This leads to the question, "How is it possible to specify the interactions among units?"

Law of Interaction Defined

The linkages among units of a model will be labeled its *laws of interaction*. Scientific law will be limited to mean a specified interaction and only that. This point is important. The term *law* or *scientific law* has come to mean many things (e.g., universal law, natural law). It is necessary to be specific about operational meanings for the term *scientific laws,* as the purpose of this volume is to make theory building an explicit set of operations for the working scientist.[1]

A lawful statement expresses a linkage or connection between two or more units. It is for this reason that laws in science may be considered interactions. That portion of a statement that has any meaning at all as a law is the statement of the relationship, not the designation of the units involved. What appears to be the connecting phrase in a sentence stating a scientific law turns out to be the *law of interaction* that links the subject (unit) with the object (unit) in the sentence. When looked at from this standpoint, the term *scientific law* undergoes an immediate clarification. It is a statement of a relationship. It is the *relationship* that is the lawful part of it and not the definition, or identification, of units that are related.

The term *law of interaction* is employed to focus attention on the relationship being analyzed. For example, consider a staple of economics, Gresham's law. You will remember that Gresham's law is the law of economics that declares that bad money drives good money from the market. Gresham's law is made up of three kinds of units—good money, bad money, and a money market. The law states what happens, when, in the same market, both kinds of money are in circulation. The statement of Gresham's law is always written with the units and the interaction explicitly set forth in the statement. The reason that one gets the sense that a law must include both the units and their relationship is that the relationship by itself does not state anything. The statement "drives from the market" does not convey the context in which this occurs. The identification of good and bad money makes no declaration of their relationship.

---

[1] It is fascinating, for example, to consult the index of current and classic works on the philosophy of science. The delightful ambiguity and downright confusion in the analysis of scientific law is enough to make a "mere empiricist" out of any budding scientist.

Only when the units are put together with the interaction is a law derived as the term *law* is usually employed in science.

It should now be clear that if you understand the *structure* of a statement labeled a *law*, you will realize that it is composed of two analytically distinct parts—*units* that are connected or linked by a *law of interaction*. It is this more restricted sense of *law* as a specification of interaction that will be the basis for dealing with laws of interaction in this book.

This is a point long recognized by leading scientists. For example, B. F. Skinner, whose work on operant conditioning has proved so seminal, has stated, "Science sharpens and supplements this experience by demonstrating more and more relations among events and by demonstrating them more and more precisely.[2] It is a relationship that one sets out to demonstrate in a scientific investigation.

In every formulation of a scientific problem beyond the description of units, the heart of the statement is the interaction, or relationship, among units. Until such interactions are built into the models, they are only taxonomic models of units.[3] Once, however, interactions are included, the model is cranked up to operate and is ready to show associations among the units when values are assigned or ascribed to the model's units.

The phrase *of interaction* is used to modify the word *laws* in order to denote laws of a particular kind. It is a matter of indifference whether the word *law* is applied to other classes of phenomena, as it usually is in talking about science. From this point on, laws of interaction will be meant if the word *law* is used by itself.

Causality

It is necessary to find a place for causality before treating laws of interaction.[4] Implicit assumptions are often made that a statement of relationship may also be taken to be a statement of causality. Thus, if Gresham's law states a relationship—bad money drives good money from the market—then the appearance of bad money in the market is the cause

[2]B. F. Skinner, *Science and Human Behavior* (New York: Macmillan, 1953), p. 13.

[3]A great deal of sophisticated scientific attention is directed to the development of taxonomic models, as we saw in the first chapter. The word *only* in this sentence means incompleteness, not inadequacy.

[4]For a more extended discussion of causality see: Robert Dubin, "Causality and Social System Analysis," *International Journal of General Systems,* 2:107–113 (1975).

of good money disappearing. Care is necessary to be certain what Gresham's law really states. There is here *only* a statement of relationship, not of causality. When good and bad money simultaneously appear on the market, one kind of money will remain, the other kind will flee the market. Now it is sensible immediately to recognize that it is not bad coins that chase the good ones from the market. Indeed, to assume this is to anthropomorphize money. A model that attempts to say *why* good money becomes scarce when bad money appears must include the unit *people* who possess and use money as well as the unit *value*, plus laws of interaction connecting each of these units with each other and with good and bad money. Even adding these new units to the model does not introduce causality into it. Gresham's law is *not* a statement of causality, only of a relationship.

For the scientist, the analytical problem involving laws of interaction among units is

1. Given variation in the values of a unit (A),
2. what other units (B, C, ... K) can be linked to the first (by laws of interaction)
3. so that the variance in values of the original unit (A) may be accounted for by the linked variations of values in the other units (B, C, ... K)?

The scientist's problem of interaction among units is one of accounting for variance in one unit by specifying a systematic linkage of this unit with at least one other. This systematic linkage is the law of interaction.

What, then, is the meaning of *account for* in the analysis of variance? It is to account for the *variation in the measured values on one unit by a system based on its assigned relation to at least one other unit, whose measured values are employed.* The analysis of variance has empirical meaning only when values are measured on each unit lawfully related in a system. Having said that, we are now in a position to attach meaning to the term *accounted for* in the analysis of variance.

To account for variance in the values of a unit is to narrow the range of values measured on that unit by associating them with values measured on other units. To grasp this notion visually, you will note that in Figure 5-1 a moderate relationship between X and Y is represented in a scatter diagram. We could state the law of interaction as follows: "Values of unit Y are positively associated with values of unit X." We could be more specific by declaring an average relationship between X and Y to be represented by the best-fitting trend line for these data in the following form: $Y = a + bX$. This is a more precise law relating units Y and X, for,

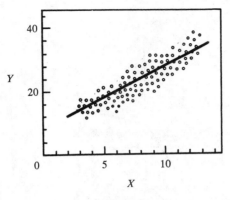

Figure 5-1

in addition to stating that they are positively related, the formula also shows the average rate at which values in Y change with each measured change in X. We note immediately that this more exact statement of relationship does not accurately represent all the points on the scatter diagram of measured values of X and Y, and to use this average relationship will produce errors because of the differences between the estimated values derived from the equation and the actual values of X and Y measured in the real world. These differences are the variance in the values of Y as they might be predicted from the values of X and from the law by which X and Y are related.

Given this variance, we want to narrow its range. Suppose we introduce another unit into the system, W. We may now find that the values measured on W and X are associated with values of Y in such a way that predicting the Y values from a plane determined by W and X values will reduce the sum of the differences between the predicted values of Y and their measured values. This is illustrated in Figure 5-2. Now, the fact that the differences between the predicted and measured values of Y are less in the three-unit model than in the two-unit model means that the three-unit model accounts for more variance in Y values than does the model employing only X and Y.

Note that we have not said anything about the values of Y being *caused* by the values of W or X or both. All we have said is that given measured values of W and X we can predict values of Y that will be closer to the actual values of Y than we could have predicted by guessing. It does not improve our understanding (resolve the power paradox) or make more accurate our prediction (resolve the precision paradox) to say that our law of interaction, $Y = a + bX + cW$, is a causal law. The *operations* by which we test the relationship between theoretically predicted values and empirical values differ in *absolutely no respect* whether we label the

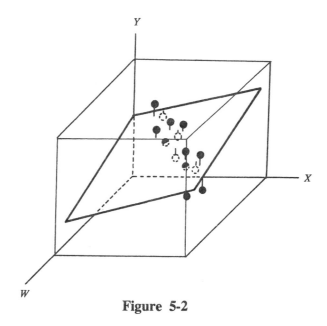

Figure 5-2

relationships among units of a model as *laws of interaction* or as *causal laws*. We conclude that no purpose is served by gratuitously employing the label *causal law*.

   The law of interaction itself is never measured. This seems self-evident. Its very obviousness has been a central source of confusion in the scientist's preoccupation with causality. In the contemporary phase of this confusion, structures of correlation coefficients are employed in an effort to tease out causality. As will presently be shown, these efforts have the more modest consequence of establishing sequential laws of interaction and *not* causality.

   What is self-evident about the fact that laws of interaction are never measured? It is this: Any scientific law is tested empirically if, and only if, values are empirically assigned to the units employed in the law. There is absolutely no way to assign values to the linking clause in the statement, the law of interaction. Consider Boyle's law as described and analyzed by Pierre Duhem, the late, distinguished French theoretical physicist.

   Let us take one of these laws, Mariotte's law [Boyle's law], and examine its formulation without caring for the moment about the accuracy of this law. At a constant temperature, the volumes occupied by a constant mass of gas are in inverse ratio to the pressures they support;

such is the statement of the law of Mariotte. The terms it introduces, the ideas of mass, temperature, pressure, are still abstract ideas. But these ideas are not only abstract; they are in addition, symbolic, and the symbols assume meaning only by grace of physical theories. Let us put ourselves in front of a real, concrete gas to which we wish to apply Mariotte's law; we shall not be dealing with a certain concrete temperature embodying the general idea of temperature, but with some more or less warm gas; we shall not be facing a certain particular pressure embodying the general idea of pressure, but a certain pump on which a weight is brought to bear in a certain manner. No doubt, a certain temperature corresponds to this more or less warm gas, and a certain pressure corresponds to this effort exerted on the pump, but this correspondence is that of a sign to the thing signified and replaced by it, or of a reality to the symbol representing it. This correspondence is by no means immediately given; it is established with the aid of instruments and measurements, and this is often a very long and very complicated process. In order to assign a definite temperature to this more or less warm gas, we must have recourse to a thermometer; in order to evaluate in the form of a pressure the effort exerted by the pump, we must use a manometer. . . .[5]

Note that what are measured are the volume, temperature, and pressure of the gas. The term *inverse ratio* is the law of interaction linking these units. If, under constant temperature, the *measured* volume is inversely proportional to the *measured* amount of pressure on the gas, then it may be concluded that Boyle's law (the French, naturally, call it Mariotte's law)—the inverse ratio of volume to pressure—is an accurate statement of the relationship. Only the value of units is measured in a relationship, *never* the form of the relationship itself.

The relational format for the statement of the law of interaction does not impair the power of prediction. The psychologist builds many models of behavior based upon a "black box" into which are put the intrapersonal processes that connect measured imputs with measured outputs. All that can be determined by observation, and measured, are the inputs and outputs. This is a good example of outcome rather than process analysis, as set forth in Chapter 2. The inputs and outputs can be shown to be related by laws of interaction that depend only upon a statement of relationship and not of causality. It is interesting that when the psychologist attacks the causal problem, he puts all his ideas about causal mechanisms inside the black box. This is no different in structure and form from the

[5]Pierre Duhem, *The Aim and Structure of Physical Theory* (New York: Atheneum, 1962), p. 166.

theologian's law of interaction that it is "God's will."[6] Sociologists do the same thing when, for example, they assume some process like internalization as the "cause" of a person's guiding his behavior according to a socially defined set of values, or when they piously assert that particular types of institutions are "caused" by the need of any society to manage tensions inside people and among people and groups. The sociologist has his own peculiar black boxes that are not as honestly labeled as those of the psychologist. The anthropologist who emphasizes functional determinism ends up with comparable black boxes into which he puts such causes as "universal functional requisites of a society" or "diffusion of cultural elements," as though universal functional requisites "cause" societies to develop particular social institutions or as though diffusion "causes" cultural elements to spread from their point of origin.

Empirically relevant theory in the behavioral and social sciences is built upon an acceptance of the notion of relationship rather than of the notion of causality. This characterizes the laws of interaction employed. We may insist on employing a causal rhetoric in our laws of interaction, such as "broken homes cause (spawn, create, encourage, produce, make possible, facilitate) delinquency among children." Our evidence, however, makes clear that many broken homes do not result in the delinquency of the children in them. Further, many delinquents do not come from broken homes. The law of interaction that best fits the empirical evidence linking home solidarity and delinquency is "A greater-than-chance proportion of delinquents comes from broken homes." This statement of relationship clearly avoids a causal format. It says nothing about delinquents who do not come from broken homes. In short, it avoids the necessary and logical consequences that must follow from the causal rhetoric. By virtue of this, it is empirically more accurate.

Forms of Interaction

The quotation at the head of this chapter states, "Law in the scientific sense is thus essentially a product of the human mind and has no meaning

---

[6]The form and structure of coherent theology and scientific theory are identical. This makes sense of the fact that some of the very early greats of science were consummate theologians. What distinguishes theory from theology, of course, is the necessity of empirical test to qualify as scientific theory and the abhorrence of empirical test in theology, whose foundation is faith and whose empirical questioning is heresy.

apart from man." This is a revolutionary position.[7] It must be contrasted with the earlier view that science was the pursuit of God's laws governing the universe or of the "harmony of the spheres." Many leading scientists still believe in the older view. This does not, in fact, change the operations they employ when they are doing science, in spite of their ruminations about its ultimate purpose.

That scientific law is the product of the human mind has two important implications: (1) The forms of such laws are limited by the capacity of the human mind to invent ways of denoting relationships; and (2) laws are not absolute and may be changed as man's needs are changed. We will consider only the first of these two implications.

What constitutes the range of possibilities for formulating a relationship? This is a central philosophic problem best summed up in the title of Boole's seminal treatise on mathematics, *The Laws of Thought*. Mathematicians have been most explicit in working out ways in which units may interact with each other. The operations of arithmetic, for example—addition, subtraction, multiplication, and division—describe relations among things, whether quantities or qualities. Following the lead of Boole, a contemporary preoccupation of mathematicians has given to scientists, and especially social scientists, finite mathematics as a tool in developing laws of interaction. The finite mathematics, graph theory, and matrix algebra, to mention but three of the technologies available for expressing relationships, are particularly adapted to social science data in which cardinal measures are less prevalent than ordinal ones.[8]

At this point the task is to answer the question, "What general categories exist among the laws of thought for expressing interactions among units?" From these general categories will be derived the explicit forms of law of interaction employed in social scientific theory. The conclusion is that there are three general categories that encompass all forms for expressing relationships. These are

[7]Einstein is very clear on this point. "For the scientific method can teach us nothing else beyond how facts are related to, and conditioned by, each other." "Science is the century-old endeavor to bring together by means of systematic thought the perceptible phenomena of this world into as thorough-going association as possible." Albert Einstein, *Out of My Later Years* (New York: Philosophical Library, 1950), pp. 21 and 24.

[8]For social scientists it is evident that the laws of induction and deduction constitute the rallying points for the opposition of the axiomizers seeking deductively coherent theory and the empiricists whose belief is that theory may be inductively generated from funded facts. Karl R. Popper has a long polemic against induction that must be taken into account here. See his *The Logic of Scientific Discovery* (London: Hutchinson & Co., 1959), especially Chap. 1.

1. Categoric interactions.
2. Sequential interactions.
3. Determinant interactions.

Each will be examined in detail in succeeding sections of this chapter.

Categoric Laws

A categoric law of interaction is one that states that values of a unit are associated with values of another unit. The association is in the form of the presence or absence of the respective values for the two units. An example of such a law is "There is a greater-than-chance probability that juvenile delinquents will come from broken homes." Another example is "Jews tend to vote Democratic in the United States." In the first example the character of a home and the delinquent behaviors of the children within it are said to be associated. In the second example ethnic background and voting preference are said to be associated. This type of law of interaction is the most common in the social and behavioral sciences. I estimate that probably three-quarters of all laws of interaction in the literature of the social and behavioral sciences are expressed as categoric laws of interaction.

What is often not recognized when categoric laws of interaction are employed is that four laws are usually required for a complete specification of the associated values of two units joined by the laws. Consider a fourfold table like Table 5-1. The first law of interaction between units A and B may be stated for cell #1. It takes the form "Nonzero values of A and B are associated with a probability of P_1." This, of course, cannot be the full statement of the association between unit A and unit B. Two general cases are visible.

Table 5-1

		UNIT B	
		NONZERO VALUES	ZERO VALUES
UNIT A	NON-ZERO VALUES	(cell #1) P_1	(cell #2) P_2
	ZERO VALUES	(cell #3) P_3	(cell #4) P_4

$$P_t$$

Case 1. In the first case we may assume that the probability of association between zero and nonzero values of A and B units totals one. That is, P_t equals one. We then have three degrees of freedom and would have to assign probability values to three of the four cells. Thus, the full statement of laws of interaction between unit A and unit B involves three independent statements like the following:

1. Nonzero values of A are associated with nonzero values of B with a probability of P_1.
2. Nonzero values of A are associated with zero values of B with a probability of P_2.
3. Zero values of A are associated with nonzero values of B with a probability of P_3.

From these three independent statements it may be concluded that zero values of A are associated with zero values of B with the probability of $1 - (P_1 + P_2 + P_3)$. It is clear, of course, that any triplet of P values may be chosen as the independent ones. The total of four laws of interaction completely specifies the relation between values of unit A and values of unit B, on the assumption that the sum of probabilities for the table as a whole equals one.

Case 2. In the second case we may choose to subdivide our 2×2 table into four 1×2 tables. Thus we may consider the first row as a separate table. If we now assign to cell #1 the probability P_1, then the probability P_2 is equal to $(1 - P_1)$. Thus, knowledge of the probability in cell #1 permits us to predict automatically the probability of an entry in cell #2. But we can also do more than this. If we consider the first column of the original table as a 1×2 table and cell #1 still retains the probability value previously assigned, then the probability for cell #3 becomes $(1 - P_1)$. The value of P_1 then also determines the value of P_3. But if we now know the values of P_2 and P_3 or either one of these, we can then automatically secure the value of P_4 by considering either the second row or the second column as a 1×2 table and perform the standard subtraction of the value of either P_2 or P_3 from one to secure P_4.

In general, if we set the probabilities of the column or row totals equal to one, then we have only one degree of freedom in assigning values to P_1, P_2, P_3, and P_4. In Case 2 we then have to specify only one crucial value of the probabilities for the association between values of unit A and values of unit B, namely, the probability in any one of the four cells. Usually we specify the probability for cell #1.[9]

[9]It is evident in the second case that $P_2 = P_3$ and $P_1 = P_4$, e.g., $P_1 + P_2 = 1$ and $P_2 + P_4 = 1$, hence, $P_1 + P_2 = P_2 + P_4$ or $P_1 = P_4$.

It is absolutely essential in employing categoric laws of interaction to know which of the two cases is intended. The two cases differ by the number of degrees of freedom in assigning values to the probabilities. The two cases give identity for P values in only one of the four cells of the fourfold table. Values of the probability in the other three cells must vary between the two cases.

Thus, if we employ the Case 1 type of categoric law of interaction, it is necessary to make three statements of the interaction between unit A and unit B that employ independent values of cell probability. On the other hand, if we employ a Case 2 type of categoric law of interaction, it is only necessary to make one independent statement of the interaction between A and B. A Case 2 type of categoric law of interaction is therefore more parsimonious.

Parsimony, however, is not the sole ground for making a choice between Case 1 and Case 2 in employing categoric laws of interaction. Indeed, the less parsimonious Case 1 may be much more accurate than a Case 2 statement of the law of interaction. By accuracy I simply mean here that the probabilities assigned to the four cells are more nearly in accord with empirical data.

Categoric laws of interaction sometimes have a more primitive form than the one employing a statement of probabilities. For example, "Being a Jewish voter and voting Democratic are associated." Such a statement, however, has as a minimum an implied probability, namely, that there is a greater-than-chance probability that ethnic background and party voting regularity are related. This implied probability is a threshold at the lower end of possible probabilities. For if it is true that the association between being a Jew and voting Democratic is purely a chance association, then there is no law connecting Jewishness and Democratic voting behavior. This more primitive statement of a categoric law of interaction has therefore the exact form of a precise statement of the law. It has an implied probability, namely, a threshold probability above that of a chance association.

Categoric laws are symmetrical. It does not matter whether one or the other of the units comes first in the statement of the law. Thus, "Juvenile delinquency and broken homes are positively related" is identical with "Broken homes and juvenile delinquency are positively related." The symmetry of categoric laws is emphasized, for this fact buttresses the conclusion that a law of interaction is not a statement of causality. What, indeed, is the meaning of cause if the units *juvenile delinquency* and *broken homes* can be interchanged without restriction in the law of interaction between them? Before you jump to the conclusion that the broken-home condition preceded in time the juvenile delinquency and therefore caused it, reserve your judgment until you have read the following discussion of sequential laws.

The recognition of a categoric law of interaction is facilitated by noting that its typical form employs the words *is associated with*. Synonyms for this phrase serve, of course, to provide the same identification. As we will see in discussing the other two types of interaction, the semantic signals are important for identifying the class of law.

Sequential Laws

A sequential law of interaction is one always employing a time dimension. The time dimension is used to order the relationship among two or more units.[10] The standard format of a sequential law of interaction may be illustrated as follows: "A community disaster activates an informal community leadership structure to organize response to the disaster." "In a task-oriented group, pressure to produce from the group leader may raise the level of group morale." In both instances we have examples of directly stated or implied temporal sequences between the values of the units employed. A high positive value for the unit *disaster* is what precedes the activation of an informal leadership group in the community. The pressure from the group leader is what precedes the heightened morale of group members.

The sequential ordering of the values of the units employed is the only meaning we can attach to the law of interaction, however tempting it may be to view this temporal sequence as a causal one. The only measures available to us when we test propositions derivable from the laws of interaction of a sequential nature are measures of time differentials in the appearance of values for the units linked by the law.

One of the commonest errors made in interpreting laws of interaction is to confuse a sequential law with a causal law. I have already suggested that I find it confusing to employ the category *causal law*. It should now be clear that the source of confusion lies in interpreting a sequential law as though it were a causal one. Consider Figure 5-3. On a time scale measured from a given point of origin we may locate values of the units

---

[10]Our sequential law is what Kaplan designates a *temporal law* subdivided into three types: *interval laws, genetic laws,* and *pattern laws.* Abraham Kaplan, *The Conduct of Inquiry* (San Francisco: Chandler, 1964), pp. 109ff.

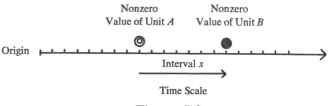

Figure 5-3

employed in a law. Thus, in Figure 5-3 it is clear that the value for unit *A* occurs in time at a point closer to the point of origin of measurement than does the value of unit *B*. The values of both units we are trying to relate by our sequential law are clearly distinguishable as to the time in which these values occur, measured from a common starting point of measurement. We can then say that specified values of *A* are succeeded by specified values of *B*. We may even more exactly say that specified values of *A* are succeeded by specified values of *B* with an interval, on the average, of time *X*. In both instances, we are stating only a temporal sequence of the appearance of the respective values of units *A* and *B*. It may be noted parenthetically that the sequential law becomes the categoric law when we cannot distinguish a temporal interval between the values of unit *A* and the values of unit *B*.

The typical usage of *cause as sequence of events* is revealed in Jevons's treatise on science, first published in 1874.

> I have no objection to use the words cause and causation, provided they are never allowed to lead us to imagine that our knowledge of nature can attain to certainty. I repeat that if a cause is an invariable and necessary condition of an event, we can never know certainly whether the cause exists or not. To us, then, a cause is not to be distinguished from the group of positive or negative conditions which, with more or less probability, precede an event. In this sense there is no particular difference between knowledge of causes and our general knowledge of the succession of combinations, in which the phenomena of nature are presented to us, or found to occur in experimental inquiry.[11]

Now, if we are clearly limiting our idea of cause to describe a sequence of events, then no difficulty is encountered. The two notions are identical.

[11]W. Stanley Jevons, *The Principles of Science* (New York: Dover, 1958), p. 224. Jevons was a broadly educated man whose contributions to political economy are classic. In this same work, Jevons quotes from Brown's *Essay on Causation: Observations on the Nature and Tendency of the Doctrine of Mr. Hume, Concerning the Relation of Cause and Effect* as follows: "A cause, he [Hume] says, may be defined to be the object or event which immediately precedes any change, and which existing again in similar circumstances will be always followed by a similar change." (Jevons, *ibid.*, p. 224).

There is only a psychological reason for preferring the term *cause* as being more in keeping with the theological heritage of the West in which the search for a first cause has made causality a familiar, if not an expected, feature of our laws of thought.

It is notable that two distinguished philosophers of science, publishing parallel treatises on the nature of science within three years of each other, come to similar conclusions in dealing with causality in the social and behavioral sciences. Nagel in 1961 devoted considerable attention to causality in the physical sciences and then turned to the same problem in the behavioral sciences under the heading "Explanation and Understanding in the Social Sciences."[12] Kàplan, publishing in 1964, did not even have an index entry under *cause* or *causality* (although he discusses them a number of times, e.g., under taxonomic laws, pp. 111ff.) and devoted an entire chapter to "Explanation" with an especially enlightening treatment, parallel to Nagel's, of explanation in behavioral science.[13] The arguments and crosscurrents of thought on the subject of causality in models of social behavior are much too detailed to summarize here. The conclusion that explanation or, as I prefer, understanding is one goal of social science, rather than causality, is amply sustained in the detailed arguments of Nagel and Kaplan and of Popper[14] before them. This conclusion has its roots in the Enlightenment, when a man-centered view of the universe contested with a God-centered orientation.

A sequential law may have two sources of specificity. The first case involves an exclusive choice of the first-appearing unit. The second case involves the transitivity of the order of appearance of values in the units.

CASE 1. In the first case, the sequential law may be made more specific by modifying a general sequential law. The modification takes the form of making the first-appearing unit the only one that is followed by the values of the second-appearing unit. The law is then asymmetrical. Thus, our first sequential example could be restated as follows: "If, and only if, a disaster occurs, will an informal leadership group arise in a community to meet the conditions of disaster." This more restrictive statement of the sequential law says that the only unit whose positive values will be succeeded by the positive values of the second unit is the one specified. The "if, and only if" clause is the restrictive statement that achieves this consequence. (This example of a sequential law of interac-

---

[12]Ernest Nagel, *The Structure of Science* (New York: Harcourt, Brace & World, 1961), Chaps. 10 and 14.

[13]Kaplan, *op. cit.*, Chap. 9.

[14]Karl R. Popper, *The Logic of Scientific Discovery* (London: Hutchinson & Co., 1959), originally published as *Logik der Forschung* in 1955.

tion may not be empirically accurate, but it certainly is logically possible.)

CASE 2. The second restrictive case of a sequential law is one that specifies that the order of the appearance of values for the units is unidirectional. Values will first appear for unit *A* before they will appear for unit *B* but not vice versa. This would then give to our second sequential illustration the following formulation: "The heightened morale of task group members always follows, and never precedes, a group leader's pressure for productivity."

It is, of course, possible to combine the two restrictive cases of sequential laws into one law of interaction. This would be a statement of interaction that makes the temporally first unit the only one whose values are followed by values on the second unit, the order of occurrence being intransitive. For example: "If, and only if, a group leader applies pressure for increased output to a task-oriented group, will there be a subsequent increase in group morale, morale never increasing prior to the application of leadership pressure for productivity."

FALSE CASE. A third, but false, case of a sequential law is one in which there is an oscillation in the succession of values of the units. Thus, given values of unit *A* are succeeded by given values of unit *B,* which are succeeded by new values of unit *A,* and so on. In this case it would appear that there is complete transitivity and therefore symmetry in the relationship. For example, the behavior of an individual may be classified as manic-depressive. Whichever state the person is in will be followed by the other state. Note that I have deliberately used the word *state* to describe the condition of the individual. This is, I think, the fundamental feature of the false case of a sequential law of interaction. It is actually a case of the state of a system. I illustrated movement of a system through its states in the first chapter and will give a detailed treatment of this feature of a model in Chapter 7.

In either the Case 1 restrictive instance or in the combined restrictive instance, there is a sore temptation to view the relationship as a causal one. The argument is simple. If the appearance of values in the temporally prior unit is the only time that values appear in the temporally succeeding unit, then why cannot we assume that whatever characterizes the earlier unit is the cause for what happens to the one that has values at a later point in time? Perhaps the analogy of a chemical formula will be helpful at this point. A chemical formula is typically written with an arrow going from the left to the right side of the formula. The wisdom of the chemical convention of using an arrow rather than an equality sign lies in the recognition that this is a statement of a sequential law of interaction and not a causal one. When two atoms of hydrogen are combined in the presence of one atom of oxygen, then the arrow pointing from the summed values of the two units says that at the succeeding moment in time the two will combine to produce H_2O, or water. The hydrogen atoms, the oxygen atom, or their combination do not "cause" water.

A more complex treatment of causality in the social sciences is based upon the analysis of a matrix of correlation coefficients. This analytical approach stems from considerations introduced by Herbert Simon, following Sewell Wright's much earlier development of path coefficients, and advanced principally by Blalock.[15] Insofar as the argument for causality rests on the analysis of correlation coefficients and regressions, it faces an insurmountable barrier. The fundamental identity of correlation, $r_{ab} = r_{ba}$, cannot be gainsaid, and any assumptions to the contrary, as made by Simon and initially elaborated by Blalock, founders on the denial of the identity.[16]

The most recent forays into the analysis of causal laws in the social sciences have taken Professor Blalock into an enlightening discussion of asymmetry in the interaction among units of a theory.[17] This formulation avoids the regression issue that Polk justifiably criticized. The essential argument is that two units may be related asymmetrically. The values of one unit may force values of the other, but not vice versa.[18] A forcing variable has the status of causing the consequent values in the response variable, which is the underlying idea in the notion of asymmetry in the interaction between two things. From my standpoint this is no more useful than to view the asymmetry as a statement of sequence in the successive appearance of values of the units being related. The time lapse is the crucial operational criterion by which the forcing variable is designated. Thus, to call the forcing relationship a sequential law of interaction

[15]See H. A. Simon, *Models of Man* (New York: John Wiley & Sons, 1957), especially Chapters 1 and 2, and S. Wright, "The Method of Path Coefficients," *Annals of Mathematical Statistics*, 5:161–215 (Sept. 1934). See also footnote 11 in the Sewell-Shah paper cited in footnote 19 of this chapter for a complete set of references on path analysis especially as applied in the social sciences.

[16]See the exchange of correspondence between Professors Polk, Robinson, and Blalock in *American Sociological Review*, 27:539–548 (August 1962).

[17]See Hubert M. Blalock, Jr., *Causal Inferences in Nonexperimental Research* (Chapel Hill, N.C.: The University of North Carolina Press, 1964). See also Chapter 1, "Some Methodological Problems," in his *Toward a Theory of Minority-Group Relations* (New York: Wiley, 1967).

[18]The notion of forcing variables as derived from J. D. Trimmer, *Responses of Physical Systems* (New York: John Wiley & Sons, 1950), and is employed in sociology by Blalock, *op. cit.*, pp. 7–8. See also Hubert M. Blalock, Jr. (ed.), *Causal Models in the Social Sciences* (Chicago: Aldine-Atherton, 1971).

rather than a causal one is the more accurate description of what is actually done in the operations of science.

My sequential law is distinctly an asymmetrical interaction between two units of a theory. The asymmetry is time-determined. The added advantages of calling this a sequential law of interaction rather than a causal one lie in the fact that a host of philosophical problems with murky solutions may be safely ignored by setting aside the causal formulation. In addition, the precision of prediction and the power of understanding secured from a theory that incorporates a sequential law of interaction is in no way impaired because the law is not called a causal one.

Path coefficients, on the other hand, depend upon a temporal sequence of a and $b,$ and the directionality assigned to r_{ab} rests on the fact that the value in the unit b comes after the appearance of the value in the unit $a.$ Thus, Wright's path coefficients provide one statistical technology for testing sequential laws.[19]

Sequential laws of interaction assign a temporal ordering to the appearance of values for two or more units joined by law. In the special case in which there is no temporal difference in the appearance of values for two or more units, we have a categoric or a determinant law rather than a sequential law of interaction. The temptation is strong to interpret sequential laws of interaction as though they were causal in structure. This gratuitous assumption of causality adds nothing to social science, however much it satisfies psychological needs.

Determinant Laws

A determinant law of interaction is one that associates determinate values of one unit with determinate values of another unit. Boyle's law, encountered earlier in this chapter, is a determinant law since it states that under conditions of constant temperature the volume of a gas is inversely proportional to the pressure bearing upon the gas. This law declares that a given volume is associated with a given value of the

[19]A recent and excellent use of path coefficients in social analysis is W. H. Sewell and V. P. Shah, "Socioeconomic Status, Intelligence, and the Attainment of Higher Education," presented at the Sixth World Congress of the International Sociological Association, Sept. 1966). Methodological discussions of path analysis will be found in Herbert L. Costner (ed.), *Sociological Methodology 1971* (San Francisco: Jossey-Bass, 1971), especially Parts Two and Three.

pressure. If the value of the pressure changes, then the value of the volume also changes in a determinate direction, namely, as the reciprocal of the pressure. Stouffer's law of migration, which states that the number of migrants moving from a point of origin to a destination is inversely proportional to the distance traveled and directly proportional to the intervening opportunity, is an example of a determinant law.[20] Allport's J curve of conforming behavior is still another statement of a determinant law.[21]

The essential components of a determinant law are two: (1) The specific relation is set forth, and (2) determinate values are assigned to the units related by the law of interaction.

For every determinate value of one unit there is a determinate value of the unit related to it. For example, $y = f(x)$ where for every x there is a corresponding y. The most common expression of this kind of a law of interaction currently in the social sciences is in the form of a correlation for which a best-fitting trend line is calculated to represent the relation between the units being correlated. The mathematical formula expressing the trend line is then taken as the most probable description of the relationship.

Categoric and sequential laws of interaction have limited forms, each of which has already been discussed. Determinant laws of interaction may take any form within the range of logic by which the distribution of values for one unit may be said to be related to a distribution of values for another unit. The essential feature is that these values are paired, with each value for the first unit having a mating value on the second unit (or other units), and that these associated values on the units are invariantly linked.

The most common feature that identifies a determinant law is that it may be drawn as a line, curve, plane, surface, a structure of linked points (as in graph theory), or matrices of fixed-position values (as in matrix algebra). On a geometric form will be located the points corresponding to scale values of the units that are related. Each such geometric form may be represented by a mathematical expression. Hence, the most common language for stating a determinant law of interaction is the language of mathematics.

[20]See S. A. Stouffer, *Social Research to Test Ideas* (New York: Free Press, 1962), Chap. 4.

[21]See Floyd Allport, "The J-Curve Hypothesis of Conforming Behavior," *Journal of Social Psychology*, 5:141–183 (1934).

Negative Laws

A law of interaction may be expressed in a negative form that specifies generalized nonrelationship among units. The usual statement of the negative law is the null statement. For example: ''There is no systematic relationship between the values of one unit and those of another unit.''

A negative law of interaction, or as it is often called, the null hypothesis, is employed when a hunting expedition is undertaken as a form of scientific research. Data are collected representing values for two or more units. As there is no theoretical reason for presupposing that the values of the units being measured are in any way related, it is hypothesized that there is no relationship between the values of the respective units. This is the null hypothesis. Then, if by standard statistical tests of association, the values of two or more units are found to be linked together beyond chance probability, it is asserted that the null hypothesis or the negative law is incorrect. The researcher is then presented with the problem of developing a law of interaction between the units previously assumed not to be linked together.

The form of a true negative law of interaction has the following general structure: If the values of unit A are greater than zero and determinate, then the values of unit B will be greater than zero but many-valued, no one value of which is determined by the value of unit A. This is pictured in Figure 5-4. This diagram represents a negative law of interaction, a law of nonrelation between units A and B. It is also a diagram of a correlation of value zero ($r_{AB} = 0$).

The negative law, or the null hypothesis, should not be confused with

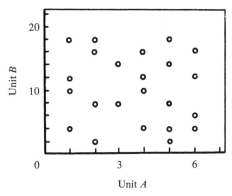

Figure 5-4

a special case of a law of interaction of any of the three general classes. This special case of a law of interaction specifies that for a given value or region of values of one unit, there may be either a zero value or many values for the other unit. For example, Parsons has asserted that the affectivity choice instead of the neutrality choice among pattern variables in the actor's evaluation of objects eliminates the possibility of a choice by him between the universalism-particularism pattern variables.[22] This is a positive law of interaction even though the values on particularism and universalism are equal to zero under the particular condition that the affectivity choice has been made.

Efficiency of a Law

In Chapter 2 a distinction was drawn between power of understanding and precision of prediction. It was there contended that prediction could be achieved, and often was, without understanding. Conversely, power of understanding is possible without ability accurately to predict. It is possible to link the ideas of prediction and power with laws of a model. This linkage is achieved through the concept of the efficiency of a law.

By efficiency of a law is meant the range of variability in the values of one unit when they are related by a law to the values of another unit. The level of efficiency of a law is determined by the narrowness of this range in unit values. Where the range of unit values is broad, the law has low efficiency.

There are four general levels of efficiency of a law. In the lowest level of efficiency are laws that state that a unit will have some values when its lawfully related unit also has some values. The highest level of efficiency is attained when it is possible lawfully to state that a direction and amount of change in value in one unit is correlated with a fixed direction and amount of change in another unit. The four general levels of efficiency of a law may be labeled

1. Presence-absence (lowest level of efficiency).
2. Directionality.
3. Covariation.
4. Rate of change (highest level of efficiency).

[22]T. Parsons, and E. A. Shils, *Toward a General Theory of Action* (Cambridge, Mass.: Harvard University Press, 1951), p. 89.

A law of the lowest efficiency is ont that states that given the presence of a positive or negative value of unit *A,* there will be corresponding positive or negative values of unit *B.* An example of a low-efficiency law would be "Masculine identification of a male child is dependent upon interaction with a father figure." Here the law merely states that the unit *masculine identification* and the unit *father figure* are linked by a statement of concurrent presence.

A law of the next higher level of efficiency is one that proclaims the directionality of a relation between the values of one unit and the values of another. For example: "Liking between two people increases with the frequency of their interaction." A law connecting liking and interaction states that as interaction *increases* liking will also increase. This is a directionality statement. Laws of this level of efficiency are very frequent in the social sciences and are accepted as representing signal advances in scientific precision. It should nevertheless be noted that this is still a low level of efficiency of the law of interaction.

The third level of efficiency is one that expresses covariation between two or more units. The law relating the units accounts for any changes in directionality of the relationship in the statement of the law itself. For example: "Conformity to a standard of behavior in a fixed population varies in the shape of a J curve from absolute obedience."[23] In a law of this level of efficiency, the covariation of the number of people conforming and the degree of obedience is declared to have a particular relationship by the term *J curve.*

The highest level of efficiency of a law of interaction is one that expresses the rate of change in the values of one variable and the associated rate of change in the values of another variable. An example of this kind of law of interaction would be the statement "Let A_i be amount of attachment by a person to a group, C_i the number of his contacts with group members, C_g the number of contacts among all group members, and C_{it} individual i's total contacts, all contacts being measured for same time period." We may then assert as a law the following:

$$A_i = \frac{2C_i/C_g}{C_{it}} = \frac{2C_i}{C_g \cdot C_{it}}$$

It will be noted that the levels of efficiency of a law are cumulatively inclusive. At level two the presence and absence factor is included. At level three the directionality and presence and absence factors are in-

---

[23]Allport's famous law. See Allport, *op. cit.* Should the formula for the J curve be substituted for its name, the law would then be at the highest level of efficiency.

cluded. At level four the previous three levels are included. Each higher level of efficiency of a law of interaction fulfills the conditions of all lower levels of efficiency.

The notion of levels of efficiency of a law of interaction is important for both scientific and psychological reasons. The scientific reason is simple: As sophistication improves in a given scientific discipline, the laws of interaction employed in that discipline move to the highest levels of efficiency. Indeed, it should be possible to measure the level of sophistication of a given discipline by the efficiency of the laws therein employed.

Relations Between Types of Law and Levels of Efficiency

There are clear relationships between types of laws and levels of efficiency. These relationships are such as to indicate why determinant laws are preferred over categoric ones, and why sequential laws usually are valued for their appearance of causality as well as for their efficiency.

A categoric law cannot rise above the lowest level of efficiency. Recall the example used in the discussion of categoric laws, the relationship between being Jewish and voting for the Democratic party. Even when the probabilities in the four cells of the fourfold table are reexpressed, the laws relating ethnic background and voting behavior state only the probabilities of the presence and absence of a relationship. There is no statement of directionality, covariation, or rate of change. This minimum level of efficiency makes prediction by categoric laws low in precision. The widespread use of categoric laws in the behavioral sciences despite low-quality predictions must, therefore, be taken as evidence that behavioral scientists are employing a strategy of building theory to improve understanding before seeking to improve prediction.

A determinant law is always at the second or higher level of efficiency, and never at the lowest level. The very idea of determinant laws is that directionality, covariation, rate of change, or any cumulatively inclusive combination of these is what is meant by *determinant*. It is clear, therefore, that there is a neat distinction between categoric and determinant laws based on their respective efficiencies. Determinant laws are always more efficient than categoric laws.

Sequential laws may achieve any level of efficiency. Thus, "If a group leader applies pressure for productivity, the work group morale will change," is a sequential law of the lowest efficiency. Contrastingly, "A unit increase in the amount of group-leader pressure for productivity will produce an increase of one quarter unit in group morale,'' (the units of each being specified) is a sequential law of the highest efficiency level. Inasmuch as it seems clear that sequential laws may be stated at any level of efficiency, we may perhaps also be asking them to do more. Can this be another reason why we find it psychologically satisfying to ascribe causality to sequential laws as a means for finding an additional function for them? Perhaps we ought to be satisfied with the knowledge that the exclusive function of sequential laws is to handle the time dimension, which cannot be incorporated in categoric and determinant laws.

The idea of efficiency of laws in a discipline often may be utilized for the imperialistic border defenses erected against sister disciplines. When scientists from other disciplines attack problems of a less well-developed discipline, its practitioners are likely to resist the invasion and refuse to give credence to the invaders' theories. This is happening increasingly as physical and biological scientists encroach upon the territory of the social sciences. It is notable in the social sciences that there is a high barrier erected against physical scientists attempting to specify laws of interaction among social units. Thus, for example, Rashevsky's mathematical models of human behavior, which employ laws of the highest level of efficiency, have been almost universally ignored by social scientists. The social scientists were quite incapable of moving up to the high level of law employed by Rashevsky, a mathematical biophysicist.[24]

Logical Relationship Among Laws

Two laws cannot relate two units of a system with inconsistent results. Either of the two laws must be discarded. Thus, if A is related to B by law L_1, an alternate relationship, L_2, is subsequently proposed, and the predicted values of B for specified values of A are different under the two laws of interaction, then one or the other must be discarded. In the three-unit case, if A and B are related by law L_1 and B and C by law L_2, and if A and C are simultaneously operative so that the predicted value of B is not identical in both A and C, then the system is not coherent. Something has to be changed in the theory to restore coherence, either by

---

[24]See N. Rashevsky, "Two Models: Imitative Behavior and Distribution of Status," and J. S. Coleman, "An Expository Analysis of Some of Rashevsky's Social Behavior Models," both in P. F. Lazarsfeld (ed.), *Mathematical Thinking in the Social Sciences* (New York: Free Press, 1954).

changing one of the laws of interaction or by dropping one of the units previously included.

A system has a *minimum* of one law of interaction. Failure to contain at least one law means there is no theory relating at least two units.

The *maximum* number of laws of interaction for a system of *n* units is the number of laws necessary to relate the units two at a time each once with all the other units. The formula for this is the formula for combinations, of *n* things taken two at a time. In the instance of the lowest power of categoric law, the maximum number of laws is four times as great since each pair of units is linked by four laws.

A system may have categoric, sequential, and determinant laws governing interaction among its units. There is no logic limiting the mixture of types of laws in the same model provided each type employed meets the criteria for its class.

Parsimony of Laws

Parsimony in the number of laws of a theoretical model is determined by the *minimum* number of laws necessary to relate all the units of the system. If the laws relating *A* to *B* and *A* to *C* are identical, then there is a reason to believe that *B* and *C* are not distinctive units of the model. The most parsimonious set of laws is the minimum set for a system.

The issue of parsimony of laws of interaction has solely to do with the *number* of laws of interaction by which units of the model are linked. Parsimony does not relate to the complexity of the statement of relationship or to the efficiency level of the law.

It should be clear that when employing a categoric law of interaction in a two-unit system, there are always four possibilities, as represented by the four laws covering each of the cells in a 2 × 2 table. On the other hand, it should also be clear that where determinant laws of interaction are used for a two-unit analysis, there is only one law of interaction that can be stated at a time. The obvious conclusion we reach is that it is more parsimonious to use determinant laws than it is to use categoric laws.

"Universal" Laws

What can be done with the ubiquitous notion of "universal" law or, as it is sometimes more modestly called, "general" law? First of all, what is a universal law, and, secondly, how does it relate to laws of interaction?

There are two senses in which we use the term *universal law*. The first is to declare that for a given collection of units there is an invariant law (or set of laws) that links these units together. In this sense the universality of the law has to do with its generality in a given universe defined by the units composing it. For example, the following may be a universal law: "All human beings in contact interact." This universal law declares that regardless of the kind of people involved or the condition of their contact, they will interact. It will be noted, of course, that the law part of the statement is "contact interact" and not the full statement. Human beings are the units that are also denoted by the statement. In some respects this kind of universal law appears wholly trivial because it is so commonsensical. Such triviality may be further underscored by considering the fact that any action, including simply remaining in the presence of the other but not verbally or gesturally responding, may be considered an interaction. Under these circumstances, contact automatically means interaction and the law is tautological. It could just as well be stated as "contact in contact" ("All human beings in contact are in contact.").

The triviality of universal laws for a given universe is both heartening and discouraging. It is heartening because it suggests that scientists need not be geniuses in order to discover laws of their respective scientific disciplines. What makes these discoveries so disheartening is that they have such a strong ring of common sense when stated. One has the feeling that the scientist has merely restated folk wisdom, and, in fact, this has been especially the case in the social sciences.

A second sense in which we use the notion of universal law is to conceive of the same law of interaction as applying to several universes made up of different complements of units. In this view of universal law we assume that quite diverse types of units interact within given spheres in the same ways. We may identify these ways of interacting as having the same form. For example, using the categoric law of functional necessity, we could assert that human personality is dependent upon interaction with other people in a functionally necessary sense, and at the same time assert that the provision of supplies of food is functionally necessary to the survival of a group. In this sense of universal law, the law has the same form. In the two instances cited, the law states the relationship between quite different pairs of units in quite distinctive universes.

It would then appear to be entirely a matter of taste and artistic preference as to whether or not an individual scientist is dedicated to the search for universal laws. In the sense of *the* law of interaction pertaining to a given universe composed of fixed units, the universal law is likely to appear and be trivial. In the instance of a law that has application in several universes, the search for universal laws focuses on form rather than on content. If the theorist-scientist is interested in universal laws in either of these senses, there is certainly no prohibition against his pursuing them. What is important to recognize is that the category *universal law* is not used here as being a law different in kind from laws of interaction. For most theorist-scientists, the primary focus of attention will be on laws of interaction, leaving the issue of universality to the great generalizers and the philosophers.

Catalyst

One of the concepts widely used in chemistry is that of chemical catalyst. The catalyst unit is defined as a chemical agent whose presence in a chemical system is necessary in order that two or more other chemicals interact. The catalyst remains unchanged in the course of the interaction for which its presence is necessary. We may now ask, "Is it possible to use the concept *catalyst* in social analysis?"

There does not seem to be any theoretical reason why we may not think of social catalysts and employ them in theoretical models. So the issue that arises is how do we incorporate such catalysts into the model? In particular, this issue becomes pertinent when we ask by what laws does a catalyst enter into relationship with other units of the model? A catalyst unit may be of any type (EARS). Its significance in a theory rests on the law by which it relates to other units and not on the type of unit represented by the catalyst. The most general case is the one in which the unit labeled a *catalyst* has any value in the system. Two or more other units interact by the law of interaction connecting them if, and only if, the catalyst unit has a value in the system. We may visualize this in a three-dimensional chart, as in Figure 5-5. The units having variable values are displayed on the X and Y dimensions. On the Z axis will be found the catalytic unit that may have an unlimited range of positive values and/or may have an unlimited range of negative values. The surface formed by unit values measured on these three axes then constitutes a description of the relation between the catalyst and the other two units in the system. At any slice at right angles to the Z axis through the surface, as at Z_i, the values of X and Y units will be the same. Thus the values of X and Y are independent of the positive or negative values of the Z catalyst.

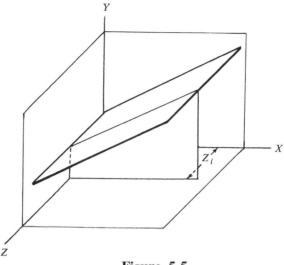

Figure 5-5

There may, of course, be more restrictive conditions on the catalyst unit. For example, the catalyst may operate in the system only when positive values are associated with it. Or the catalyst may operate only when a unit has negative values. Indeed, there may be even a more limited range of values in either the positive or the negative scale for Z over which Z is operative as a catalyst in the system containing X and Y units.

The notion of a catalyst unit in a social-science model is quite common. For example, in the study of the behavior of populations under conditions of disaster, the nature of the disaster itself is unimportant with respect to the analytical problems. The state of the system labeled *disaster* is the catalytic unit whose presence is necessary for the interaction of social or psychological units that are studied by disaster specialists. It makes no difference whether the disaster is a flood, an earthquake, an explosion, or whatnot. The unit *stress* is a comparable catalytic unit that is used in sociological analysis as well as psychological analysis. This unit of a model enters it only with some positive values that then make operative the laws of interaction of the other units composing the model.

The critical feature of the law by which catalytic units relate to the other units of a system is that the value of the catalytic unit is independent of the values of all other units to which the catalytic unit is connected by this singular law of interaction. There is only one set of values of the catalytic unit that is critical, namely, its zero value, or that range of values in which there are no relationships among the other units of the system.

Table 5-2

U_C	U_A and U_B
Nonzero Values	$U_A \xleftrightarrow{\quad L \quad} U_B$ over some values of A and B defined by L, independent of values of U_C.
= zero (or defined range of nonzero values)	U_A independent of U_B over any values of A and B, defined by L.

The law of interaction of a catalyst with other units of the system may be expressed as follows:

Given two units, U_A and U_B, U_A and U_B interact by law L if, and only if, the catalyst U_C has nonzero values (this is only a sufficient condition). The values of U_A and U_B defined by law L are independent of the nonzero values of U_C (this is the necessary condition).

This is shown graphically in Table 5-2.

In the structure of social theory it is not often recognized how frequently catalytic units are employed. It is certainly true that the law of interaction of catalytic units with other units is ignored. For example, the great insight that initiated the profound work of Hans Selye on stress was his recognition, early gained in his medical schooling, that many empirical observations over a number of different realms of medical problems stemmed from the patient being in a state of stress, thus leading Selye to identify stress as a catalytic unit in his models.[25] Once this identification was achieved, Selye was able to advance some seminal research and theory building in this area. In the same way, when Merton recognized that the catalytic unit in social theory relating individual adaptations to social expectations was that of deviancy, he was then in a position to spell out the main types of deviancy that are generated in a social system where acceptance of goals and means becomes problematical. Indeed, the very tables that Merton used, and those that I modified in extending his typology, labeled the conditions of deviancy as minus values, meaning rejection of norms or means. Thus, a catalytic unit, *deviancy*, had only minus values in this system. The types of deviancy (three in the Merton system and fourteen in the Dubin system) are determined by the number and location of the negative orientations of individuals.

We can now conclude that the catalyst unit has special significance for social analysis. This significance lies not in the character of the unit but in the character of the law by which the unit relates to the analytical system

---

[25]H. Selye, *The Stress of Life* (New York: McGraw-Hill, 1956).

in which it is employed. This, of course, turns out to be identical with the operational meaning of catalyst in physical models or theories.

Holding Constant

The common tactic in doing research is to attempt to hold the values of one or more units constant. In experimental research it is often believed desirable to hold constant by designing experimental conditions so that one or more units have a zero value. At this zero value it is assumed that the unit taking that value has no lawful relationship to the remaining units under study. When it is impossible experimentally to design the study so that a unit takes a zero value, then the alternative tactic is to assign a fixed value to a unit. Thus, if a study involves people and it is believed that maleness and femaleness may be lawfully related to other units employed, then the holding-constant approach is to limit a sample study to either males or females.

It should be recognized that underlying the tactic of holding constant is an admission that there is a real but unstated law of relationship between the held-constant units and the other units under study. The researcher assumes that he needs to eliminate the relationship of the unit being held constant to the system of other units precisely because it is believed to have some connection with the values of the other units being studied.

The tactic of holding constant should be distinguished clearly from the problem of the adequacy of empirical indicators of unit values. If empirical indicators for the values of a given unit are unreliable, then the researcher is constrained to improve their reliability. Empirical indicators are analyzed in detail in Chapter 9.

The act of holding constant as a research tactic serves to reduce the scope of the theoretical model being tested by deliberately eliminating one or more units from possible inclusion in the model. In this very operation the researcher admits that the model being tested is, by definition, incomplete, as the units being held constant are believed to be lawfully related to the units employed in the model of narrower scope. From the standpoint of the reader of research results, it then becomes crucial to ask, ''What happens to the model employed in this piece of research if we put back into it the very units that were held constant in making empirical tests?'' When this question is asked, it becomes quite evident that the particular model under investigation is necessarily incomplete, or deliberately limited.

Holding the values of a unit constant in designing a research undertaking is both an admission of knowledge and an admission of ignorance. It is an admission of knowledge because it concludes that values of one unit are lawfully related to values of other units incorporated into a given theoretical model. The admission of ignorance is the conclusion that the nature of this law of interaction between the unit held constant and the others is unknown. Because the law of interaction is unknown, it is assumed that values taken on by the unit held constant will confound the interactions among the units included in the study. The reward of holding the values of a unit constant is to clarify the interactions among the units remaining in the model. The cost of holding the values of the unit constant is an admission of ignorance—the researcher admits he is incapable of lawfully relating this unit to those employed in the smaller theoretical model.

It is always alleged to be one of the glories of the experimental approach that effective control is achieved on the values of some units by holding constant experimentally. But it is also one of the ignominies of this very research tactic that it throws out of consideration something that the researcher must be the first to admit is relevant because it is a unit lawfully related to the units under study.

Levels of Analysis

One of the troublesome features of any science is the fact that it apparently is not independent of other sciences. This becomes particularly evident when we examine a thing like a person. The sociologist may claim that he is interested in the individual only in his *inter*personal relationships. The field of inquiry for the sociologist lies outside the skin of the individual, but he uses properties of the person among the units that enter into sociological theories. The psychologist, on the other hand, is interested in the *intra*personal properties of the individual, whether these are wholly contained inside the skin or involve some linkage with the outside world, as in learning or personality theories. The physiologist, in his turn, focuses on properties primarily within the skin of the individual at the level of organs, tissues, and cells. The microbiologist may be concerned with cell and subcell structures, whereas the organic chemist may deal with the properties of the individual at an atomic level.

For any discipline dealing with units larger than those at the atomic level, there tends to be fervent defensiveness against reductionism. Reductionism is combated as an attempt to degrade the theory of a discipline using large units to the level of the theory of the discipline using small units. Thus, sociology is concerned with the possibility of the reductionism of the discipline to psychology. Psychology meets part of the threat of reductionism by retaining physiological psychology within its diverse discipline.

Reductionism may also be viewed as an analytical problem dealing with the linkages among levels of analysis rather than as a political problem having to do with the maintenance of discipline boundaries. As an analytical problem, our focus of attention may be characterized in the following questions: "Is there some systematic way in which levels of analysis may be articulated with each other? If so, what is the nature of this articulation?"

One way of attacking this problem is to consider that the summative units of one level of analysis are composed in part, but not exclusively, of any or all of the other kinds of units that are small and hence at a lower level of analysis. (By *lower level* we mean a level at which the units are smaller in scope.) From the previous chapter you will remember the conclusion that summative units are not useful in theoretical models although they do have their usefulness as heuristic devices in education. It will also be recalled that summative units are global in character and implicitly or explicitly sum up a number of properties of things.

Suppose now we were to ask the following question: "What happens if we decide to break down a summative unit into its component parts?" If we did this, we might find that some of the constituent properties of a summative unit are properties (enumerative, associative, relational, or statistical) at a lower level of analysis. For example, suppose a sociologist is concerned with the study of alcoholism. A summative unit that would be useful in defining his realm of concern would be one like *drunkenness*. For the sociologist, the unit *drunkenness* is clearly a summative one. The sociologist does not know anything about the physiology or psychology of drunkenness, nor for his purposes is this knowledge necessary. When the sociologist poses his own analytical problems, he will do so in the following manner. He will ask, "What is the relationship between habitual drinking and husband-wife interaction?" or "What is the relationship between excessive drinking and parent-child interaction?" or "What is the relationship between having imbibed X amount of intoxicating beverages and responsiveness to social norms in behavior?" For the sociologist the nature of drunkenness is not important. Whether it is the consequence of the interaction of alcohol and the chemical constituents of the blood or whether it is a consequence of the definition of the self by others as "drunken" does not really bother the sociologist. On the other hand, these kinds of analytical problems are obviously central ones to the physiological chemist or the psychologist. For the sociologist, the summative unit *drunkenness* may be spelled out in terms of such empirical indicators for a given study as "regular drinker" or "excessive drinker" or "having drunk X amount of intoxicating beverages." These properties of individuals become appropriate associative units for use in the analysis of some of the sociological consequences of alcoholism. They are not, let me repeat, the same thing as *drunkenness*.

Whatever may be found out by the physiological chemist with respect to the chemical or physiological etiology of a drunken condition would ordinarily have no influence on the sociologist's problem or the nature of his analysis and the theories he develops with respect to this problem. This is another way of saying that there may very well be an analytical hierarchy but that this analytical hierarchy does not lend itself to subsuming all phenomena under the theoretical models of that level of analysis having the most basic (smallest) units in it.

Let us now turn to the relationship between laws of interaction and levels of analysis. Laws of interaction, as we have used this phrase, mean the same things as Bergmann's *process law*.[26] That is to say, laws of interaction among units focus upon the processes of interaction at a given level of analysis. Remembering the previously established distinction between outcome and process, we are able to see that there are *not* laws of interaction that link up units *between* levels of analysis. In relation to levels of analysis, laws of interaction are always *intra*level in location. The linkage between levels of analysis derives from the fact that there is a gathering together of the units of a lower level of analysis into a summative unit at a higher level of analysis.

I conclude, then, that there are no laws of interaction connecting levels of analysis but that there are units (summative ones) that provide such linkage.

[26]See Gustav Bergmann, *Philosophy of Science* (Madison, Wisc.: University of Wisconsin Press, 1957).

INTERLUDE TWO

A Note on the Pronunciation of "Shibboleth"*

Elbridge Sibley
The Social Science Research Council

Then said they unto him, Say now Sibboleth: and he said Sibboleth: for he could not frame to pronounce it right. They they took him and slew him . . .

—Judges, 12:6

A myth appears to have gained credence in some quarters of the academic community, to the effect that failure to utter certain powerful words (without too much regard for their meaning) will be as fatal to an application for a Council fellowship as was failure to pronounce *Shibboleth* correctly when challenged by the ancient men of Gilead.

The passwords by which aspirants seek to gain admission to the guild of social scientists change from year to year. Among those currently in vogue are *model* (variously used to refer to a system of equations, a paradigm, a taxonomy, something else, or nothing in particular), *multivariate analysis* (connoting almost anything except monistic determinism), *parameter* (by which the user may or may not mean a statistical datum), *interdisciplinary* or *multidisciplinary approach* (too often connoting a general lack of discipline), and *computer* (for which read usually computer, but sometimes tabulating machine or even desk calculator).

When pressed to explain what he meant by his statement that he would use "a flexible configurational mode of analysis," a fellowship candidate avowed that his words had no definite meaning. "But," he

*From *Items,* Social Science Research Council, 19:16 (March 1965). Used by permission of the author.

went on to say, "I put them in because, according to the folklore at this university, the Council wants that kind of language." His candor was refreshing to an interviewer who has talked with great numbers of less forthright applicants. But he was only admitting explicitly what is self-evident in too many other applications.

Granted that an applicant can hardly be censured for trying as best he can to impress the selection committee; and granted that in some fields of endeavor the ritual use of language to persuade rather than to inform is appropriate; still, an applicant addressing a jury of competent and responsible social scientists ought to be aware that word dropping will not conceal an intellectual vacuum but may well make even a basically valid proposal look meretricious.

But let us not hastily lay more blame on the applicant and his mentors than they deserve. For perhaps there is here a more chastening lesson for the Council and its staff. Have we failed to communicate to the academic public a correct impression of what the Council is trying to do? Have we inadvertently encouraged our friends and their students to conjure with jargon? Have we failed to insist loudly enough that the advancement of social science must be brought about by giving meaning to some of the words just mentioned, not by using them as mere shibboleths?

Boundaries

The situation seems to be a pretty general one which presents itself whenever we try to deal with a physical situation with partial differential equations. The equations themselves can never adequately reproduce any physical situation, but always have to be supplemented by boundary conditions. The boundary conditions we have in our control. One experimental situation is different from another by its boundary conditions. We vary the initial conditions, that is, we make different experiments by varying the boundary conditions, and we measure the results of our experiment with instruments which are themselves simply a part of the boundary conditions. We never make contact with the equations themselves through our instruments, but only by calculation and through the boundary conditions. . . . We start with boundary conditions, which we impose, and we end with boundary conditions, which we measure. Our only demand is that we know how to correlate initial and final boundary conditions.

—P. W. BRIDGMAN, *The Way Things Are*

IN THIS CHAPTER the boundaries of a theoretical model are examined. In order that a model may represent an empirical system, it has to have boundaries corresponding to the empirical system. The boundaries are important to the specification of any theoretical model.

The chapter opens with a consideration of bounded systems followed by an analysis of the way in which the boundary criteria are shared by both units and laws of a model. Attention then turns to boundary-determining criteria for any system. From this follows an analysis of the methods for determining boundaries. The relation between the number of boundary-determining criteria and the domain represented by a theoretical model is then examined. The chapter concludes with an analysis of the generalization of individual models to a model encompassing a larger domain comprising those covered by the individual models.

Boundedness

A theoretical model is said to be *bounded* when the limiting values on the units comprising the model are known. The limiting values are always determinate. As will be shown presently, the determinate character of these limiting values may be derived either from the characteristics of units themselves or from the characteristics of laws by which the units interact. In each instance these limiting values are determined by criteria internal to the model. It is also possible to determine limiting values by criteria external to the model. Both these cases will be examined.

Open and Closed Boundary

It is a convention of systems analysis to distinguish between open and closed systems. A closed system is usually defined as one in which there is no exchange between the system and its environment. An open system is one in which some kind of exchange takes place between the system and its environment. The distinction between open and closed systems, as conventionally set forth, depends on *exchange over the boundary* of the system between itself and its environment. This exchange conforms to laws of interaction fully as explicit as the laws of interactions found inside the system among the units composing it. Furthermore, the boundary is just as explicit whether it is open or closed.

It follows, therefore, that the logic of a system, and the theoretical model representing this system, in nowise depends upon the openness or closedness of its boundary. The convention adopted in this volume is to view an open system as one that may be closed, i.e., have a boundary over which exchange *does not* take place, by the addition of one or more units to the existing system and of the appropriate law or laws of interaction connecting the new units with the existing ones. In this view, a system with an open boundary is one that can be translated into a system with a closed boundary by enlarging the domain through the addition to the system of one or more units with which the formerly included units interact.

Boundary Criteria

The boundary-determining criteria of a model apply with equal force to the units employed and the laws of interaction among these units. The units of a model must fit inside the boundaries before the model is complete. Thus, if a given model is sex-linked, being limited, for example, to males, then the only units that may be employed in the model are units that have the characteristic "maleness." By the same token, if maleness is one of the boundary conditions, then the units employed in the model may interact only with reference to this characteristic of the boundary.

The pervasive influence of boundary-determining criteria on both units and laws of a model was the subject of detailed consideration in Bridgman's book *Dimensional Analysis*.[1] In that volume Bridgman gave attention to the need for maintaining a common dimensionality to the analytical models employed in science. It turns out that homogeneity with respect to dimensionality is achieved by insuring that the units employed and the laws by which they interact satisfy the same boundary-determining criteria. Indeed, Bridgman made this clear in the quotation at the head of this chapter when he stated that "We start with boundary conditions, which we impose, and we end with boundary conditions, which we measure. Our only demand is that we know how to correlate initial and final boundary conditions."

A common syllogism is a good illustration of units sharing a common boundary-determining criterion. Thus: "All men think; Plato is a man; therefore, Plato thinks." Plato and men are within the same domain and share a common boundary-determining characteristic, namely, that they both fall within the domain of the unit *think*. We can see this best by diagramming the statement, as in Figure 6-1. This kind of diagram, so important in logic and mathematics, is concerned only with the location of boundaries of two or more domains.

It is possible to find examples in social science research where either there was a failure to have the units and/or laws respond to the same boundary-determining criteria or it was believed that this was improbable. For example, the standard response to the theories of Rhine and his associates dealing with ESP has been to assert that the results achieved were the consequences either of trickery or of chance. It has been considered improbable by reputable psychologists and sociologists that man could interact either with other men or with objects through a faculty called *extrasensory perception*. The very belief in this improbability in effect declares that any law of interaction that employs or implies extrasensory perception does not come within the same boundary as the unit *man*. Recent reports have indicated that a Russian psychologist claims experimental support for ESP. Perhaps now the consequence will be to

---

[1]P. W. Bridgman, *Dimensional Analysis* (New York: Harper & Row, 1931).

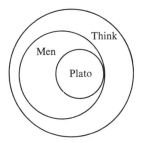

Figure 6-1

assert that ESP is really a communist plot (which might shake the foundations of Duke University, the home of Professor Rhine) or the equally revolutionary assertion that ESP *is* a quality of man and properly falls within a system boundary in which man is an appropriate unit (which would have foundation-shaking consequences for the profession of psychology!).

In model building a scientist has two courses open to him with respect to boundary-determining criteria. (1) He may use a logical test, like the syllogism, to be certain that the units employed and the laws by which they interact all satisfy the same boundary-determining criterion and therefore may be incorporated in the same model. (2) The alternative course open in model building is to employ an empirical test to determine whether a supposed sharing of boundary-determining criterion is, in fact, a reality. The second course is represented by the work of Rhine on ESP and the responses of his critics, who argue with each other about whether or not the boundary-determining criteria are, in fact, applicable both to the unit *man* and to the law by which men interact, namely, that of extrasensory perception.

Dimensional unity among the units and laws of interaction in a given model is achieved by ensuring that both satisfy the boundary-determining criterion for the model. Failure to do this, either by meeting the canons of logic or by subjecting the proposed dimensional unity to an empirical test means that the model is an inconsistent one.

Interior and Exterior Boundary-Determining Criteria

There are two general classes of criteria that may determine the boundary of a model. Interior criteria are those derived from the characteristics of the units and laws employed in the model. Exterior criteria are those imposed from outside the model. The distinction between interior and exterior criteria may be made clear by examples.

Suppose it is proposed to study leadership behavior in task-oriented *ad hoc* groups established under laboratory conditions (a very common problem in small-group research). The boundary-determining criteria are (1) that the members not be friends but be selected on an *ad hoc* basis, (2) that the group so formed by isolated from any external contact under laboratory conditions, (3) that the group be given one or more tasks to perform, and (4) that there be opportunity for leadership to develop in the group. All these boundary criteria are internal to the group itself. The units employed in building a model under these boundary conditions (e.g., leaders, followers, interaction behaviors of authority and compliance, task behaviors) and their laws of interaction (e.g., leaders initiate interaction more frequently than followers) must all conform to the boundary criteria.

Suppose, however, we now turned attention to studying leadership behavior in task-oriented groups among employees in a bureaucratic organization. This would result automatically in changing one internal boundary criterion, namely, that the persons in the group be selected on an *ad hoc* basis. In a bureaucratic organization members of a task-oriented group would know each other and have longtime working relations with each other. But more important, by moving the group within an organized setting larger than itself, we introduce an external boundary-determining criterion that includes functional linkages between the particular work group and other groups in the larger organization. Indeed, it may very well be that the linkage of the work group with other such groups may materially influence leadership behavior inside the work group. The mere fact of linkage among work groups shifts the domain of the model by shifting the boundaries from the laboratory-bounded model to the organizationally embedded model. These may be models of totally different phenomena, even though superficially related by sharing the characteristic "small group."

It is possible to specify the particular methods available for determining model boundaries. We will deal respectively with methods for determining the interior criteria of boundaries and the exterior criteria.

Interior Boundary Criteria

The most common boundary-determining criterion viewed from the interior of a model is what the logician calls a *truth table*. A syllogism may be placed into a truth table as we have already seen. More complex truth tables may also be developed.

A simple truth table would be one examining the values of p and q that would satisfy the statement "$p \wedge q$." This statement is the shorthand way of saying, "If p is true and q is true, then $p \wedge q$ is true, otherwise $p \wedge q$ is false." The units of this model are p and q. The law of their interaction is "$p \wedge q$ is true only if p is true and q is true; in all other instances, $p \wedge q$ is false." The truth table would look like Table 6-1. Thus, there is only one combination of the values of p and q that places them inside the boundaries of $p \wedge q$, namely that they both are true.[2]

What is notable about a truth table is that once units and the laws of their interaction are established, then certain things must follow in accordance with the rules of logic. The essential feature of a truth table is to reveal those things that must be true given the starting specification of units and their laws of interaction, as well as those things that must be false by the same criteria.

Truth tables may be used in connection with both units and laws of a model. Indeed, this must hold for all methods of determining boundaries, as we have already concluded that units and laws of a model must conform to the boundary conditions of the model.

A second general procedure in finding boundaries is to establish a limit of probability (and therefore the boundary between the probable and improbable) on the values taken by units employed in a model. If the empirical value measured on the unit exceeds the limit so established, it is then assumed that the measured value does not lie within the domain of probable values of that unit when used in that model. This is an interior boundary-determining criterion employed when tests for homogeneity are used *to eliminate* sample values because they lie beyond a predetermined limit of probability. Thus, in sampling variables, whether or not the parent population is normally distributed, the sampling distribution for large samples may be represented "by a range of 3σ on each side of the mean [that] includes the major portion of the distribution."[3] Any sample values that exceed $\pm 3\sigma$ are considered improbable values that do not belong within the parent population from which the sample was drawn. Hence, we feel confident in throwing out the sample value on the assumption that it does not come from the parent population. This is another way

[2]An especially pertinent discussion of truth tables valuable for the scientist will be found in John G. Kemeny, J. Laurie Snell, and Gerald G. Thompson, *Introduction to Finite Mathematics* (Englewood Cliffs, N.J.: Prentice-Hall, 1957), Chapter 1.

[3]G. U. Yule and M. G. Kendall, *An Introduction to the Theory of Statistics,* 11th ed. (London: Charles Griffin & Co., 1937). p. 380.

Table 6-1

p	q	$p \wedge q$
true	true	true
true	false	false
false	true	false
false	false	false

of saying that the boundary that we have drawn depends upon the belief in the improbability of a value occurring in a sample of a population if that value deviates beyond a chosen value from the statistic of the population. A sample value must conform to the population values and the limits contained therein in order for the sample legitimately to be assumed to be drawn from the parent population.

There is a third method using interior criteria to determine boundaries consisting of what Lazarsfeld calls *subsetting the property space*. Subsetting depends on using an affirmative criterion to distinguish a unit or a law of interaction from other possible types. Thus, one may, following Merton, define deviant forms of individual adaptations as rebellion, retreatism, ritualism, and innovation. It will be noted that each of these categories of deviant response may be defined only with respect to itself and not with respect to the definition of the other categories. Thus, it would not be possible to know what rebellion is by defining all other forms of deviant individual adaptation. The definition of rebellion requires a positive explication of its own characteristics.

A subsetting operation for determining a model boundary may be best understood by remembering that it takes a positive set of criteria to determine the characteristics of a category and that all other or residual categories may simply be designated by the term *not_____*. Thus, if we can define category *A,* then all other categories may be defined as *not-A*.

Subsetting operations to determine the limits of a model are characteristically employed. For example, in psychophysical research a common analytical problem is that of determining thresholds. A threshold value, for example, the threshold value of auditory perception, is a very limited range of perception or response. A model is built with respect to such thresholds by subsetting a range of response and the laws governing response at the threshold. These may turn out to be different from the units and laws employed above and below the threshold to model the empirical behavior encountered in those domains. A subsetting is often employed to deal with the problem of discontinuity when either the units or the laws or both need to be changed in order to model the phenomenon being studied at the points of discontinuity. Thresholds, of course, are not only psychophysical. In psychology they are an essential concern. However, there are many other kinds of thresholds in social behavior. For example, the diplomatic relations between nations when broken off and transformed into a war relationship represent the moving of one type of interaction to another type of interaction through a threshold giving rise to the second type.

Still another interior boundary-determining criterion is one built into the law of interaction employed. Suppose two units are viewed as interacting in a manner represented by a curve that has one or two asymptotes. The value of the asymptotes approached by the curve may be calculated from the knowledge of the curve itself. It follows that the model employing this kind of interaction between the units contemplates no interaction or a different kind of interaction beyond the values of the asymptotes. Should such deviant values be found, they would have to be accounted for by a different model. In exactly the same way, the directionality of a relationship between two units, or among several units, is an interior criterion that determines the boundary of interaction among or between these units. Constants in a law of interaction operate in precisely the same way as limits or asymptotes or directionality in establishing interior criteria for model boundaries. If two units are asserted to be negatively related or inversely related, then relationships that are not negative or inverse are excluded from the domain of the model.

The various methods suggested in this section illustrate the range of possible ways in which interior criteria determine boundaries of theoretical models. The following section examines external boundary-determining criteria.

Exterior Boundary Criteria

The most frequent instance in which an external criterion determines the boundary of a model occurs when either a new unit or a new law or both are required to close the domain of the model. When either a new unit or a new law must be introduced into the model, it is clear that the unit must be designated affirmatively as must be the law. What may have been a *not-A* category from the standpoint of interior boundary-determining criteria must now be translated into a *B* category in order that a new unit or law may be incorporated in the old model. It is because of the need to specify the new unit or law that it is viewed as exterior to the old model.

The sense of external criteria determining boundaries is revealed in the following statement describing a closed system: "A system is *closed* if there is no import or export of energies in any of its forms such as information, heat, physical materials, etc., then, therefore, *no change of components,* an example being chemical reaction taking place in a sealed insulated container."[4] The pertinent phrase to note in the quotation is the one stating *no change of components.* There is no need to add a unit or law in order that the model be bounded when the model is considered closed. By the same token, there is no need to subtract a unit or law in order to maintain the boundary of the model.

The most commonly encountered circumstance in which an exterior criterion determines the boundaries of a model is the one in which the model builder admits, after testing the model empirically, that he cannot account for the empirical results without introducing what he calls *an intervening variable* into the model with which he started. The conclusion that a variable has intervened to produce the empirical results not predictable from the starting model is the investigator's way of saying, "I did not know that this unit was necessary in my model and/or that this law needed to be included in order to account for the empirical reality." This particular use of the concept of intervening variable as a new unit added to an existing model is a common signal in the literature that a new boundary has been established for an older scientific model; it has been established by adding a newly defined unit and the law connecting this unit to the others comprising the initial model.

There is a special feature of an exterior boundary-determining criterion that distinguishes it from an interior criterion. Often an exterior criterion is employed to establish the boundary but then plays no further role in the model. Such a criterion is only for the purpose of determining the boundary. The following is an illustration. Suppose a model is built to study interaction in a two-person group. Suppose further that the investigator, a family sociologist, is interested in limiting the two-person group to a male and female who are married. He may further restrict the boundary of his domain to married people with no children who have been married no longer than three years. If one examines the boundary restrictions drawn around the domain, namely, that of bisexual pairs, who are

[4]A. D. Hall and R. E. Fagen, "Definition of System," *Yearbook,* Society for General Systems Research, 1:18–28 (1956), p. 23.

married, who have not yet produced children, and who have been married for no longer than three years, each of these boundary criteria serves to narrow the domain of the model but enters into it in no other way.

We may, therefore, think of benign exterior boundary-determining criteria as distinct from active exterior criteria. The benign criteria do not enter into the dynamic model but only determine boundaries; the active criteria, as in the case of the addition or subtraction of a unit from a model, do enter into the dynamic model itself as well as function to determine the boundary of the domain represented by the model.

It is important to specify the boundary of the theoretical model because comparability among studies depends on insuring that the domains of separate studies are, in fact, overlapping domains. If the models being tested by the studies do not have overlapping domains, then the studies are not replications of each other in any meaningful sense, nor can the conclusions from the test of one model bear any necessary relation to the conclusions about the other model. For example, if a model of the ecological structure of cities with populations of five to ten thousand that lie outside a Standard Metropolitan Statistical Area is developed, then it does not follow that the same model will be applicable to cities of larger size or to cities of the same size that lie within a Standard Metropolitan Statistical Area. A change in the size of units or in the ecological location of units may require a different kind of model to analyze the internal ecological structure of the urban unit.

The usual caveat with which the typical study ends, namely, that "our empirical conclusions apply only to a model with the boundary conditions we have specified," is not an expression of modesty. It is an affirmative declaration that the empirical investigation extended only up to the boundaries of the theoretical model being investigated. There is no logic by which it may be concluded that the tested model has a domain larger than the boundaries built into the model. The problem of extending the domain of a model and thereby generalizing it will be examined later in this chapter.

Size of Domain and Number of Boundary-Determining Criteria

There is an inverse relationship between the number of boundary-determining criteria employed in a model and the size of the domain covered by the model. The word *domain* has been left undefined up to this point. I now define the domain of a model as being the territory over which we can make truth statements about the model and, therefore, about the values of the units composing the model.

The most universal model that can be constructed is one that has only a single boundary-determining criterion. As each additional boundary-determining criterion is added to a model, either a unit is dropped from the model or a greater restriction is placed on the number or character of the laws of interaction remaining in the model. This narrowing of the domain of a model is precisely the tactic employed when the investigator attempts to hold constant the values of one or more units in the process of doing research. What happens in the holding-constant process has not only an empirical consequence but also a theoretical one. By holding constant, additional boundary restrictions are placed upon the empirical situation that can only have the consequence of making the same restrictions hold for the theoretical model being tested. Thus, the investigator who sees himself as satisfying the highest canons of scientific behavior by experimentally, or through research design, holding constant the impact of variation in values of given units is, at the same time and to the same degree, also constricting the domain of the theoretical model being tested. This latter point is seldom recognized by the empirical investigator.

It has become an accepted doctrine of faith in the social sciences that the twentieth century is a century in which social and behavioral scientists will operate in what Robert Merton has called *theories of the middle range*.[5] The sense or meaning that can be given to the term *theories of the middle range* is that they are models having not too few and not too many boundary-determining criteria. Merton's insistence on theories of the middle range was largely a reaction to global theories of social behavior that had minimum boundary-determining criteria. He was also partly reacting to the fragments of research that dealt with tests of models of such narrow domain that their results did not appear to add up to much in the way of theoretical knowledge.

Whether or not the growth of theory is facilitated by the simultaneous presence of models with narrow domains, medium-size domains, or very large domains is essentially a problem of analyzing the growth patterns of given scientific disciplines. In the classical sciences, the historical landmarks most celebrated are the ones at which models of very broad domain were developed. The theoretical models of Galileo, Newton, and Einstein are landmarks in the development of physical science, and the models developed had very broad domains. The Newtonian models were developed largely from an incomplete set of empirical data. The Einsteinian

[5]R. K. Merton, *Social Theory and Social Structure* (New York: Free Press, 1949).

model was developed from a much broader base of empirical knowledge. Indeed, it might be fair to say that the Einsteinian model is a synthesis of the empirical confirmation of many models of much narrower domain.[6]

Homogeneity of Domain

The number of boundary-determining criteria has an influence on the homogeneity of the domain of a model. In general, the more boundary-determining criteria there are, the greater the homogeneity of the domain covered by a model. Conversely, the fewer the number of boundary-determining criteria, the more heterogeneous is the domain. The meanings of homogeneity and heterogeneity can be readily understood.

By homogeneity I mean that the units and laws satisfy the conditions contained in a single boundary-determining criterion and are therefore homogeneous on the criterion. Thus, if maleness is a boundary-determining criterion, then any units employed in a model for which this criterion determines the boundary must conform to maleness, as must the laws employed.

Suppose, now, two conditions are considered simultaneously as boundary-determining criteria. In order that units and laws conform to both criteria, they must satisfy each. Therefore, if a unit or a law satisfies only one criterion but not the other, it must lie outside the domain defined by the criterion it fails to match. On the other hand, if a given unit or law satisfies both criteria, then it must lie inside a domain smaller than that defined by the more extensive criterion or by the total domain, including overlapping and nonoverlapping domains defined by all criteria. Thus, a boundary determined by two criteria bounds a domain necessarily smaller than one determined by only one of these criteria. For example, if maleness is the initial criterion, then the addition of a second criterion like adolescence will further restrict the domain to the age range represented by adolescence. Maleness plus adolescence has a narrower domain than either one alone, as shown in Figure 6-2.

The process of successive addition of boundary-determining criteria is a familiar one. The more criteria added to the model, the more homogeneous are the units and laws contained within the boundary of the model. That is so because they share more conditions defining member-

[6]See, for example, M. Born, *Experiment and Theory in Physics* (New York: Dover Publications, 1956), p. 14.

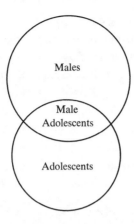

Figure 6-2

ship in the domain than would be true if fewer boundary-determining criteria were employed.

The limiting case is to impose so many boundary-determining criteria that the end result is a population of exactly one. This, of course, becomes the analytical problem for the biographer and the historian. We have already noted in Chapter 3 that the analysis of a population of one is an analysis of event and not, therefore, subject to any sort of theoretical model building.

As more boundary-determining criteria are added to a model, the units and laws satisfying the criteria become more homogeneous. Consequently, what is lost in the size of the domain of a model when additional boundary-determining criteria are used is compensated for in the increased purity of the units and laws of the model.

Another meaning may now be added to Merton's notion of theories of the middle range. Not only are these theories that have a moderate number of boundary-determining criteria, but by virtue of this they are also models of phenomena that are only moderately homogeneous. For the experimentally-minded behavioral scientist, this moderate degree of homogeneity in the units and laws of the model is inadequate. Such criticism of inadequacy is valid only insofar as the critic recognizes that he is demanding more restrictive boundaries on the models. Criticism is invalid if the critic assumes that there may be no linkage to reality in models of the middle range. There are no logical rules by which the usefulness of a particular scientific model can be determined from knowledge of the domain it represents. Indeed, as already noted, some of the classic landmark models in the exact sciences have been models with the broadest domains. It is a psychological absurdity that experimentally inclined behavioral scientists pay homage to the classical physical-science model builders at the same time that they condemn their theory-building colleagues who make use of models in the middle and broad ranges. This is one of the macabre jokes that derive from analogies rather than understanding.

Generalization of Models

The generality of a scientific model depends solely upon the size of the domain it represents. This, therefore, suggests that the fundamental process for coming to general models in any science is a process involving expansion of the boundaries of models with narrower ranges. We have already seen, however, that the expansion of a boundary depends upon reducing the number of boundary-determining criteria. Consequently, to produce a more general model (i.e., one with a larger domain) necessarily involves subtracting one or more boundary-determining criteria.

In a practical sense the circumstance under which this is done is as follows. Two models with relatively narrow domains are examined to determine which units and laws of the two models are isomorphic with respect to each other. For those units and laws that are isomorphic the boundary-determining criteria that are common to these units and laws are then determined. These will often turn out to be fewer in number than the sum of the boundary-determining criteria for the two separate models. By employing only those units and laws that are isomorphic from the two models, a third model is built. This third model will generalize aspects of the two narrower-range models. By this process generalization is achieved.

It should be obvious that a model builder may put together more than two models of narrow domains in order to generalize. Indeed, many models may be combined by this process.

For example, the analysis of a doctor-patient relationship may generate one model. The analysis of a parent-child relationship may generate another model. The analysis of a husband-wife relationship gives rise to still another model, and the examination of a teacher-student relationship to a still different model. A theorist-researcher now turns his attention to a two-person interaction. He might very well build a model for a two-person interaction from the isomorphic parts of the separate models just listed. A more general model would have a larger domain because the boundary-determining criteria would probably be two persons, in mutual presence, interacting meaningfully. These criteria would all be satisfied by the special models, but each special model would in addition have other restricting boundary-determining criteria.

Historically, in a given discipline, there is no certainty that the models employed will be ones of small domain or ones of large domain in the initial phases of the development of the discipline. In sociology, for example, Georg Simmel dealt with models of large domain in treating two-person groups. Subsequently, analytical attention in the field turned to models of narrower domain. On the other hand, in psychology the work of Skinner started with models of rather narrow domain and came to be generalized as a broad learning theory under the title of operant conditioning. In which direction the model building goes probably does not make any difference to the development of a scientific discipline. It is more pertinent in comprehending the additivity of knowledge in a discipline to recognize the crucial role that boundary-determining criteria play with respect to the coherence of theoretical models within the discipline.

The relations among disciplines may also be viewed as an analytical problem dealing with model boundaries. Two disciplines are unrelated if the boundary-determining criteria of their respective models do not produce units and laws that are isomorphic with respect to each other. From this standpoint, the disciplines of geology and sociology have no common boundaries. None of the boundary-determining criteria that may be shared between these disciplines produces simultaneously isomorphic laws of interaction and units that will be found in the separate models inside each of the disciplines. This issue is dealt with in another context in Chapter 11, ''Research.'' There the conclusion is reached that the additivity of knowledge in a discipline, and among disciplines, depends on what is labeled *contiguous-problem analysis*.

In the relations between psychology and sociology, sociology and political science, and political science and psychology, there may be a number of models that span the traditional boundaries between these disciplines. Indeed, some of the leading figures in these disciplines have reached positions of prominence by noting the overlap among models. For example, Lasswell in his book *Psychopathology and Politics* stirred the field of political science to a behavioral orientation by applying psychological models to political behavior. The viability of these applications subsequently came into question, but the unanticipated consequence of Lasswell's contribution to a subdiscipline of behavioral political scientists is beyond question. Behaviorally oriented political scientists freely use models from sociology and psychology for what appears to be a fruitful shift in analytical attention among political scientists. In a similar way, Homans has moved psychological models into the center of sociological attention in his book *The Human Group* and its sequel, *Social Behavior: Its Elementary Forms*. Homans did this fully recognizing that he was going to be accused of reductionism. Homans has insisted that this is an irrelevant charge and that the test of his psychologically oriented models is whether or not social behavior can be brought within the boundaries of such models and be shown to share the boundary-determining criteria of the psychological models. In this respect, Homans is accurate, and his critics must be considered obscurantists when the grounds for their criticism rests solely on the charge of reductionism.

Theoretical and Empirical Boundaries

Research reporting usually contains a standard caveat. It is typical for the scientist to state that the conclusions drawn from his data do not necessarily apply beyond the boundary of the domain from which he drew his data. For example, in Martin's study *The Rural-Urban Fringe,* conclusions are drawn with respect to the sample in a small Western metropolitan area, Eugene-Springfield, and the author says, ". . . there is, at the present time, no basis in the data for generalizing outside the universe studied."[7] Such a standard caution in a research report is the consequence of recognizing two limitations: (1) that the sample of units studied may or may not be representative of the universe from which it was selected; and (2) that the universe represented by the sample may be quite different from other universes defined by boundary-determining criteria of other kinds of models.

The first issue to which such cautious conclusions are directed is an issue in sampling. It is not relevant to our present consideration.

The second basis for this caution by the researcher is to warn the reader that he should not extend the conclusions reached in the research beyond the boundaries of the model and its predictions tested by the assembled data. In short, the caution expressed here is in clear recognition of the fact that other models will have different boundary-determining criteria.

[7]Walter T. Martin, *The Rural-Urban Fringe: A Study of Adjustment to Residence Location* (Eugene, Ore.: University of Oregon Press, 1953), p. 74.

In most of the research reporting in the biological and physical sciences, this kind of caution is not employed. This is probably true because scientists in these disciplines clearly recognize the boundaries of the scientific models being tested and the boundary-determining criteria employed. Perhaps in the social and behavioral sciences these cautions are necessary in order to alert the reader to the boundary-determining criteria and the domain covered by a particular model being tested.

When a research report concludes with a catalog of problems representing future research projects, there is often included within the list a set of research topics involving the study of models of larger domain to find out whether the results of the particular study are consistent with a more general model. There is also usually included in the list of projects for future study the admonition that replication of the present study is desirable. The necessary condition for replication of an existing study is that the boundary conditions of the subsequent studies be the same as those of the initial study. In addition, the replication study will follow the initial study by employing the same laws of interaction and units.

When the theoretical model is constructed in the absence of any prior empirical knowledge, the boundaries of the model are determined logically. As a result this, in turn, theoretically specifies the domain over which the model operates as a system. The boundary of the theoretical system specified by the model is the furthest extension over the empirical world that the model is expected to operate. The domain of the model is that portion of the empirical world included within the boundaries. The domain of a model is always bounded. Therefore, to determine the domain of a model requires the determination of its boundaries.

Empirical Test of Boundaries

When a model is empirically tested, one consequence is to determine the actual location of boundaries and, thereafter, the extent of the empirical domain.

The empirical tests of boundaries and domain result in three possible consequences for the model. (1) The domain logically specified turns out to be identical with the domain empirically discovered. (2) The domain empirically specified is greater than the theoretically revealed domain. This can be discovered either through "accidents" in carrying out the research operation or because the sample of the empirical world is deliberately chosen to be greater (drawn from a wider domain) than that which is logically specified by the model. Tightly planned research that seeks to eliminate accidents (inadvertently including data not demanded by the theoretical model) and that refuses to include data lying beyond the theoretical boundaries of the model cannot produce this second result. It can at best show only that the theoretical and empirical boundaries are identical or that the former is greater than the latter. (3) The theoretical domain is greater than that which was anticipated empirically.

In the first instance—identity between theoretical and empirical domain—the model remains unaltered (because its boundary predictions are not disproved) and in this form is subjected to further tests.

For the two cases where the theoretical domain differs from the empirical one, a modification of the model is immediately called for. If the model predicts boundaries beyond its empirical range, then it has to be further restricted to correspond to the empirical world. This means introducing additional boundary-determining criteria so as to reduce the domain of the model. If empirical data exceed the boundary of the theoretical, then one or more of the boundary-determining criteria may be dropped in order to increase the size of the domain.

Tests of the boundaries of a model are among the important empirical tests made of it. Any need for modification of boundaries in the light of empirical evidence not only shifts the boundary of the model but also requires the modification of its units, its laws of interaction, or both. The feedback to the model of tests of its boundaries therefore provides critical tests of the model itself.

CHAPTER SEVEN

System States

The commonsense notion of such systems is that of an objective situation involving material objects and having both constant and variable characteristics. While the identity of the system is, as it were, preserved by the constancy of the former, the variable characteristics of the system may undergo continuous changes in time and thereby cause the given system to pass through a sequence of successive states.

—G. SOMMERHOFF, *Analytical Biology*

UP TO THIS POINT we have developed an image of a scientific model composed of determinant units, interacting by specified laws with each other within defined boundaries. This system is given the task of predicting the values of all the units composing it at any point within the boundary. However, it will be made clear presently that all regions within the boundary of a model are not identical. We need one more building block of a scientific model, namely, *system state,* in order to handle the fact that all regions within the boundary of a system are not homogeneous with each other.

It is the task of this chapter to define system state and to distinguish a state of a system from the outcome of a unit. There then follows a discussion of the criteria from determining the states of a system. Attention will then shift to the analysis of the special characteristics of those units of a model that determine the system states. A section will be devoted to the discussion of the format and language for indicating system states. Finally, the significance of system states for the empirical test of a model will be examined.

System State Defined

A state of a system may be defined by three features.

1. All units of the system have characteristic values.
2. The characteristic values of all units are determinant.
3. This constellation of unit values persists through time.

The essential notion of a system state is that the system *as a whole* has distinctive features when it is in a state of the system. The manner, however, in which we are able to designate a system state is through the recognition of the characteristic values of the units when the system is in that particular state. Thus, a system state is apprehended only by knowing the characteristic values of all the units of the system. These values, in turn, must be determinant. If any of the values of any units are indeterminant, then an analytical problem arises as to whether the system as a whole is in a system state or whether the system is in transition between system states. Should the system be in transition, then the values of one or more units may vary so widely that the practical outcome is to declare that the values are indeterminant.

Nagel has a telling statement of the need to insure that the values of units in a system are determinant in order to designate a system state.

. . . proposed explanations aiming to exhibit the functions of various items in a social system in either maintaining or altering the system have no substantive content, unless the *state* that is allegedly maintained or altered is formulated more precisely than has been customary. It also follows that the claims functionalists sometimes advance (whether in the form of "axioms" or of hypotheses to be investigated) concerning the "integral" character or "functional unity" of social systems produced by the "working together" of their parts with a "sufficient degree of harmony" and "internal consistency," or concerning the "vital function" and "indispensable part" every element in a society plays in the "working whole," cannot be properly judged as either sound or dubious or even mistaken. For in the absence of descriptions precise enough to identify unambiguously the states which are supposedly maintained in a social system, those claims cannot be subjected to empirical control, since they are compatible with every conceivable matter of fact and with every outcome of empirical inquiries into actual societies.[1]

[1]E. Nagel, *The Structure of Science* (New York: Harcourt, Brace & World, 1961), p. 530.

When all units of the system have characteristic and determinant values, and when these constellations of values persist through some time interval, we can designate this a *system state*. The length of time over which the system state persists is the state life. The time interval of a state life is relevant to the laws of interaction among the units of a system. In some physical and chemical systems, a system state may persist for only a very small fraction of a second. In biological systems the time interval is more extended for the state life of a system. Social systems are usually characterized by much longer periods of time for the state life of the system. Indeed, this very fact has led to the development of models of social phenomena that are viewed as having but a single system state, as we shall see in the subsequent discussion of the one-state system.

System States and Unit Outcomes

At this point an important distinction needs to be drawn between *states of a system* and *outcomes of a system* in operation. This distinction is not always easy to maintain in actual analysis of a model. Nevertheless it needs to be drawn, for in the distinction lies the difference between focusing on the status of the system as a whole or on one or more units and their values.

An outcome of a model is defined as a region of values (or a single critical value as well) for one (or some) unit of a model that gives to that unit (or units) a distinctive analytical character. An outcome, then, is a special condition of one or more units, but not of all units, of the system that, when achieved, distinguishes the condition of that unit from other of its possible conditions.

An example of an outcome would be to consider a system of persons whose interactions are characterized by laws of activity, social response, and affective state. In such a system we may describe a single person (but none of those with whom he interacts) as exhibiting high frequency of physical and verbal activity, insensitivity to cues from other persons, and an excited affective demeanor. To this combination of values we might give the name *manic*. This manic condition would be an outcome of the interpersonal system in operation but would describe the condition of only one unit of this system of interpersonal relations. Another example of an outcome may be labeled *the condition of juvenile delinquency,* the outcome condition for a juvenile when he breaks an organizational rule or societal law. He may do this once or several times, or he may do it with varying degrees of severity (truancy, shoplifting, burglary, assault with a deadly weapon, rape). Over this range of frequency and severity values, we would define the outcome condition for the adolescent as juvenile delinquency.

Outcomes of a model are the distinctive conditions of one or more units employed in the model, this distinctive condition being analytically useful, meaningful, or important for the model.

From the standpoint of the usefulness of any model, the outcomes that are distinctive in the individual units employed are one central content of the predictions that flow from the model. I will examine this more generally and in more detail in the succeeding chapter dealing with propositions. In particular, I will distinguish between trivial and significant outcome conditions of the units as one basis for sorting critical from trivial propositions. This in turn will serve to highlight the criterion by which critical experiments or critical research is marked off from routine research.

A system state is a state of the system as a whole. It is defined by the unique combination of values of *all* units composing a system. This combination gives to the system as a whole a distinctive condition. Outcomes, on the other hand, are conditions of one or of several units of a model but not of all of them simultaneously.

Examples of system states follow. In economics there is a system state called *pure competition* in which no individual competitor, by any action chosen, can affect the market value of a product. This is contrasted with another system state called *imperfect competition,* and both are different from a third system state called *monopoly.* In the system state of imperfect competition, several competitors do affect the selling price of a product by their own marketing decisions. In the monopolistic state, a single seller determines the selling price of a product. These three states of an economic system (from the standpoint of a single product) are characterized by unique marketing behaviors of the selling units in each of the separate states and by distinctive price structures.

For some models of social life, the system state of stability is distinguished from the system state of instability or change. Again, all units of the social system contained in a model are presumed to be affected as to their values by the stable or unstable state of the system. At the level of the individual as a system, the two states of social maturity and social immaturity may be characterized by the distinctive values in each state of the quantity and quality of interpersonal relations.

Criteria of System States

The first criterion of a system state is that all units of the system have a value or distinctive range of values in that state. This is the criterion of *inclusiveness*. The inclusiveness criterion is especially useful because it serves to insure that the system as a whole is being kept in the focus of attention. It follows, then, that the only genuine states of a system are those conditions of a system in which all units composing it have distinctive values. Where less than all units are affected or where individual units have similar values in several regions, we may properly conclude that we are not dealing with system states but, rather, with outcome conditions of individual units. Thus, the inclusiveness criterion, which demands that all units of the system have special values in a given system state, serves to draw a line between outcome conditions for individual units and system states as a whole.

The inclusiveness criterion applies only to those units of analysis incorporated into the model. Although this may seem obvious, there is a devious tendency in social-science discourse to argue by changing the model and then insisting that units not incorporated into the initial theory do have determinant values and are lawfully related to the units originally employed. The inclusiveness criterion demands only that the theory builder, when specifying the system states of his model, declare that all units included in the theory have special values when the system is in its various states.

It must be recognized that there may be some arbitrariness in distinguishing between system states. This occurs especially where values of individual units of a model form continuous scales. Under such circumstances the boundary of a particular system state, for which the unit values are unique, may be drawn with some arbitrariness between two adjacent values. It may be hard to establish on which side of a given value the boundary between states should lie.

A second criterion of a system state is that the individual units have *determinant values* in it. The determinant values of the individual units have two characteristics: (1) They are measurable for the particular state of the system; and (2) they are distinctive or unique for the state of the system.

By the first determinant criterion is simply meant that the values of all units of the model may be measured, at least in principle, by instruments that give *real* values, at least within the particular state of the system.

The second determinant criterion means that the values so obtained by measurement for each unit are *distinctive* values for that state of the system.

To illustrate the consequences of the determinant criterion for designating system states, and how this serves to differentiate a system state from a unit outcome, let us reconsider the example of the manic person. The analytical problem is to determine in what states of the system of interpersonal relations the person displays the manic outcome. Let us assume that manic behavior is related to isolation from social contacts that results in the excited behavior as a form of substitute sociability, taking the place of easy social relations. This law of interaction predicts the manic outcome under conditions of determinant low levels of social interaction between the person and his social environment. In testing this prediction (the unit condition of the individual, called *manic phase*), we would attempt to reconstruct the individual's life history, using measures to determine the volume and quality of his social interactions with other people in his environment. Our law of interaction predicts that regardless of the areas of social relations, the measures should reveal minimum interaction in all areas at a time when the manic phase occurs, or just prior to it. If our data should establish that the individual was, in fact, withdrawn in his relations with family members, peers, and people casually contacted in his daily round of life, then we have those determinant values as characteristic of the state of the system in which the outcome "manic behavior" occurs. If, however, upon examination of the life histories of a sample of manic-behaving persons, it is determined that only in close personal relations does withdrawal seem to be characteristic (measures of interpersonal interaction give low values) but in casual contacts manic individuals appear prior to their manic phase to be able to interact normally (i.e., with a modal amount of interaction), then the system state of minimal interaction between the individual and his environment no longer has unique values associated with it for all units of the system.

The consequence would be one of two possibilities. (1) The model would be reconstituted so as to include only close interpersonal relations, thereby changing the units included in the model. (2) The model would be reconstituted by changing the original law of interaction to one linking manic outcome with withdrawal from only close personal relations and further reconstituted by adding another law by which the manic person interacts with casual contacts in his environment. In the first instance, the state of the system in which minimal interaction occurs in close personal relations also is accompanied by the manic phase. In the second instance, however, we would still predict the outcome "manic" but we would not specify the system state in which it occurs because there would *not* be determinant values for casual contacts at the time that close personal relations are minimized and followed or accompanied by a manic behavior pattern. The point of this example is that the determinant criterion forces the theorist-researcher to recognize whether or not he is dealing with a system state.

The third criterion of a system state is that the state *persist* through some period of time, i.e., have a state life. The minimum period of time that is sufficient to be called *persistent* is highly flexible. In some chemical and physical systems, the time period may be as small as milliseconds. For most social systems, or systems involving people, the time period over which a system state persists is usually of considerable duration (subliminal perception may be a system state of the individual of relatively short duration, however).

The expectation that system states persist for a relevant time period is based on the experience of man with his environment. Most systems observed by man do have states that can be observed and described because they do persist long enough to be apprehended.

It should be clear that not all models specify system states. It is possible to build models in which system states are overlooked or models that have only one system state, for which, therefore, the notion of system state may be properly ignored. Indeed, it is this latter fact that has produced some serious controversy in the behavioral sciences regarding those who theorize about only one system state. Thus, so-called "functionalists" are often accused by their detractors of dealing only with the system state of stability, and these detractors allege that it is equally important to deal with social systems as dynamic and state-changing systems. There is no logic that demands that a particular theory or theoretical model have more than one system state. When system states are employed in models, then their characteristics will be as set forth here and their scientific utility will follow the lines to be developed in the last section of this chapter.

The three criteria of system states—*inclusiveness* of consequence for values of all units of the system, that the values are all *determinant* values, and the *persistence* of the state over some relevant time period—together describe the conditions that must be met to deal with system states. What is most important to understand is that the focus of attention of system states is itself an important feature of the system or model being examined. A system state that meets these three criteria is by virtue of that fact a description of the *system as a whole*. As has already been indicated, there is an important distinction between an outcome condition of a unit of a system and the state of a system as a whole. When it is possible to delineate the system state, its very description is a description of the system in its entirety and not of the outcome condition of a single or several units of the system.

Recurrence of System States

In the analysis of many aspects of social life there is a more or less regular recurrence of system states. Indeed, it is this very feature that gives to social analysts their feeling of confidence in being able to make predictions about social behavior, for they focus their attention on predicting the order of succession of social system states and the time period over which a given system state will persist. The daily round of life in all its aspects has been a regular focus of attention of anthropologists and sociologists as well as psychologists. Anthropologists order much of their description around the daily and seasonal cycle of activities, a habit often emulated by sociologists. Predictions may be made very accurately about human behavior by noting and describing the system state in which the behavior occurs. In the more obvious instances, traffic flow into and out of a metropolis may be accurately predicted for the point of transition between the work state and the nonwork state of the economy; TV audience number and composition may be predicted with precision by periods of the day, representing different states of the social system; recreational patterns are highly correlated with the work and nonwork states of the economy; and childhood behavior is predicted with great reliability in Western society depending on whether the child is in a school or nonschool system state.

It therefore becomes a matter of genuine analytical significance to specify for any model its system states and their recurrence, for this will provide the grounds upon which important predictions may be made about the system. The repetition of system states is one of the dynamic features of the model, as Sommerhoff suggested in the opening quotation of this chapter. When social scientists claim they are searching for social uniformities, one such uniformity may be the recurrence of states of the social system under analysis.

System states may appear only once in the history of a system. Thus, a biological system often has a life history in which successive states are nonrepetitive with preceding states. The directionality of successive states and their nonrepetition do not deny the fact that they may still be states of the system as a whole, as indicated in the biological states of the individual: infancy, adolescence, adulthood.

In some kinds of systems it may be important to direct attention to rare system states. Such states may be crucial in the history of the system, even though they occur infrequently. For example, most crowds never panic. Should a crowd panic, the social consequences are usually serious. Thus, a system in which a crowd is a unit could be analyzed to include as one of its features a state of panic. The empirical analysis of a sample of crowds may only rarely reveal the system state of panic. Nevertheless, because of the magnitude of behavioral change that accompanies this system state, it would be crucial for analyzing a system of which a crowd was a unit.

The opposite may also be true. A system state that occurs frequently may not be an important or crucial state of the system. Thus, the state of sleep of the individual may tell us almost nothing about his waking-hours behavior (unless, of course, the theorist is convinced that dream content is highly relevant to waking behavior).

Special Units as "State Coordinates"

It is sometimes considered useful to designate certain of the units of a model as the ones that exemplify the characteristics of the system state. These are what Nagel calls the *state coordinates* of a system.[2] The state coordinates are often used as the descriptive terms for the particular system state. Thus, in the Marxist analysis of social systems, a capitalist state of an economy is one in which the means of production are in the hands of a small class of capitalists. The capitalist ownership of the means of production is the value for the ownership unit of the economic system, and gives to that state of the system its particular name. At the same time, in the capitalist state of an economic system there are determinant and persisting values of all other units of the system.

Those units of a system that are given the characterization of state coordinates are the ones that name the particular state of the system. In a more exact sense, these are the units often used as the so-called independent units (or variables) in an analytical statement. Thus, if a capitalist class owns the means of production, then a working class will be ex-

[2]See E. Nagel, "A Formalization of Functionalism," in his *Logic Without Metaphysics* (New York: Free Press, 1956), especially pp. 254ff.

ploited by the owners, according to the Marxist doctrine. This form of statement gives determinant values to capitalists and to workers and states a law of interaction between them. The exploited position of workers is an outcome condition for the unit *worker,* which in the context of this model is dependent upon the fact that capitalists own the means of production. In this sense, state-describing units of a model have fixed values, or a fixed range of values, which are viewed as characterizing the special values of other units.

From the standpoint of the orientation of this book, it is not important to draw the distinction between dependent and independent units. It has already been indicated that the discussion of causality is not central to theoretical models and that the relations among the units of a system may be expressed in categoric, determinant, or sequential laws of interaction. Therefore, state-coordinate units, those which give to the system state its characteristic name, gain special significance for this reason and this reason alone. They have no special logical importance in a model.

Format for Indicating System States

It is easy to see the format in which system states are designated in a model by examining states containing the three types of laws of interaction.

A system characterized by a categoric law of interaction typically has the following format: "If... , then... under conditions of.... For example: "As the size of a human group increases, then the division of labor within it is elaborated, provided the group has (continuity; established goals; purposes, either singly or in any combination) but not when the group is transitory." The state-determining coordinates are *continuity, goals,* and *purposes* in one state of the system or zero values on all of these units in the second state of the system characterized by the label *transitory.* For both states of the system, the size of the group may change, but in only one of the system states will the division of labor be elaborated if the group size increases, whereas in the other it will not. All units of the system have determinant values and these are persisting values.

A second example of a system employing a categoric law would be Merton's model of individual adaptation in a social system: Individuals follow one of four courses of individual deviant adaptation to social circumstances—rebellion, retreatism, ritualism, or innovation—under conditions where there is a disjunction between social goals and the means for their attainment. In this statement, the disjunction between social goals and means gives to the units *social goals* and *institutional means* the role of state coordinates in the system for the system state of individual deviant adaptation. Their noncongruent values determine one of four possible unit outcomes for the individual. Merton, of course, also specified another system state, that of concordance between social goals and institutional means for which there is only one adaptive response by the individual—conformity. Thus, Merton's paradigm is a two-state system. The four nonconforming individual adaptations are unit outcomes and not states of the system of persons responding to social goals and institutional means.

To see how the system state is characterized, we may also examine a system employing a determinant law. The general format for a determinant law is "A change in value of *A* (in a given direction; by a given amount; in and by both) is accompanied by a change in values of *B* (in a given direction; by a given amount; in and by both) under conditions. . . ." An example would be the Stouffer-Ravenstein model of migration: "Migration to a given area (or point) is inversely proportional to the intervening opportunities and the distance from point of origin, where the opportunities at the destination, and intervening, are known."[3] The state-describing unit is the opportunities (intervening and at destination) which have determinant and known values to the migrant. Here again, all units of the model have determinant and persisting values. The specification "where the opportunities at the destination, and intervening, are known" designates a system state, the other state being one in which the opportunity values are not known to the migrant and for which there will be another law of interaction, not specified by Stouffer in his studies.

The general format of a system employing a sequential law of interaction is "A change in the value of *A* (in a given direction; by a given amount; in and by both) is followed in time by a change in the value of *B* (in a given direction; by a given amount; in and by both)." An example would be "Revolution as a struggle for governmental power results only when a society is so disorganized that the historic power holders lose control of the instruments of force and they transfer to the possession of a challenging group."[4] The state-describing unit is the coherence of social

---

[3]See the original and revised versions of this model in Samuel A. Stouffer, *Social Research to Test Ideas* (New York: Free Press, 1962), Chap. 4, pp. 68–112.

[4]Taken from James C. Davies, "Toward a Theory of Revolution," *American Sociological Review*, 27:5–19 (Feb. 1962).

organization. When in the condition of disorganization, or possessing this value, then revolution may occur. The sequential character of the law in this model is revealed by the statement that the traditional power holders must lose control of the instruments of force before revolution will occur.

The systems represented in these examples are very simple systems chosen for this reason so that the state-describing units could be readily displayed. Most systems are much more complex, having a number of states, many more units interacting, and many more laws of interaction among them. Indeed, as we shall see in the next section of this chapter, one of the analytical-empirical problems in system analysis is to determine whether states for the system exist that have not been theoretically specified. This may be an important empirical question for which the analysis of data provides the answer.

When more complex systems are set forth as theoretical models, the number of system states usually increases with the model complexity. Thus, Parsons, in attempting to characterize a social system as a whole, designates four basic system states in which any social system operates.[5] These he labeled the *social-system problems:* G, goal attainment; A, adaptive; I, integrative; and L, latency or tension management. What Parsons calls a *system problem* is his inexact way of designating a state of a social system that, when entered into by a social system, is accompanied by special values of its behaving units. The bulk of the analytical statements made by Parsons are concerned with the values attaching to the units of his model in each of the four system states he specifies.

System States as Analytical Features of Models

There are four analytical problems for which the notion of system state is relevant. These analytical problems generate some but not all answers to the question, "What happens when the theoretical system operates?"

The first analytical problem is to answer the question, "Under what conditions will a given system state persist?" Thus, a viable prediction about any theoretical model is to predict the state life over which a given

[5]First set forth in Talcott Parsons, Robert F. Bales, and Edward A. Shils, *Working Papers in the Theory of Action* (New York: Free Press, 1953), and revised and clarified in Talcott Parsons and Neil J. Smelser, *Economy and Society* (New York: Free Press, 1956), pp. 33–38.

system state will persist, or the values of the units in that state that will maintain that state.

Nagel has illustrated this analytical problem in the following fashion.

> ... once a system *S* and a state *G* supposedly maintained in it are adequately specified, the task of the functionalist is to identify a set of state variables whose operations maintain *S* in the state *G,* and to discover just how these variables are related to each other and to other variables in the system or in its environment. In the actual conduct of social inquiry, however, this sequence is usually reversed: some variable (e.g., a religious ritual) is first identified; and inquiry is then directed toward ascertaining what functions it has ... and whether it does in fact contribute to the maintenance of some state *G* (e.g., emotional solidarity) which is suspected of being fairly stable. It is therefore quite easy to overlook the requirement that the system *S* and the state *G* with which the analysis presumably deals must be carefully delimited, and in consequence to omit explicit mention, in the teleological explanation finally proposed, of the specific system within which the variable allegedly maintains a specific state. It is then easy also to forget that even if the variable does have the function attributed to it of preserving *G* in *S* (e.g., the performance of a religious ritual having the function of maintaining the state of emotional solidarity of *each* primitive tribe in which the ritual takes place), it may not have this role in some *other* system *S'* (e.g., in a confederation of tribes, where the ritual may have a divisive force) to which the variable may also belong; or that it may not have the function of maintaining at the same system *S* some *other* state *G'* (e.g., an adequate food supply), with respect to which it may perhaps be *dysfunctional* by obstructing the maintenance of *G'* in *S.*[6]

A second analytical problem dealing with system states has to do with when a given state of a system ceases to exist. The answer to this question usually involves determining the critical values of the units of the system in a given state that, when exceeded, characterize the system in another state.

The third analytical problem has to do with the answer to the questions, "Is there any patterning in the succession among system states?" and "Does the knowledge of the present state of a system permit a specific prediction about the particular states that will succeed it as to their individual probability of occurring next, their order of occurrence, and/or duration of existence?" This kind of analytical problem was noted

[6]E. Nagel, *The Structure of Science* (New York: Harcourt, Brace & World, 1961), p. 532. Reprinted by permission of the publisher.

in Chapter 2 where we used as an example the oscillation of an economic system from a capitalist to a socialist state. As was pointed out there, the possibility of chance accuracy in making predictions increases as the number of states in which a system may operate decreases.

A fourth analytical question of system states has to do with determining when a given state of a system makes the system permeable. By permeable we mean a breach of the system boundary so that one of two unit outcomes may occur: (1) One or more units of the system fall out of the system; or (2) one or more units enter the system for the first time. Thus, some states of a system may be lethal for the system as a whole in that they lead to the transformation of the *system* into another one.

The first three analytical problems deal with a closed system; the fourth deals with transforming or destroying a system. It is clear that in each instance that we are dealing with a dynamic system and that even though the system may be closed, the analysis of system states is one feature of a system's dynamic quality.[7] It is especially noteworthy that with respect to the third analytical problem, that of sequence of states, such predictions as are made about the system are governed by sequential laws. This becomes apparent when one examines what the global historians of mankind have said about various epochs of its history. Spengler, Toynbee, and Sorokin all have models of successive states of society that represent literal analogs of the life cycle of the biological individual. The order of the successive states of a society characterizes its life history for these historians.

Empirical Search for System States

One of the descriptive tasks of empirical research is to delineate the observable states of a system. When this is done, it is likely that there will be significant feedback to the model from which the research was generated. In particular, the feedback may force modification of the starting model by introducing states of the theoretical system that were not previously recognized. Several examples will serve to illustrate this point.

Sutherland, in his study *White Collar Crime*, made it clear that criminal behavior resulted in states of the system linking the individual with his social milieu that were not previously conceptualized by criminologists.

---

[7]See Chapter 6, ''Boundaries,'' for a discussion of open and closed systems. There the difference between them is viewed as having no consequence for the *structure* of a theoretical model.

Clinard's study *The Black Market* as an extension of the analysis of white collar crime added further complexity to the states of the individual-social system that produce criminal behavior. Subsequently, Yablonsky, still working in the area of criminal behavior, analyzed the delinquent gang as a near group and came to the conclusion that there was a state of relationship among members of a delinquent gang that was different from the states usually postulated by the students of delinquency. In this example of the work of Sutherland, Clinard, and Yablonsky, each described system states that required revision of extant theoretical models in order to incorporate the empirically determined system states.[8]

In the field of human ecology, the original formulation of the structure of a city being best represented by concentric circles of land use, as set forth by Burgess, was subsequently modified by imposing a sector developmental structure on top of the concentric-circle model. The sector-circle states of the ecological system differ from those originally conceptualized by Burgess and resulted from the empirical description of Hoyt and his associates.

In the field of group process, the original formulation of Likert and others that worker autonomy and work-group morale were positively correlated had to give way in the face of subsequent empirical work that indicated a two-state system in which over one range of values for worker autonomy there was a positive relationship with morale, but over another range of autonomy values there was a negative relationship. In other words, the shift from an increasing to a decreasing set of values for morale indicated that the system relating a group of workers to the amount of work autonomy they possessed and the amount of morale they exhibited is a two-state system.

These examples should be sufficient to indicate that the empirical study of system states is a significant contribution to the test of a theoretical model.

System states are an important feature of a theoretical model. Not all models specify multiple system states, but this does not disqualify them from meeting the full requirements of a theoretical model. When system states are built into a model, they serve the purpose of specifying a condition for the system as a whole. When the system as a whole is the focus of attention, then the system states become the features of the system of analytical importance.

[8]See E. H. Sutherland, *White Collar Crime* (New York: Dryden Press, 1949); M. B. Clinard, *The Black Market: A Study of White Collar Crime* (New York: Holt, Rinehart & Winston, 1952); and L. Yablonsky, "The Delinquent Gang As a Near Group," *Social Problems*, 7:108–117 (Fall 1959).

CHAPTER EIGHT

Propositions

Consider now a variable of which ... we know how to find the (smallest) closed system among whose relevant variables it occurs.... Thus, we know all the other variables with which our variable "interacts." ... We know, in particular, how to compute the future as well as the past values of our variables from what we can now measure (provided we also know the past or future boundary conditions). Retrospectively we know, furthermore, what the present value of our variable would have been if some earlier state of the system had been different from what it actually was. Prospectively, we know how to influence its (and other relevant variables') future values by present interference with the system from the outside; and we also know the limits of such interference. What else, I ask, could we possibly want to know about this variable in a scientific way?

—G. BERGMANN, *Philosophy of Science*

IN THIS CHAPTER we are concerned with the ways in which a theoretical model is put to use. One purpose of any scientific model is to generate predictions about the empirical domain it represents. We have now come to the point in theory building at which predictions occupy a central role for the first time.

To begin this chapter a proposition is defined. Then a distinction is drawn between a proposition and the assignment of an element to membership in a set. Propositions are shown subsequently to be concerned with predictions about the values of units in the system. There follows a discussion of the number of propositions in any given model. Attention then turns to a consideration of critical propositions as distinct from trivial ones. The contrast is then amplified between a law of interaction and a proposition of a model. Finally, the role of negative propositions is examined.

Proposition Defined

A proposition may be defined as a truth statement. It is a truth statement of a special and limited kind. The limitation is that we will consider propositions to be only those truth statements that may be made about a theoretical model. The governing principle for all such limited truth statements is that they conform to some systematic canons of logic for distinguishing true and false to which the model builder subscribes. All the propositions about the models he builds are true by the criteria of the system of logic by which he thinks. This definition of a proposition of a scientific model rules out of consideration all truth statements having to do with the correspondence between the predictions of the model and the empirical domain it purports to represent. This latter issue will be taken up in the next three chapters.

A proposition, then, is a truth statement about a model when the model is fully specified in its units, laws of interaction, boundary, and system states. Any truth statement that can be made about such a system is a proposition of the system.

The term *truth* should not cause any trouble if it is kept clear of its metaphysical connotations. We could just as well employ the term *logical consequence* in place of *truth statement* in the definition of proposition. Care has been taken to state that any system of logic may be employed to establish a truth statement about a theoretical model. This relativity with respect to the system of logic employed makes clear that *the* truth statements about a model may be changed if the system for defining truth is changed. The only criterion of consistency that propositions of a model need to meet is the criterion that their truth be established by reference to only one system of logic for all the propositions set forth about the model.

It is fashionable in the social sciences to present propositions as the starting point of investigations. This is a useful place to start any empirical investigation. The habit, however, has had a time-wasting consequence. Through the past several decades propositional inventories have been the work of a number of investigators. The goal has been to add up theory by organizing the propositions of a field into subject-matter categories. These inventories have been uniformly useless, and for a now obvious reason. The propositions of one scientific model do not necessarily add up, fund, or bear coherent relationship to the propositions of any other model. To inventory propositions of a field and to try to give order to the totality is to commit the sin of adding noncomparable things.[1]

[1]An example of a propositional inventory that proved useful is contained in Robin Williams, *The Reduction of Intergroup Tensions* (New York: Social Service Research

There is no logic by which the truth statements about one model may be brought into congruence with those of a different model. There may, indeed, be such congruence or identity. If it is found, it results because of some concordance between the different models whose propositions turn out to overlap or to be congruent. This is one of several considerations already set forth in this volume that will be brought together in Chapter 11, where I examine research.

I will simply assert here that a collection of propositions is *not* a theory or scientific model. This is, perhaps, a jolting conclusion to some social scientists who claim special status as theorists and whose principal output is propositional statements. It may also dismay empiricists who like to believe that their research is theory-linked and who use a proposition as their theory anchor. To theorists I offer the challenge to discover the implicit models from which their propositions derive as truth statements. To researchers I offer the same suggestion. To both I point out their shared interest in scientific models.

In a later section of this chapter that distinguishes propositions from laws of interaction, I will show how a group of propositions may be analyzed to discover the underlying law of interaction from which they are derived. This should prove useful as support for the conclusion that a collection of propositions is not a theory.

Propositions versus Set Membership

It is necessary to make an important distinction between truth statements about a model and truth statements about set membership of units. Much of logical analysis is concerned with establishing the class, or set population, of which elements are members.[2]

The classical syllogism illustrates the problem of set membership: "All men are mortal; Socrates is a man; therefore, Socrates is mortal." The conclusion here is that the set defined by *men* plus *mortal* includes

---

Council, 1947), Bulletin #57. This particular propositional inventory was useful precisely because Professor Williams attempted to search out the underlying models from which the collected propositions derived as truth statements. The manner for accomplishing this is discussed in the later section of this chapter entitled "Proposition and Law of Interaction."

[2]Set is here used in the same sense as *set theory*. "A set is a collection of definite distinct objects of our perception or of our thought which are called elements of the set." "Elements belonging to a set are determined by the distinguishing characteristics of the set." Both of these definitions are from Joseph Breuer, *Introduction to the Theory of Sets* (Englewood Cliffs, N.J.: Prentice-Hall, 1958), p. 4.

Socrates even though we have only established that he is a man and assumed that he must be mortal because "man" and "mortal" go together to define the set in which we are interested. If one portion of the definition is satisfied by the particular case, then the other must be because we assert an invariable connection between "man" and "mortal" in the definition of the basic set. It should be noted that the statement "Socrates is mortal" is not a prediction about Socrates but only a statement of his location within a particular set. It is a truth statement about membership of an element in a set. In this instance, we are locating the element "Socrates" in the set "man," which in turn is wholly included in the set "mortal." This conclusion is not a prediction but an assignment of an element to its appropriate set. If we know the characteristics of the set, and this we must know by definition, then *all* elements which make up the set possess the set characteristics. Furthermore, *any* element having the set characteristics is a member of the set.

Much of the statistical procedure is concerned exactly with the problem of locating the appropriate set from which a statistic comes or to which a given element may be assigned. All tests of significance are concerned with locating the universe of which a given statistic is a member. Statistics like differences between means that exceed limit criteria, e.g., a given T value, are considered to lie outside the universe of similars. That is, the measured difference is so great that there is larger-than-chance probability it lies *outside* the set of differences. In the same vein, if we examine the statistical techniques employed in handling distributions, a given element is considered to be a part of a set if its value lies within a predetermined sigma value of the mean of the universe. If the value lies outside this predetermined sigma value, then we consider that the element is not a member of the set defined by the characteristics of that universe. In a similar way the logical tests used by Zetterberg in his book *On Theory and Verification in Sociology*[3] are tests designed to reduce redundance in propositional statements by demonstrating that the units of several propositional statements are really members of the same set and that therefore several propositional statements may be reduced to a single one.

The problem of set, of boundary, and of the elements included within the boundary or excluded from the set is an appropriate concern when considering the definitions of units, laws of interaction, boundaries, and system states. It is always presumed that one does not mix elements from

---

[3]Hans L. Zetterberg, *On Theory and Verification in Sociology*, rev. ed. (Totowa, N.J.: Bedminster Press, 1963).

different sets and measure their values as though they were elements of the same set. This is a problem we will examine in the next two chapters when we deal with hypotheses and empirical indicators. It is important to know that elements alleged to be from the same set are, in fact, truly so. To reach the conclusion that they are, however, is not a prediction. It is a statement of location of the element with respect to its parent set.

It is obvious that a truth statement may be made about the set membership of a given element. This is not a propositional statement about a model.

A proposition of a theoretical model is, therefore, a truth statement about the model in operation. As we shall presently see, there may be both positive and negative truth statements. In either event, however, they are always statements about the system or the values taken by system units. Propositions are not about the location of the system components in their respective sets.

Proposition and Prediction

All predictions contained in a scientific model take the form of propositional statements about the values of units in the model. The propositional statements are predictions because they tell us what must be true about the model in operation if we know the components, units, laws of interaction, boundaries, and system states that characterize the model. Having intellectually constructed his scientific model, the theory builder's curiosity must, of necessity, be turned to a consideration of how the model will function as a dynamic system.

Quite simply, the use of the model is to generate predictions or to make truth statements about the model in operation. Indeed, it is at this point that theory building becomes exciting and thoroughly interesting. The design of a model is, of course, an exacting task. However, to put the model to work, to see what it can do in operation, is the feature of theorizing that makes the game more than worth the effort.

The distinction between process and prediction that was drawn in Chapter 2 may be further clarified at this point. The idea of process is incorporated in the laws of interaction by which the units of a model relate to each other. These laws of interaction are unequivocal statements about how the units are related to each other. As we have seen in Chapter 5, the efficiency of the laws of interaction may vary, but their exactitude of statement is unquestioned. The predictions with which we are now concerned when we examine the propositions of a model are all the truth statements we may make about the conjoined values of two or more units whose relationship is expressed in the laws of interaction of the model.

Campbell[4] pointed out that science always produces synthetic truth statements, and he meant that these are statements that follow as true from the model about which they are made. Since the model itself is a synthetic product, being constructed logically and intellectually by the theorist, all truth statements about the model must also be synthetic. It is important to emphasize the synthetic character of the propositions of a theoretical model. This synthetic quality of the propositions makes clear that we are not talking at this point about the empirical accuracy of the propositional statements.

The sole test of the accuracy of a proposition is whether or not it follows logically from the model to which it applies. Thus, all propositions of a model satisfy logical rules and not empirical rules to establish their truth.

Prediction and Unit Values

I have already indicated that the problem of prediction is a problem of establishing unit values. That is to say, the only thing that can be predicted are the values of the units that are employed in a model. This is so obvious as to need little elaboration. Nevertheless, its very obviousness leads many scientists to overlook this simple and astonishing fact.

It will be recalled from Chapter 2 that a stress was placed upon the distinction between process and outcome. We may now restate this issue in the following terms. The analysis of process is the statement of the law of interaction between two or more units. The process statement is always the lawlike linkage between two units. By contrast, a statement of outcomes is always a statement of a value of a unit or of the values of a number of units. It is the values of the units of a model that are the content of the truth statements represented by the propositions of a model.

The most usual form in which the proposition states the values of two units is the classic "if . . . then" format. For example: "If an individual is frustrated, then he may become aggressive." This proposition states that

[4]Norman Campbell, *What is Science?* (New York: Dover Publications, 1952). First published in 1921.

a positive value of frustration is associated with a positive value of aggression in a person's behavior.

"If... then" statements abound in science. These are properly labeled *propositions*. The reason is that the specification of the *if* clause is always limited to one or a small range of variables, and the same is true of the *then* clause.

It is even possible to link a number of "if... then" propositions. This is done by employing the value of the unit in the first *then* clause as the value of the unit in the succeeding *if* clause. Thus, a chain of propositions would look like the following:

If (*a*), then (*b*);
If (*b*), then (*c*);
If (*c*), then (*d*); etc.

There are those in social science, and Zetterberg is one important proponent of this view, who assert that linked propositions of this sort constitute a theory or theoretical model. We examined one such linked system in the last section of Chapter 2. It should be clear by now, however, that a linked system, no matter how elegant it appears, is no more than a group of logically related propositions. This group of propositions is definitely not a theory or theoretical model. Indeed, it is a difficult analytical problem to construct a model or theory from the statement of a linked set of propositions. This difficulty is serious and may be the very reason why many social science researchers prefer to start their investigations with a proposition, or a series of propositions, rather than with a theoretical model.

Propositions of a model, then, are truth statements, or predictions, of the values taken by one or more units of a model.[5] This may be stated as a concern with the outcomes of a scientific model because the values taken by the units are the outcomes that are observable and measurable on the model.

Types of Propositions

We have now agreed that a propositional statement is a prediction about the values of units in the model. There are three general classes of such predictions, or propositional statements.

---

[5]Since system states are defined by the values of the units of a model, this conclusion holds for system states as well.

1. Propositions may be made about the values of a single unit of the model, the value of that unit being revealed in relation to the value of other units connected to the unit in question by a law of interaction.
2. Propositions may be predictions about the continuity of a system state that in turn involves a prediction about the conjoined values of all units in the system.
3. Propositions may be predictions about the oscillation of the system from one state to another that again involves predictions about the values of all units of the system as they pass over the boundary of one system state into another. (A special case of this third class of prediction is the case in which the system is destroyed or modified by virtue of penetration of the system boundary.)

These three classes of predictions, or propositions, exhaust the logical possibilities. All propositions about the system fit into one or the other of these three classes. This conclusion makes clear that the task of developing the propositions of a model is more readily undertaken by recognizing that the full range of truth statements is expressed in only three general types.

Number of Propositions of a Model

In principle, every model may give rise to an infinite number of propositions. This may readily be seen by examining a linear relationship between two units. The line segment representing the statement of relationship or law of interaction between the two units may be infinitely subdivided so that however great is the number of values on either of the units, it can be made even greater by subdividing those values still further. In the example $Y = a + bX$, there would then follow an infinite number of statements of the order "If the value of X is k, then the value of Y is m."

In most social-science models the scales employed in measuring the values of units are not infinitely divisible. Therefore, we may give a practical answer to the question, "How many propositions may be derived from a given model" The number of propositions is the sum of different ways the values of all the units in the model may be combined with the values of all other units with which they are lawfully related. This turns out to be a large number even with a moderate number of units in the model and values for each unit.

Consider, for example, a model composed of two units, in which unit *A* has five possible values (e.g., the empirical indicator of the unit is a five-interval Likert scale) and unit *B* has nine possible values (e.g., the empirical indicator[6] of the unit is an age-class interval of five years between the ages of 20 and 65). There are forty-five different possible combinations of the values of the two units. If there is a lawful relationship between the two units (as must be true, otherwise they would not be incorporated in the same model), then the number of propositions is reduced by eliminating those cells of the 5 × 9 table for which the prediction is a zero frequency. (We shall shortly see that the empty cells are the locale of what I call *negative propositions,* described in the last section of this chapter.) But even this may leave a large number of cells for which the model, to be exhaustive, must predict nonzero frequencies.

We may move further to reduce this number by asking the model to predict only the means of each value of the scale measuring unit *A* for the corresponding values on the scale measuring unit *B*. There would then be only as many predicted values as there are separate scale intervals on unit *B*. In our example, if we took the mean score on the Likert scale for each of the age intervals, we would have to predict the relationship among only nine mean values from the law relating units *A* and *B*. But let us further suppose that the theory predicts that there is a linear relationship between *A* and *B* and that this may be represented by the succession of mean values of *A* for each interval of *B*. Then one crucial prediction of the theory would be the slope of the line representing the linkage between *A* and *B*. We have thus reduced the number of propositions from a potential forty-five to a single one that satisfies our sense of what is important to test in determining whether or not the theory accurately models the empirical domain it purports to represent.

In the process of following through this example, it should be clear that we have successfully turned attention away from the full range of possible truth statements we may make about the relationship between the values of *A* and *B* in order to seek out those conjoined values, or that single value, that satisfies us as expressing best their relationship. In short, we have moved toward the strategic proposition by eliminating the trivial ones.

Some kind of parsimony needs to be introduced in the task of looking for and stating the propositions of a model. What is needed is some way deliberately to ignore the trivial propositions. I mean by trivial those propositions that give substantially the same results or outcomes because

---

[6]See Chapter 9, "Empirical Indicators."

the values in successive "if . . . then" statements differ only very slightly from each other and no sensible significance may be attached to these minor differences. This consideration leads immediately to strategic propositions.

Strategic Propositions

Strategic propositions are those that state critical or limiting values for one of the units involved. A critical value may be one at which the value of a unit reaches a maximum or minimum point. This would occur, for example, if the law relating to units could be expressed in a curve of a second degree or higher. Another type of critical value may be the value zero for the units. Still another type of critical value may be the value of the unit for which surrounding values on either side change from decreasing to increasing amounts. Critical values are therefore notable because something more than the usual increment of change in value occurs at the critical points.

Limiting values may be the most extreme values beyond which the model predicts that the unit will have no values. In psychophysics the search for auditory and perceptual thresholds requires models that will predict values below which there is no perception of sight and sound. Such limiting values may be absolute or they may represent a limit approached but never reached, as in the asymptote approached by a curve. Limiting values, like critical values, are notable values of the units.

Consider, for example, Figure 8-1. Assume that the formula for the line expresses the law of interaction between A and B. Now what are the areas of significant propositions and what are the regions of trivial propositions that may be made about units A and B lawfully interacting as determined by the specification of the curve of their relationship? The answer to these two questions has to do with where something significant is happening on the curve.

Some significant areas are (1) the point $A_j B_h$, where the curve inflects or changes from increasing at an increasing rate to increasing at a decreasing rate; (2) the region $B_d - B_e$, where significant changes in value of B are accompanied by very minor changes in the value of A, and the similar region $B_x - B_y$; and (3) the values A_c and A_k, which are limiting values of the relationship. At all these points and regions of values, something significant or attention-attracting is happening in the relationship between A and B. Those propositions telling us what the values of A and B are at

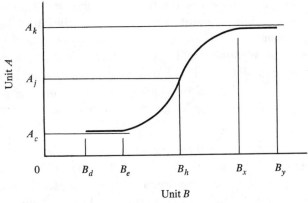

Unit B

Figure 8-1

these points and in these regions of values are the strategic propositions of the model in which A and B are related.

Some insignificant areas in which trivial propositions may be generated are the regions of values between B_e and B_h, and between B_h and B_x, where small differences in values of B are associated with small differences in values of A and where the direction of shift in values remains unchanged. The propositions describing the values of A and B in these regions are all true but trivial precisely because they say just about the same thing.

In choosing the propositions of a model for empirical testing, it is desirable in the interest of parsimony to select strategic propositions. There is, however, another good reason for testing strategic propositions in preference to trivial ones. The strategic proposition points out where something notable is happening to the values of one or more units. Such notable values readily command attention because they are distinguished from the mundane surrounding values. Therefore, insofar as the theorist-researcher can distinguish strategic from trivial propositions, he is armed with a useful means for zeroing his research attention on critical tests of a model. Whether or not a model will be corroborated or need modification after making the empirical test is more easily determined if strategic propositions have been tested.

Proposition and Law of Interaction

The distinction between a proposition and a law of interaction must be understood for several reasons.

1. The form and content of the two statements are different.
2. The uses to which a law of interaction is put differ from the uses of a proposition.
3. There is an asymmetrical linkage between a law of interaction and propositions of a model such that the propositions are logically derivable from the model of which the law is an integral part, but it takes an inductive leap to go from propositions to laws of interaction.

We shall consider these three points in order.

From the standpoint of form and content, a law of interaction states the relationship between two or more units of a model for the entire range of values over which the units are related by the law. The units are named in the law, but the statement of their relationship covers the full range of values over which the law holds. On the other hand, a propositional statement sets forth the value of one unit that is associated with a corresponding value of another unit. The same units are designated as would be true in a law of interaction. The proposition has specificity with respect to the given value that each unit takes, whereas the law of interaction has generality with respect to all values of the units linked by the law. For example, the statement "Family income and family social status are positively related" is a statement of a law, and the particular family income and particular family status derivable from this law of interaction would take such a form as the proposition "Families with low income have low social status." The proposition is limited to the prediction that low income and low status are positively associated, but is silent on average or high income.

A law of interaction and a proposition have different uses. The law of interaction functions in a theoretical model to provide the statement of the lawful relation between units of the system. By contrast, propositional statements about a model are predictions of the value of one or more units from a knowledge of the value of one or more other units. The law of interaction states the general relationship among units, whereas the proposition predicts the specific values that one unit will have in relation to the values of another. In other words, the law of interaction tells *what the relationship is,* and the proposition states *what the predicted values of the units will be.*

The asymmetry in the connection between a law of interaction and a proposition is revealed by the fact that a proposition is logically derivable from a theoretical model of which the law of interaction is an integral part. Given a theoretical system, the application of a set of logical rules will produce the propositional statements that must be true of the system.

Given, however, the problem of determining what are the laws of interaction in a theoretical system for which only the propositions are known, a process of induction is required. This is a generalizing operation for which the rules of logic are much less clear and precise than they are for deducting the truth statements, or propositions, of a theoretical model. In short, the intellectual operations involved in going from theoretical model with its laws of interaction to proposition as a prediction about the model are different intellectual operations from those involved in going from a set of propositions to a model and especially to its laws of interaction. The difference makes the relation between laws of interaction and propositions asymmetrical.

An illustration will best serve to draw out the distinction between a law of interaction and a proposition. Homans has set forth the following proposition: "A person of higher social rank than another originates interaction for the latter more often than the latter originates interaction for him."[7] We may add to this a number of related propositions in the following fashion.

1. A person who receives more than he initiates from person *A* and who initiates more than he receives from person *B* is in an intermediate rank between *A* and *B*.
2. Persons are in the same rank who initiate interactions for each other with equal frequency.
3. In an *n*-person group in which all members are ranked and no two of whom are of the same rank,
   a. One person will originate interaction for all others more than they will originate for him,
   b. One person will originate least for all others, and
   c. Some members will originate interaction more than they receive from others of lower rank and will be recipients of interaction more than they originate for others of higher rank.

Each of these propositions, starting with Homans's original one and including those I have added, represent truth statements about an unspecified model dealing with origination of social interaction among members of a social group. The analytical problem is now to specify the model, and particularly the law of interaction of that model, that generates these propositions.

The model may first be specified as bounded by a group size such that

---

[7]George C. Homans, *The Human Group* (New York: Harcourt, Brace & World, 1950), p. 145. Homans properly labels this a *proposition* in his discussion of it.

all members of the group have opportunity to originate social interaction with each other. Any group for which this is not true does not fall within the purview of the model. The model has only one system state, namely that in which interaction between pairs of members takes place. The units of the model are members of a group distinguished from each other only by their differential rank in the system, there being as many distinctive types of individuals as there are ranks. There may be plural memberships in any rank, but the propositions stated deal only with the relations among pairs of individuals according to their rank.

The most challenging task in constructing the model from which these propositions are derivable is to state the law of interaction for the model. One formulation of the law of interaction could be "In a pair relationship, social rank and origination of social interaction are positively related." All the propositions, both Homans's and mine, may now be derived from this model. Each proposition assigns determinant values to the origination of interaction between any two people in the system.

It is readily apparent that this system may be made into a two-state system by permitting interaction in triads rather than in pairs. At least one new law of interaction would have to be introduced to generate interaction relations among three people to take into account the possibility that they may not interact hierarchically, as the initial law for two persons demands.[8]

We have not, of course, exhausted the number of propositions that may be derivable from the stated model employed in this illustration. It should be clear, however, that a compendium of propositions like these five, or others supplementing their number, does not constitute a theoretical model and that the sum of nonredundant propositions does not constitute a theoretical system.

Negative Propositions

A negative proposition is a prediction of a range of associated values precluded by an affirmative proposition. A negative proposition is therefore based upon the prior ability to formulate a regular proposition in order to negate it. If, for example, it may be asserted that "high family income is associated with high social status," then a negative proposition

[8]Cf. Theodore Caplow, "A Theory of Coalitions in the Triad," *American Sociological Review*, 21:489–493 (Aug. 1956).

like "high family income is associated with low social status" may be stated as one of its opposites. The difference between these two propositions lies in the fact that a range of values on one unit cannot be associated with a stated range of values on the other unit. If high income and high status go together, then high income and low status *cannot* be associated values for these two units.

Negative propositions have an important use in research. Under some often-encountered circumstances, it is difficult to secure empirical indicators for the range of values of a unit that are predicted by a model. At the same time, there are available empirical indicators of unit values that lie outside the range of the model's predicted unit values. By stating the propositions of a model in negative form, it then becomes possible to test empirically its usefulness.

Consider the example of the OSS staff during World War II. It was necessary to develop screening tests to select the most able and reliable candidates for positions as secret agents. As described in the book detailing the work of selection, the tests were negative rather than positive ones on the whole.[9] The model of the good secret agent predicted that he must be decisive, fearless, orderly, and unexcitable, among other attributes. However, it was much more difficult to secure empirical indicators of these attributes than to measure their opposites. Consequently the tests and selection programs were based on eliminating candidates who had undesirable values on these attributes on the assumption that they would not make good agents and spies.

A comparable situation occurs in determining loyalty to country. The proposition "A good citizen is loyal to his country" is difficult to test, however true it may be. The negative proposition "A good citizen cannot have the value *holds membership in subversive organization*" is a readily testable proposition. For that reason the test of loyalty may rest on the negative rather than the positive proposition because it is so difficult to find direct empirical indicators of loyalty.

The test of the positive proposition by using its negative is one important strategy in doing research. This strategy is dictated by the availability of an empirical test of a negative proposition that may prove just as useful in evaluating a model as a test of one of its positive propositions.

The negative proposition must not be confused with the null statement. The null statement is an assertion of *lack of any relationship* between two units. The disproof of the null statement leads to a search for a

[9]OSS Assessment Staff, *The Assessment of Men* (New York: Holt, Rinehart & Winston, 1948).

lawful relation between the units. The confirmation of the null statement leads to an abandonment of the search for a meaningful relation between the units. The negative proposition, on the other hand, declares a range of values of one unit that cannot lawfully be associated with given values of another unit. The disproof of the negative proposition requires that the model from which it was derived be modified in order to generate the negative proposition as a positive one. The confirmation of the negative proposition leaves the model intact as having been supported by the empirical test.

INTERLUDE THREE

All games have an important . . . influence on the destinies of the players under ordinary social conditions; but some offer more opportunities than others for lifetime careers. . . .

—ERIC BERNE, *The Games People Play*

THE CLICHÉ EXPERT TESTIFIES ON THE SOCIAL SCIENCES*

Bernard Berelson
The Population Council, Inc.

Q. Mr. Arbuthnot, I understand that you have undertaken a career as a social scientist.

A. That statement conforms in a high degree to its truth value in terms of reality testing.

Q. What's that again?

A. Yes.

Q. Just what do you do as a social scientist?

A. Oh, many things, some of us hypothesize and others hypothecate.

Q. And what about the others?

A. There aren't any others—except, of course, those who analyze the general context of action.

Q. You mean observe how people act?

A. Well, if you want to put it that way. However, we prefer to see behavioral manifestations in their context of acts, either objective or subjective. That allows us to relate them, of course.

*From a manuscript privately circulated *circa* 1950s. Used by permission of the author.

175

Q. What to?

A. Why, to ongoing theoretical developments.

Q. I'm not sure, Mr. Arbuthnot, that I know what you mean by a context.

A. You mean a general context.

Q. Do I?

A. I think so, You see, all contexts are general.

Q. Pardon me.

A. By context we mean culture, or attutudinal atmosphere, or behavioral climate, or the situation mode—in short, just general context.

Q. I suppose it is quite complicated.

A. Oh, yes, it has several dimensions.

Q. And what are they?

A. Well, there can be the personal dimension, or the group dimension, or the cultural dimension. Then, of course, there's the intensity dimension, but that dimension runs off in another dimension.

Q. And what do you do with these various dimensions?

A. Usually we analyze them at various levels.

Q. Levels?

A. Oh, yes, there are a lot of them, too. There are, for example, the latent and manifest levels, or the structural and functional levels, or the descriptive and analytical levels, or, if you want more differentiated levels, there are the individual level, the group level, the organizational level, the institutional level, and the societal level. Of course, some of these levels are on a higher level than others.

Q. Of course.

A. For example, all of them can be found on either the concrete level or the abstract level.

Q. Are there any other levels?

A. Well, only the most pervasive level of all.

Q. What's that?

A. The level of generality.

Q. The level of—

A. Excuse me. I mean, of course, the level of generality/specificity.

Q. I don't see how you can handle all of this.

A. We can do so only through pilot, exploratory, preliminary, tentative, and suggestive studies—all, of course, as related to basic research.

Q. Of course.

A. You see everything relates to something else.

Q. That figures.

A. For example, right now you are relating to me in a certain role.

Q. Well, I thought we were just talking.
A. Not in terms of the role structure or group dynamics of our subculture. That requires a different kind of relationship. You see, certain kinds of antecedent relationships always lead to certain kinds of consequential relationships in terms of communication.
Q. They do?
A. Well, they tend to.
Q. In your studies I suppose you collect a lot of interesting information.
A. It may be interesting, but it isn't information. It's data. Or, to be more precise, they are data.
Q. And how are the data expressed?
A. Oh, quantitatively, of course, except when that mode is inappropriate.
Q. And then?
A. Then the data are qualitative.
Q. I suppose the data prove a lot of things.
A. Well, they don't always exactly *prove* things. Usually they suggest, indicate, reveal, or reflect. Sometimes, of course, they aren't even statistically significant.
Q. By that, I suppose you mean they aren't important.
A. No. By statistically significant I mean *statistically* significant. You see, there are all kinds of significance.
Q. There are?
A. Yes. You see, there is statistical significance, and then there is, well, as you say, importance.
Q. It must be difficult to keep all these matters correlated.
A. Correlated! Why, I didn't know you are a social scientist.
Q. I guess I meant keep them all together in your minds.
A. Oh, it's not so hard when you have systematic theory of component hypotheses.
Q. I should think not. Do you?
A. No. But then, no one does.
Q. Well, then, just to summarize to this point, as I understand it you study these problems and collect information on them.
A. Oh no. We undertake a scientific analysis of urgent theoretical problems based upon available and systematic data.
Q. And when you are through—
A. Then we have (1) a suggestive study contributing to ongoing theoretical developments, (2) a potentially useful methodological innovation, (3) a systematic body of rigorously collected data, (4) an evaluated and interpreted summary of the material, (5) an article for the learned

journals, and (6) a set of exploratory hypotheses for someone else to verify.

Q. Mr. Arbuthnot, I'm impressed with how rich and complex your field is. Every noun seems to require some adjective in modification.

A. Oh, not just adjectives. Sometimes whole nouns. See what I mean: role differentiation, process analysis, aggression expression, authority status, goal attainment, drive states, and all of these, you see, lead to problem saturation.

Q. It certainly is complicated.

A. Yes, but then everything is integrated in terms of a reference frame or a frame of reference, or a conceptual framework, or if you prefer, ongoing theoretical developments.

Q. I suppose everything has to have a frame of reference.

A. At least one.

Q. That way you find out what's good and bad in behavior, I suppose.

A. Please! Don't use valuation variables or preference statements.

Q. I'll try not to. But then, you certainly are tempting me to. But now tell me something of how you do all this.

A. Through specific and concrete investigations that employ relevant methodologies leading to the integration of substantive areas and appropriate conceptualizations.

Q. I suppose that takes a lot of attention.

A. Only concentrated attention.

Q. And how do the problems get concentrated attention?

A. Through systematic attack at both the substantive and methodological levels. All of this, of course, within a conceptual framework that is oriented in terms of selected general areas that carry important implications at both the psychological and social levels as they relate to personality structure, personality patterns, and personality development. This usually yields substantial returns.

Q. How?

A. By laying a firm foundation for coherent substantive research— assuming, of course, that the problem is well-structured.

Q. I suppose all this is a pretty highly organized activity.

A. Oh, it has a highly developed hierarchical structure, if that's what you mean. You may, however, be referring to the functional patterns.

Q. I guess I was.

A. They're highly developed, too.

Q. Where does all this go on?

A. In various settings—laboratory experimental settings, field settings, participant-observation settings, or Navajo reservations.

Q. What comes of all this, Mr. Arbuthnot?

A. Well, we sharpen our tools, make our hypotheses more insightful, clarify our conceptualizations, refine our differentiations, improve our dynamic formulations, orient our situational tasks more realistically, maximize intercommunication, and contribute to the decision-making process—all, of course, on focal points of interest.

Q. But do you learn anything?

A. You mean relatively? We always mean relatively.

Q. I guess I do.

A. Within the limit of statistical significance, we do.

Q. Could you give me a few examples?

A. What do you think I've been doing?

Q. Well, I really must thank you for this tour through the field of the social sciences.

A. Not at all. I hope it has performed its therapeutic function of transference.

Q. Oh, counter, counter.

CHAPTER NINE

Empirical Indicators

Although operationism was originally a program of concept formation aimed at quantitative sciences, the term "operationism" nowadays tends to connote the empiricist postulate that any descriptive term, whether quantitative or not, which is cognitively significant must either designate something that is directly observable or else be definable in some way on the basis of terms of the latter kind.

—ARTHUR PAP in C. W. Churchman and P. Ratoosh (eds.), *Measurement: Definitions and Theories*

In the case of measurement . . . it has not always been clear whether the term means an operation *involving an observer and a more or less complex apparatus, or whether it means the* number *that emerges as a result of such an operation—whether, in other words, a measurement produces a result or an operation produces a measurement.*

—PETER CAWS in *ibid.*

THIS CHAPTER is concerned with finding the empirical indicators that produce the values on the units employed in a model. From the preceding chapter, we now know that all propositions are predictions of the values on one or more units in the model. In order that a unit be measured to indicate a value on it, the thing itself must be apprehended by an empirical indicator.

The chapter opens with a general discussion of empirical indicators that leads to a definition. There then follows a brief discussion of operationism and the reliability of indicators. Since units being measured and their empirical indicators are fundamentally linked, each type of unit and its appropriate indicators is next examined. A subsequent distinction is then drawn between absolute and relative indicators, and each is analyzed separately. The possibility that a single unit of a model may have more than one empirical indicator measuring it is taken up, followed by an examination of compound indicators made up of a combination of several indicators. The chapter closes with a brief consideration of validity.

For the first time, we now turn analytical attention systematically outward from the model to confront the empirical world. In previous considerations of the empirical world, useful results were obtained as a basis for discovering and describing the units of a model (Chapter 4), its laws of interaction (Chapter 5), its boundary conditions (Chapter 6), and its system states (Chapter 7). These descriptive features of the empirical world, however, provided only suggestions for the theory builder. Once these suggestions entered into his consideration, there was no need to have further reference to the empirical world in building the theoretical model.

We are at that point in the theory-building–research cycle at which the propositions or predictions of the model must now be put to the test of their empirical accuracy. This, of course, requires the answer to the basic question, "Can my model make any sense out of the real world?" The first step in answering this question is to find for each unit employed in every proposition to be tested an empirical indicator that will measure the values of the unit. Whereas this conversion to empirical indicators is the necessary condition for making the empirical test, the sufficient condition is to convert the whole propositional statement into an hypothesis in which each unit is represented by its empirical indicator. This second step in the test of a proposition will be examined in Chapter 10.

Empirical Indicator Defined

An empirical indicator is an operation employed by a researcher to secure measurements of values on a unit. An empirical indicator is therefore a procedure employed by a researcher when he says, "This value, which I am measuring by the following procedures, stands for the value of the thing, or unit, I have built into my model."

If we refer back to the opening quotation from Professor Caws, the empirical indicator is the "operation involving an observer and a more or less complex apparatus," and the score or number that results from this operation is the value measured on that unit by the empirical indicator. It should be clear, then, that the process of measurement contains both the *operation of measuring* and the results or *value produced* by this operation.

The value of the unit produced by an empirical indicator is most often a number like a dial reading, a test score, or an ordinal position on a scale. The measured value of a unit may also be a category like *present* or *absent, central* or *peripheral, dominant* or *submissive,* and *sociometric star* or *sociometric isolate.* In each instance, it is possible unequivocally to sort a sample of identical units into these categories so that the units have the values described by the categories.

There are, then, two principal criteria of an adequate empirical indicator.

1. The operations involved in the relation between observer and the apparatus used for observing are explicitly set forth so that they may be duplicated by any other equally trained observer.
2. The observing operation produces equivalent values for the same sample when employed by different observers.

These two criteria of an empirical indicator have been treated in other contexts under the names (1) *operationism* and (2) *reliability.*

Operationism

Operationism owes its basic formulation to Percy Bridgman, the physicist. Bentley, writing in 1954, suggested that

> Bridgman was a worker with high pressures. What he did he did with his hands. What he talked about he wanted to talk about competently . . . his method in getting his answers was very simple, he just pushed away all the rubbish he found around him without any feeling of awe for it at all; he made fresh, direct observations of the way physicists actually work; and he asked the kind of questions the worker in the laboratory wants, and needs to have answered. Then he established procedures for answering with a minimum attention to spooks of any kind. In doing this he gave "empiricism" a modernized dress, both physically and psychologically, and set up programs which are deeply influencing psychologists as well as physicists, and which by all signs will grow greatly in influence. . . . To develop his interpretation Bridgman adopted two key-words with which everyone today is acquainted, "concept" and "operation." What the world has to be thankful for and in my judgment will appreciatively acknowledge is that instead of hunting out meticulous definitions for these words, and then doing his best to degrade himself to the level of his definitions, Bridgman shook the two words out like two signal flags, and planted them, one on each side, to mark out the territories that must be taken into account.

The word "operation" indicates the thing-happening, a specific case of the physical fact as it is taken up by Bridgman for interpretative inquiry. The word "concept" indicates any specific case of the presence or registration of the fact-as-known. In a way, then, but not at all in any of the ordinary ways, "operation" represents the empirical, and "concept" the rational element of the older disputations. The great difference is that the two are not split apart, detached; they are stresses in the one common situation of man-experiencing-fact. And right here is the point at which the primary Bridgman "feel" for his problem is sympathetic, physically and psychologically, to the great requirements of the understanding.[1]

The essential feature of Bridgman's contribution was to demonstrate that the empirical indicator of a unit of a theoretical model is an operation performed by an observer with some kind of observing instrument. The result produces a value on the unit. What Bridgman did *not* do in his basic works, *Dimensional Analysis* (1922) and *The Logic of Modern Physics* (1927), but what some of his enthusiastic disciples in the behavioral sciences insisted upon, was to reach the conclusion that the only legitimate models of science were those in which all the units employed could be operationalized.[2]

Bridgman emphasized that when a model is being tested empirically, those units composing the model and involved in the proposition under test must be measured by some kind of empirical indicator to determine their values. Bridgman, in short, insisted that there be empirical indicators only when the proposition was subject to the test, but not before. This conclusion is consistent with the analytical development of this volume.

It should be clear, then, that the central importance of operationalism relates to the empirical test of a proposition and not to the formulation of the model from which the proposition is derived. I have asserted in Chapter 3 that the units chosen for a theoretical model are not limited and restricted by their potential for being measured by an empirical indicator. It is still possible, for example, to use the unit *id* in psychiatric theory and

[1]Arthur F. Bentley, *Inquiry Into Inquiries* (Boston: Beacon Press, 1954), pp. 117 and 119.

[2]Bentley points out that Bridgman in his later book *The Nature of Physical Theory* (1936) bent under the criticism of his earlier work and unnecessarily gave ground. See Bentley, *ibid.*, p. 116. The position advanced by Bridgman was not readily accepted, as Bentley notes in his footnotes on p. 117 of *Inquiry into Inquiries*. The uncritical acceptance and distortion of Bridgman is well illustrated in the behavioral sciences by the work of the late Professor George Lundberg. See his *Social Research* (New York: Longmans, Green & Co., 1942).

practice without an empirical indicator being available for its measurement.

Reliability

The second criterion of an empirical indicator is that it produce reliable values. Reliability of any operation for measuring the value on a unit depends upon the identity of the values produced when a single observer repeats a measurement or when different observers use the same measuring instruments. The reliability of a given empirical indicator is, therefore, a measure of the degree to which the operation involved in securing the value is independent of a particular observer and his idiosyncratic relationship to the measuring apparatus. Just as important is the stability of the measuring apparatus in repeated use. The former is called *observer reliability,* the latter *instrument reliability.*

The results of all scientific research have to be reproducible if they are to gain credibility. The reliability of empirical indicators is what guarantees the reproducibility of a given piece of research. When an empirical indicator is reliable, it produces values of a unit that differ little if at all from one observer to another. If the operation of employing the measuring instrument is a reliable one, such variations in values as may be produced may be ascribed to measurement errors and not to instability of the instrument.

The statistical procedure for establishing observer reliability, test reliability, instrument reliability, and measurement-scale reliability are well known and are not the primary subject of this chapter.[3]

The normal manner of indicating an empirical indicator takes the standard form "The value of unit X as measured by..." The term *as measured by* and what follows it should describe the operation of the particular empirical indicator employed to generate the value on the unit. This phrasing is important to keep in mind because, as we shall presently see, there may be several or even many empirical indicators for the same unit. It therefore becomes essential in the proper description of any empirical test of a proposition to state the specific empirical indicator that produces the value being measured in the particular study.

---

[3]See, for example, the important early work of L. L. Thurstone, *The Reliability and Validity of Tests* (Ann Arbor, Mich.: Edwards Bros., 1937), or standard research-methods books like L. Festinger and D. Katz, *Research Methods in the Behavioral Sciences* (New York: Dryden Press, 1953).

Empirical Indicator and Units

It is worth repeating in this chapter what has been previously asserted, i.e., that the only portions of a theoretical model that are ever measured are the values of the units employed in the model. The most important implication of this assertion is that the laws of a model are never made the subject of empirical indicators or measured in a scientific study. Laws of interaction are specified but not measured.

The initial assertion of this section must be qualified by pointing out that the boundaries of a model may also be determined empirically. Where external or benign criteria of boundary are employed, it will be necessary to establish the values of those units that define the boundary. This constitutes a special case in which units of a model incorporated in laws of interaction of the model are not the only units whose values are measured. Those units that are boundary-determining for the model, but that never enter into the functioning of the model, must also have their values measured in order to establish the empirical location of the model's boundaries. This special exception to the general rule that empirical indicators deal only with values of units of a model should give no trouble to the theory builder.

Because empirical indicators are employed to measure values on units of a theoretical model, it should prove useful to determine whether or not the empirical indicators are in turn unique to the particular classes of units set forth in Chapter 4. Are empirical indicators of enumerative units different from those that measure values on associative units? Are the empirical indicators that measure values on relational units different from those employed in statistical units? We will also consider summative units and the empirical indicators employed to stand for summative units.

Enumerative Unit

As it was defined in Chapter 4, an enumerative unit is a characteristic of a thing in all its conditions. This definition suggests that any empirical indicator used to establish the value of an enumerative unit has to generate nonzero values for that unit in whatever condition the unit is found. This condition of universal nonzero values is readily met by many empirical indicators. Thus, the chronological age of a person, though variable, is always a nonzero value. Similarly, the sex of a person is either male or female but never neither. Empirical indicators that, like those just mentioned, always produce nonzero values measure values on enumerative units.

The actual number of empirical indicators used for enumerative units is unlimited by virtue of the characteristics of such units. The only condition that needs to be met is that the indicator never produce a zero value. The age of a person may be obtained by observing him and estimating his age; it may be ascertained by direct questioning of the subject; or, when the determination is critical, it may be made by reference to records of the date of birth. Each of these three different empirical indicators produces a number that is taken as the age of the person. This number can never be zero. In the same way, the size of a group may be determined by observation, by questioning its participants, or by counting the names on its membership rolls. Each is a separate empirical indicator and each gives rise to a number that is the value measured on the unit *group size*. This number, of course, can never be zero, for it would then be a nongroup.

Associative Unit

It will be recalled that an associative unit is a property characteristic of a unit in only some of its conditions. In all respects save this one, it is identical with an enumerative unit. The difference is that there is a real zero for associative units. As was pointed out in Chapter 4, the fact that an associative unit may have zero value has important consequences for the measurement of values on it. The first consequence is that the measuring instrument must be capable of producing a zero value on the unit. Secondly, it may also be that the unit has both positive *and* negative values. The empirical indicator must therefore be able to produce, by passing through a zero value, negative values on the unit as well as positive ones.

As we have already seen with enumerative units, there are empirical indicators that neither go to zero nor have the possibility of producing negative values. This does not mean, however, that an empirical indicator becomes a measure of an enumerative unit because only the positive portion of values produced by the empirical indicator is employed. For example, if the affective response of a person was being measured and values ranging from weak positive responses to very strong positive responses were taken, this would not mean that *affective response* was an enumerative unit. Indeed, the same empirical indicator used to measure the limited range of positive values of affective response could be extended to measure neutral affectivity and negative affectivity. The unit *affective response* is therefore an associative unit because it can have zero and negative values, even though the range of measured values may be restricted by the researcher to positive ones.

In distinguishing, therefore, between associative and enumerative units, the entire *possible* range of values produced by the empirical indicator must be examined to determine whether the unit is in one or the other class. The range of *possible* values is different for the two classes of units. This means that propositions employing associative units may be stated for zero or even negative values of these units. The full test of the model containing associative units may depend on setting forth those propositions over the full range of values for the units. On the other hand, for enumerative units, the range of values is more restricted, and therefore the number of propositions necessary to test the model employing such units may also be limited.

Relational Unit

A relational unit is a property characteristic of a thing that can be determined only by the relation among properties of the thing. It will be recalled that a relational unit may be based upon either the interaction among properties or the combination of properties. These two possibilities indicate clearly what must be the fundamental features of empirical indicators of relational units.

Where the relational unit is based upon an interaction among properties, the empirical indicator of this relational unit must apprehend this interaction. Whether this will be done by measuring the properties that interact or by measuring the outcome of the interaction will depend upon the nature of the model constructed. Thus, the unit *sibling rivalry* would have to be measured by an empirical indicator that determines the value of the rivalry, i.e., the outcome of the relationship. On the other hand, a unit like *perceptual threshold* would depend upon the value of the stimulus as related to the value of the response above some zero point. In this second instance, it is the value of the two properties in the relational unit that is the focus of attention rather than the outcome of the interaction.

Similarly, in relational units made up of a combination of properties, either the outcome or the value of the properties involved in the combination may be measured by the empirical indicator. For example, *ethnocentrism* is a relational unit that may be measured by an empirical indicator counting the number of a respondent's preferences expressed for members of his own group and preferences expressed for nonmembers of the group. If the sum of his preferences for his own group members exceeds half of all his expressed preferences, this relationship between these measured numbers constitutes one way of establishing the value for the unit *ethnocentrism*. The unit *sex ratio*, on the other hand, is one in which the number produced by relating the size of the male group to the size of the female group in a given population produces an empirical indicator in which the outcome so measured is the appropriate value.

Relational units are rather tricky to employ, for there are four basic types involved: those based on interaction, those based on combination, and those based on each of these two types in turn being subdivided into empirical indicators that measure value on the properties so related or measure the outcome of the relationship. An examination of individual studies usually makes quite clear in which of these four ways a particular empirical indicator of a relational unit is employed.

Statistical Unit

I have already defined a statistical unit in Chapter 4 as a property summarized by some description of its distribution. An empirical indicator of a statistical unit must therefore meet this criterion.

The three classes of statistical units are: (1) those summarizing a central tendency in the distribution of a property; (2) those summarizing the dispersion of the distribution of a property; and (3) those locating the position of a unit relative to the distribution of the property in a population. A measure of median income in a population would be an example of the first class of statistical unit; the interquartile range of income would be an empirical indicator of the second class; and low income would be an indicator of the third type.

There is no particular difficulty in distinguishing and recognizing the empirical indicators of statistical units. The actual title given to these units is often the key to their identification.

Complex Units

It will be recalled that in Chapter 4 the possibility of complex units satisfying the criteria of several classes simultaneously was examined. Let us take an example of this and follow it through so as to learn how complex are many social-science empirical indicators.

Suppose in a given study it is desired to examine the category of college students called *underachievers*. What sort of empirical indicator may be developed to measure the value of underachievement in a group of college students? The first conclusion is that an underachiever must be a student whose performance is less than might be expected on the basis of his ability. Therefore, the first approach to developing an empirical indicator for *underachiever* is to consider the discrepancy between some measure of ability and some measure of performance. If performance level is much lower than ability level, then below some point of increasing discrepancy between these two measures the researcher might want to classify all members of a population as underachievers. This simple measure of underachiever is a statistical unit showing relative position in a population distribution of a property, but it is also a relational unit because the empirical indicator employed depends upon the relation between ability and achievement.

Suppose now the researcher wishes further to complicate his empirical indicator by reference to the distribution of ability and the distribution of performance in a large population from which his sample population of students may be drawn. Thus, college freshmen in an introductory sociology class who are underachievers may be defined with reference to all college freshmen in the particular university. When this comparison is employed, it will be found that within the larger populations there is a distribution of discrepancies between ability and performance. For the sample population of sociology freshmen, the measure of ability and the measure of performance are each standardized on the distribution of these attributes in the parent population of all freshmen. For example, if ability is measured by an IQ test and performance is measured by grade-point average (GPA), then the values on these two measures in the sample population are located in the distribution of these values in the parent population (i.e., standardized on the parent population distribution), before the measure of underachievement is calculated. This has the effect of minimizing the effects of the peculiarities in the distribution in the sample population.

The empirical indicator as now developed is still a relational-statistical indicator, but is once removed from the direct measures on the sample population because each of these measures is first located in the respective distribution of the parent population. The empirical indicator is removed by an intervening measurement step from the actual values determined for the sample population. Whether an individual in the sample is considered an underachiever or not depends, first, on the measures of his ability and performance and, second, on the relationship each of these measures has to the distribution of these measures in the parent population.

An empirical indicator of the sort just described turns out to be very complex. It is a complexity that may be encountered with any type of empirical indicator, although it has been illustrated with an example of one measuring a statistical unit. This kind of complexity should constantly be kept in mind when one examines the results of another's research and especially when designing one's own research. It is sometimes possible to lose sight of the theoretical unit being measured when the empirical indicator used to measure it is complex.

Summative Unit

We have previously ruled out summative units as being unacceptable in theory building. This ruling out, however, does not stand as a barrier to the employment of such units in past and future work. Many theorists will continue to use summative units, and many teachers of the social-science disciplines will continue to teach research results as though summative units have been measured. I therefore will examine summative units again, hoping to demonstrate on still another ground why they may not be employed in theory building.

It will be recalled from Chapter 4 that a summative unit is a global unit describing, for example, a complex phenomenon like an entire society or an industrial system or a total personality structure. The distinctive feature of any study purporting to use summative units is that usually one, or at the most several, empirical indicators are employed to stand for the complex summative unit. There is nothing wrong with this process except its unwarranted assumption that one or even several empirical indicators can measure values on the complex known as a summative unit. What, for example, is the empirical indicator or indicators that may be employed to measure the values in a classification of societies into capitalist and socialist? What, indeed, other than literacy, is the empirical indicator usually used to distinguish between preliterate societies and all others? How much more do we really mean by the unit *preliterate society* than is captured in the one empirical indicator used to determine a value for this kind of unit? Does the idea of an underdeveloped, or developing, society gain accurate description if the empirical indicator ''per capita capital investment'' or ''per capita income'' or ''infant mortality rate'' or even any combination of these measures is used to provide empirical indicators for this type of society? Each one of these empirical indicators may indeed differentiate among various societies. There may even be a relatively high correlation between the empirical indicators in the manner in which each does distinguish among an array of societies. But the designation *underdeveloped society* or *developing society* connotes much more than is revealed by these or other single empirical indicators.

The general fact of the matter is that when summative units are used in theory building, only limited empirical indicators are ever employed in testing theoretical models in which these units are included. I would therefore conclude that the impossibility of getting adequate empirical indicators for all the facets, or even for a significant collection of the facets, of a summative unit makes such units practically useless in theory building.

The units actually measured by the empirical indicators employed to stand for summative units are much more modest and smaller in scope than the summative units for which they are taken to stand. It adds nothing to a theory to incorporate units into it that should be measured in order to test the theory, but cannot be assessed. It is much more useful to reduce the breadth of the summative units to a smaller dimension and be satisfied with the more modest theories that emerge as a result.

A good example of a simple indicator standing for a summative unit will be found in a recent article by Sewell and Armer. Their analytical problem was to determine whether or not the neighborhood climate or social atmosphere had consequences for educational aspirations of high school students. *Neighborhood atmosphere* is a summative unit representing a general notion about style of living, class identification, levels of aspiration, and motivation to seek the rewards of the larger society. To capture this very complex type of analytical unit the authors employed as empirical indicator "the proportion of males fourteen years and older in the given area who follow white collar occupations."[4] The minimum empirical statement that may be made about the subsequent analysis is "Neighborhoods with high, medium, or low proportions of adult males following white collar occupations are related with . . ." But that is also the maximum statement that may be made, as the proportion of adult males following white collar occupations is only with the greatest difficulty taken as an indicator of neighborhood social atmosphere.

It will invariably be found that when an attempt is made to develop an empirical indicator for a summative unit, the result is unsatisfactory. At

[4]W. H. Sewell and J. M. Armer, "Neighborhood Context and College Plans," *American Sociological Review,* 31:159–168 (April 1966).

best only a portion of the features of a summative unit will be measured by the chosen empirical indicator. Neither logic nor artistic license justifies asserting that any single empirical indicator stands for a whole complex unit. The research may still be useful, however, if the model that initiated it has its units restrained and constricted to a more modest dimension so as not to exceed the features of the unit that are measured by the empirical indicator chosen.

The empirical indicators employed in a study should be homologous with the class of unit built into the theoretical model. This is a logical test that the empirical indicator must meet. Should there not be this kind of correspondence between theoretical unit and its empirical indicator, then one must change in order that the homology be preserved. Should the theoretical unit have to be changed in order to continue employing the empirical indicator, then the theoretical model of which it is a part must also be modified. If, on the other hand, the theoretical model is retained intact, then another empirical indicator needs to be chosen to measure values on the theoretical unit.

Absolute Indicators

There are many empirical indicators employed in the behavioral and social sciences that have an absolute quality about them. They are absolute in the sense that there can be no question as to what they measure. The very definition of the indicator is sufficient to guarantee that it has one and only one referent. Numerous examples may be given. Race is an absolute indicator; sex is an absolute indicator; age is an absolute indicator. The resultant values of employing these absolute indicators, such as white, Negro, Oriental, or male, female, or 21 years, 33 years, 47 years, can have no other referent than race, sex, and age, respectively. In a similar way, place of residence, occupation, income, education, and, in general, the demographic features of a population are all measured by absolute indicators.

We should not confuse the reliability of the particular measures that may be employed to determine values on the absolute indicator with the absolute character of such indicators. For example, it is notorious that householders in replying to census questions about their own age and that of family members tend to round the response to five-year intervals. This is a feature of the unreliability of the method of determining age by asking respondents to report their own age or that of others whom they know. A more accurate way of measuring age would be to require substantiation with a birth certificate. However, whether the birth certificate or the verbal response is used as the way of getting a value for the unit *age,* there is no question that what is being measured is age and nothing else.

Absolute indicators are, of course, not limited to the demographic features of populations. Man, the subject matter of the behavioral sciences, has the special capacity to respond when asked questions. The respondent can tell what he has done in the past, what he is presently doing, and what he anticipates doing. Furthermore, he is able to tell how he felt about what he did in the past and how he feels about what he is doing presently. Consequently, there is a richness in the possibility of modeling man's total activities that leads to ambitious theories about them. Thus, we may be interested in morale at work and build theories about the relationships between liking work, finding it interesting, enjoying its variety and complexity, and the consequence of all of these for level of morale. It is even possible to secure absolute indicators for liking for work, interest in work, level of complexity of work, and the degree of variety in work performance. The unit in such theories for which it is difficult to find an empirical indicator is *morale.* Here we are often satisfied with simple measures like "How do you like this company?" or "How do you like your supervisor?" each response being measured on a Likert-type response scale. Or we use indicators of behavioral withdrawing from work like turnover rates or absentee rates to determine the levels of morale.[5] Any one of these measures of morale is not an absolute one. We would have more meaningful models to test if the empirical indicators and the units for which they are providing measures had a closer correspondence than does morale with turnover or with liking a supervisor.

Because they have this absolute characteristic, there is a strong temptation to employ absolute indicators in the role of so-called "independent variables." For example, an individual is born a Negro or a white person. This at-birth characteristic obviously antedates any subsequent history of the individual. Should Negroes and whites come together and their interaction result in discrimination against the Negroes, it seems safe to infer that race differences, because they temporally precede discriminatory behavior, "cause" discrimination. This view of the direction of influence is further buttressed by the fact that if you reverse the statement it

[5]See, for example, V. Vroom, *Work and Motivation* (New York: John Wiley & Sons, 1964), or an English example, R. W. Revans, "Management, Morale and Productivity," in *Proceedings of the National Industrial Safety Conference, 1963* (London: Royal Society for the Prevention of Accidents, 1963), pp. 84–97.

becomes ludicrous: "Discrimination causes race differences." The asymmetry here derives from the fact that race may be measured by an absolute empirical indicator that is unaffected by temporal or locality considerations. Discrimination, on the other hand, may vary as to place and time of occurrence. We cannot, however, argue from the fixity of values produced by absolute empirical indicators to the conclusion that this fixity means that the units represented by absolute indicators are causally linked to the variable values produced on other units of a theoretical model for which there are no absolute empirical indicators.

Absolute indicators have two general characteristics: (1) The unit for which the indicator stands is unequivocal; and (2) the value measured on the unit tends to be fixed at a point in time. A special case of the second characteristic of an absolute unit is one in which the value may be fixed permanently in the unit and never be subject to change, as with race, for example.

Relative Indicators

Another general class of empirical indicators may be called *relative indicators*. The primary characteristic of a relative indicator is that it may be employed as an empirical indicator of several different theoretical units. It is for this reason that it is designated a *relative* indicator.

A relative indicator has possibilities of being homologous with several theoretical units. This is not an uncommon situation in the social sciences. For example, income may be used as an index of economic position, or it may stand for social-class position. Worker absenteeism in an industrial plant may be taken as an empirical indicator of morale, of health status, or of community social practices, as when the absenteeism is associated with the opening of the hunting or fishing season. Religious affiliation may be taken as an empirical indicator of the possession of a set of values, or it may be used as an empirical indicator of a degree of social conservatism.

The issue posed by relative indicators is a simple one to state and a difficult one to solve. There is a degree of reasonableness by which the same empirical indicator may be considered homologous with different theoretical units that it purports to measure. It seems reasonable to assert that people with low morale will avoid work and that therefore absenteeism is one measure of their morale because it represents an avoidance of work. It seems equally reasonable to believe that people who are incapable of going to work because of illness will protect their health status by being absent from work during the period of their illness. It is even reasonable to assume that strong local community approval exists for participation in the opening days of a hunting or fishing season and that therefore absenteeism may be taken as an index of the high but temporary social sanctioning of absenteeism from work in order to enjoy a preferred activity. Each of these links between the same empirical indicator and a different theoretical unit has an equal probability of being considered reasonable.

The solution to this kind of problem is *not* a definitional one. The individual researcher may have his own preference and choose to make a given empirical indicator the measure of a particular theoretical unit. The test of any proposition in which he gives this special significance to his chosen empirical indicator then must continue in the following direction. Another empirical indicator is selected for the same theoretical unit. If the two separate empirical indicators give the same results, then there is some reason to believe that the theoretical unit that both stand for has the predicted relationship with some other theoretical units. Thus, if one way of measuring morale is to use absenteeism, then another way might be to use turnover rates. Both empirical indicators are now taken to stand for the same theoretical unit, *morale*. Suppose the theoretical model leads to the prediction that there is a positive association between the morale level of a group of workers and their level of output. Then, if morale is measured by turnover rate (low turnover rate = high morale) on the one hand, and absenteeism rate (low absenteeism rate = high morale) on the other hand, we should expect that there would be a negative association between each of these empirical indicators and a measure of productivity. If this theoretical prediction is not verified for both of the empirical indicators of morale, we have reason to believe that the theory is wrong. If the predicted result is obtained with both empirical indicators of morale, we have confidence that the theory is accurate and may choose on the basis of convenience or taste which indicator of morale we may use in a future test of the theory. (We would expect, of course, that the intercorrelation between the two empirical indicators of morale would also be high.) If the theoretical prediction is substantiated by one measure of morale but not by the other, then the most likely consequence is to discard the indicator of the unit that fails in the test.

We are now suggesting that there is a process of convergence of several empirical indicators with respect to the test of a single proposition. It is this convergence in *results* that gives added confidence in the employment of those empirical indicators that have converged toward the same result in several research undertakings. It should be noted very carefully that we are not making the usual assumption that underlies an often-used notion of instrument validity. I am not asserting that the convergence of results when two different empirical indicators are used means that either one of these indicators is a valid measure of the theoretical unit. Indeed, the focus of attention is not upon the empirical indicator at all. Rather, the focus is upon the theoretical unit, for we are concerned with measuring it and not with the measuring operations themselves.

To summarize, then, the issue of a single empirical indicator having a reasonable linkage with two or more theoretical units is solved by determining whether additional empirical indicators chosen to measure one of the theoretical units produce results that converge with the results of the initial empirical indicator of that unit. When such convergence occurs, we have an added reason for believing that the first empirical indicator did, indeed, measure values on the theoretical unit. This does not, however, tell us how good a measure it is, nor does it tell us whether it is a better measure than the second empirical indicator employed.

Multiplicity of Indicators

It is one of the vexing problems of the social sciences, not wholly unknown to the physical and biological sciences, that the same theoretical unit may be measured by more than one empirical indicator. The operational problem is to determine what to do about such a situation.

There are two general cases to consider: (1) the case in which the population sample is ordered in the same way by the values measured by the several empirical indicators, and (2) the case in which the employment of each empirical indicator produces a different ordering in the population sample according to the values each indicator measures on it.

In the case of an identical ordering of the population sample by the values measured on it, we may immediately conclude that the empirical indicators are duplicating each other. Thus, if in a sample of families, economic status is measured by reported annual income of the family head, on the one hand, and is estimated by the researcher's evaluation of home furnishings during a visit, on the other hand, these are identical measures of economic status if they produce the same ordering from high to low economic status for the sample population.

When two measures are identical in ordering the sample population, their correlation is high, even though nonlinear. The fact of a high correlation means that the two empirical indicators are *not* independent of each other. Indeed, the common feature they share is that both are measuring the same theoretical unit (in the example, the economic status of family groups). It will be noted that the higher the correlation, the more nearly perfect is the correspondence in the ordering of the sample population on both empirical indicators. Almost never is the correlation a perfect one, however.

In the interest of economy, there now occurs the question of which of the several empirical indicators producing substantially the same ordering of the sample population will be employed. Assuming that they do produce nearly identical results, the selection among them depends upon purely pragmatic considerations. One empirical indicator may be employed more readily than another; one may be cheaper to use than another; or the investigator may simply have an artistic or idiosyncratic reason for preferring one empirical indicator over the others. These are all grounds on which the choice may be made.

The second case of multiple indicators is the one in which two or more empirical indicators produce different orderings of the sample population. When this situation occurs, the researcher is required to admit that the empirical indicators no longer measure the same theoretical unit. This circumstance leads to a low or zero correlation among the values measured by the respective empirical indicators. These indicators must be independent of each other because of the lack of correlation among them. But this also means that they cannot be measuring, or standing as indicators for, the same theoretical unit.

Obviously, under these circumstances it is necessary to decide which of the empirical indicators measures the theoretical unit contained in the model and to discard the remaining empirical indicators that do not measure this unit. If we return, for example, to a previously used illustration, it may very well be that absenteeism is a poor measure of morale, whereas attitude toward boss may be a good measure. I have already indicated that absenteeism may be a better measure of health status than of morale, and it may even be a good measure of community norms if it has a periodic character associated with the opening of hunting or fishing seasons.

The decision about retaining or discarding an empirical indicator depends upon a scientific judgment of the homology between the theoretical unit and its empirical indicator. By the homology test alone, it may be possible to call into question a particular empirical indicator and thus discard it. The homology test may be difficult to make, however, if the researcher is in any way wedded to his measuring instruments. He may then simply contend that "intelligence is what my test measures" or any analog of this statement. The effect of this conclusion is to insist that the theoretical unit be determined by the empirical indicator, rather than the other way around. It is surprising how frequently this is done in the behavioral sciences.

The problem of several empirical indicators being employed to stand for the same theoretical unit is usually only encountered when two or more studies are being compared. One empirical indicator is used in the first study, but another is made to measure the same theoretical unit in the second study. Each author asserts the propriety of his particular choice. There is no way to test the merits of either claim unless an identical sample population is measured by the several empirical indicators. This is seldom done.

The following is an example in which the identical population was measured in two distinctive ways to determine the distribution of social-class membership in the sample. An occupational classification to measure socioeconomic status, based upon a modification of Edwards' scheme, was cross-tabulated with a measure of social class employed by W. Lloyd Warner. This was done for the basic employed population in "Yankee City," the data coming from the Warner study. These data are presented in Table 9-1. The coefficient of mean square contingency is .608 with a maximum possible value of .913. There is, therefore, a moderately high correlation between a measure of socioeconomic status based solely on occupation and one based, as Warner's is, on occupation, income, place of residence, and source of income.

Table 9-1. *Relation Between a Revised Edwards Classification of Occupations and Warner's Index of Social Status for a Sample of "Yankee City" Residents**

	WARNER'S SOCIAL STATUS						
EDWARDS' SYSTEM	UPPER UPPER	LOWER UPPER	UPPER MIDDLE	LOWER MIDDLE	UPPER LOWER	LOWER LOWER	TOTAL
Prof. & Mgrs.	15	24	202	115	26	4	386
Merchants	0	2	50	91	55	15	213
Clerks	3	2	49	241	86	20	401
Skilled Wkrs.	0	0	17	145	119	25	306
Semi-skilled	0	0	7	227	756	433	1243
Unskilled	0	0	0	18	74	50	142
Total	18	28	325	837	936	547	2691

*From R. Dubin, "Factors in the Variation of Urban Occupational Structure," (unpublished master's thesis, department of sociology, University of Chicago, 1940), p. 13. These data were made available through the courtesy of Professor Warner even before the publication of his "Yankee City" studies.

The problem of two or more empirical indicators producing different results in ordering a sample population gives rise to a great deal of controversy in interpreting social-science research. One researcher, employing a given empirical indicator, will argue for the empirical results he secured, which differ from those of another researcher who employed a different empirical indicator for the same theoretical unit. Rather than consider the separate empirical indicators they used in measuring the common theoretical unit, they will both argue simply from the assumption that the same theoretical unit has been measured. This is a fruitless argument, for there is no reason to believe that the researchers are measuring values on the same theoretical unit. The only viable solution to such an argument is for each researcher to admit the limitation of his own results by stating his conclusion as follows: "The [theoretical unit] employed in my model, *as measured by* [the empirical indicator I have employed] results in . . ." It will then become obvious that a common empirical indicator *has not* been employed in the several studies and that variations in their results may be attributed to this simple fact. Beyond this resolution of the particular controversy, the degree of divergence in results attributable to the difference in empirical indicators employed may only be determined by using the different indicators on an identical sample population and then observing the divergence in their respective ordering of the values measured on this population.

Validity Revisited

The fundamental sense given to the term *validity* is that there is consensus that an empirical indicator measures values on a stated unit. This consensus is a man-made consensus and is nothing more than a conventional agreement among a group of interested students and spectators that the empirical indicator and theoretical unit whose values it measures are homologous. We may therefore expect that what is a valid measure at some time may lose this status if the consensus upon which it is based is supplanted.

The breakdown of a consensus usually occurs when an investigator raises questions about the empirical indicator based upon evidence that is independent of the circumstances of its employment. For example, Professor Allison Davis became concerned with the fact that standard intelligence tests regularly measured Negro IQ lower than that of whites. Professor Davis was not satisfied to draw the conclusion that the races had different levels of inherent intelligence. He rather asked if there was something exceptional about Negroes that might produce this result other than their level of intelligence. His conclusion was that their culture was significantly different from that of whites and that this difference showed up in the culture-bound intelligence tests usually employed. Dr. Davis then designed culture-free tests to measure intelligence in order to remove the culture component from existing tests.[6]

The impact of Davis's work was to suggest that two units were being measured by standard intelligence tests: intelligence and cultural experience. He attempted to purify such tests by eliminating the cultural unit. He did this, of course, by bringing into consideration independent knowledge about the way of life of Negroes. This is what I mean when I conclude that consensus on the validity of a given empirical indicator is destroyed by evidence independent of the circumstances in which the indicator is used.

The independence of the outside factor employed to disturb a consensus on the validity of an empirical indicator is also the starting point employed in the classic rationale of tests of validity.

Consider the following situation. A given theoretical unit (U) is measured by a stated empirical indicator (EI). The investigator then asks, "Is EI a valid measure of U?" To test this he searches for another empirical indicator that he will call the criterion measure (CM). There follows a line of reasoning having this general format:

1. The values measured on U by EI
2. and the values measured on U by CM
3. are highly correlated.
4. As we assume that CM does stand for U,
5. therefore EI must be a valid measure of U.

Diagrammatically this looks like Figure 9-1, in which the correlation between the measures of U by EI, m_1, and the measures produced by CM, m_2, is high. To make this a more specific example, suppose *dexterity* (U) was the theoretical unit under consideration. A dexterity test (EI) is devised to measure this characteristic in a sample of people. From this sample is then drawn a representative group of people with varying measured dexterity who are then given an assembly job in which dexterity is an essential requirement for success (CM). It is subsequently found that those scoring high in dexterity on EI are much more likely to be success-

---

[6]See Allison Davis, *Social Class Influences Upon Learning* (Cambridge, Mass.: Harvard University Press, 1948).

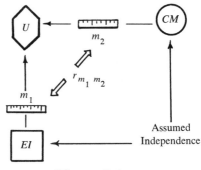

Figure 9-1

ful assemblers (CM) than those who score low. It is then concluded that this test is a valid measure of dexterity.

The argument rests on the presumption that EI and CM are *independent* of each other. But the logic of correlation tells us that a high correlation between them is obvious evidence that they are not independent. It therefore makes no sense to conclude that the validity of a test can be determined by this method.[7] This classical test of validity turns out to be a special case of the multiplicity of empirical indicators measuring values on the same unit. We have already examined that issue.

It is curious that the issue of validity of empirical indicators is raised only in the behavioral sciences and not in the natural sciences. This probably has its source in two factors. The first is the philosophical tradition that distinguishes between essence and appearance, and the second is the certain knowledge that man as a subject of investigation has the highly developed ability to dissemble. Therefore, the behavioral-science investigator has to be constantly on the alert to be certain he is catching the symbolic, or true, meaning of the words and acts he observes, because the image projected and the reality underlying it may differ. It seems worthwhile to note that if reality and image differ, then each is a separate theoretical unit to be employed under appropriate circumstances in building theoretical models. It may be thoroughly worthwhile to study

[7]The development of this kind of validity test goes back to the widespread use of tests during and after World War I. The method did not show any material change in analytical depth until the 1950s, when the American Psychological Association made the problem a matter of professional concern. See "Technical Recommendations for Psychological Tests and Diagnostic Techniques," *Psychological Bulletin,* Supplement, Part 2, 51:1–38 (1954); Lee J. Cronbach and Paul E. Meehl, "Construct Validity in Psychological Tests," *Psychological Bulletin,* 52:281–302 (July 1955); and the earlier work of Cronbach, *Essentials of Psychological Testing* (New York: Harper & Row, 1949).

image-making in society, as with political personalities. But there is no issue of validity arising here, even though the political image and the real man may be distinctive personalities.

An issue of reality in contrast with validity may be raised about empirical indicators that measure values in discrete intervals. Consider the following situation.

Suppose we have a scoring situation in which there is a binary choice, like present or absent, win or lose, tall or short, right or wrong. Suppose further that there is a sequence of events in which these outcomes are possible. Suppose finally that each event is scored on a 0 or 1 (or 0 and +) basis. For any given series of events we score the individual or unit by adding the score for each successive event and dividing by the number of events. This will inevitably produce total scores that mixed fractions.

For example, for a total of seven events, one person wins five times and loses twice whereas another person wins four times and loses three times. The first person has a score of 5/7 or 0.71429, whereas the second has a score of 4/7 or 0.57143. For all scoring situations involving seven and only seven trials, there are no scores between 0.57143 and 0.71429. On exactly the same test, a third individual has eight trials instead of seven and wins five times for a score of 5/8 or 0.625. May we now array the three individuals according to their winning scores in Table 9-2 and conclude that their relative success is revealed by this ranking?

It will be noted that persons one and two could never attain the score of person three so long as they were limited to seven trials. Similarly, neither of the scores of persons one and two could be achieved by number three in his eight trials. The conclusion seems sensible that the array is not a valid ordering of all three persons because they do not share equal opportunities to achieve the scores by which they were ranked.

The generalization about the validity of interval measures is that members of a sample population should not be ranked or measured by such empirical indicators unless all members of the sample population have some likelihood of securing the same possible scores. If some scores may be achieved by only a portion of the sample population, then the empirical indicator that produces this result is not a valid one. It is to this

Table 9-2

Person one	0.71429 (5 wins out of 7)
Person three	0.62500 (5 wins out of 8)
Person two	0.57143 (4 wins out of 7)

much more restricted case that I limit the meaning of invalid as employed in theory building. Empirical indicators are valid if all members of a sample studied have the possibility of securing any of the scores measured by the indicator.

CHAPTER TEN

Hypotheses

Another essential function of scientific theories... consists in the fact that such theories provide us with socially relevant and dependable information about objects which are observable by man.... In other words, scientific theories provide us with knowledge of things observable because that is what socially relevant and reliable information about such things comes to.

—H. Mehlberg, "The Theoretical and Empirical Aspects of Science," in E. Nagel, P. Suppes, and A. Tarski (eds.), *Logic, Methodology and Philosophy of Science*

IN THIS CHAPTER we come to the final stage in the formulation of a theoretical model. This last step is the point at which the theory is made to confront the "things observable." The object is to determine whether the theory makes sense of, and therefore provides knowledge about, "objects which are observable by man."

The chapter opens with a definition of an hypothesis, followed by a discussion of its relationship to a proposition. The number of hypotheses that are determinable for any given proposition is discussed. Finally, the strategies available for hypothesis testing are set forth.

Hypothesis Defined

In the normal discourse among scientists, any study other than a descriptive one is undertaken to test an hypothesis. The word *test* employed in this phrase denotes a scientist in contact with the empirical world. It is through the test that he relates the facts he finds in the empirical world to his theoretical predictions about them. We can safely assume, therefore, that the hypothesis is the feature of a theoretical model closest to the "things observable" that the theory is trying to model.

An hypothesis may be defined as the predictions about values of units of a theory in which empirical indicators are employed for the named units in each propositions. This is a simple definition. It says that every time the name of a unit appears in a proposition, there must be substituted for it an empirical indicator that measures values on this unit. Thus, for example, if one proposition of a two-person interaction system is "Friendliness of interaction is directly related to frequency of interaction," then one hypothesis testing this proposition could be "Expressed liking between two people as measured by the Dubin Interaction Love and Liking Yardstick (DILLY) is directly proportional to the number of hours spent in contact." The hypothesis tells us what the empirical indicator is for *friendliness* and what the empirical indicator is for *frequency of interaction*. It should be immediately evident that employing one other empirical indicator for at least one unit of the proposition produces an additional hypothesis testing the very same proposition.

We have now finally established the linkage between the empirical world and our theories about it. This linkage is to be found in the hypotheses that mirror the propositions of the model. We have come a long way from the initial chapters dealing with units, through the discussion of laws of interaction and of the other features of a theoretical model. Most of what has preceded this chapter has been devoted to a consideration of the components composing a theoretical model and the manner of their articulation. In this chapter we are now concerned with answering the basic question, "What is the reality test we can make of this theoretical model?"

It should be clear that when a scientist asserts that he is testing an hypothesis, this in turn is a test of a model from which the hypothesis may be derived. It is often confusing to read scientific literature because the author of an article may simply state his hypothesis without any reference to the underlying model from which the hypothesis derives. Therefore, it often appears that the hypothesis stands alone without any scientific backdrop. It further appears that each hypothesis is an *ad hoc* prediction that may be determined on the spur of the moment and from which there automatically flow some research operations to test its accuracy.

If the ideas so far presented provide an accurate picture of the structure of a scientific theory, then an hypothesis is not an *ad hoc* question to be answered by research but is rather a prediction of values on units that in turn are derivable from a proposition about a theoretical model. It is often instructive, for example, to start with an author's statement of an hypothesis and attempt to reconstruct, from only that piece of evidence, what was his underlying theoretical model. It is especially useful on occasion to do this for several pieces of research to determine whether there is any convergence among the separate hypotheses that lead to the conclusion that they may be derivable from the same theoretical model. Indeed, this is one of the manners in which secondary analysis of published works proves useful in theory building.

Hypothesis and Proposition

Every hypothesis is homologous with the proposition for which it stands. The homology is determined by the dimensionality of the theoretical definition of the units contained in the proposition. Each empirical indicator has to meet the necessary and sufficient conditions of the theoretically defined unit. However, should the empirical indicator exceed the sufficient condition, then it is no longer an indicator of the theoretical unit. Obviously, if it fails to meet the necessary condition of the theoretical definition, it also is an inappropriate empirical indicator. These points, already made in the previous chapter, can, perhaps, best be seen through an illustration. Suppose in a small-group research project the following proposition is derived from a model of group activity: "High member participation and strong identification with a group are positively related." If it is proposed to make an empirical test of the proposition, then the two units *participation* and *identification* need to be measured by empirical indicators.

Let us focus attention on participation. The necessary condition for measuring participation is "presence in." That is to say, a member must be present in the group in order to participate in it. The sufficient condition for defining the unit *participation* is that there be "interaction with" other members, for it is clear that if a member is present but does not interact with other members, he is not participating, a situation in which the sufficient condition is not satisfied. Thus, an empirical indicator like "amount of time spent in the group" would only satisfy the necessary condition but fails to satisfy the sufficient condition and therefore would be an inappropriate empirical indicator for participation. On the other hand, if the empirical indicator "affective response to" is used to measure participation, this clearly exceeds the sufficient condition of "interaction with." This, too, would be an inappropriate or nonhomologous empirical indicator of participation.

It will be noted that the necessary and sufficient conditions defining a unit of a theory are logically determined and not empirically established.

This is important to recognize, for the homology of the empirical indicator of a unit depends upon satisfying the necessary and sufficient conditions theoretically defining that unit. We may take as an example the idea of social class and class structure. A necessary condition for the definition of social class is that those who constitute its members share in a broadly recognized characteristic. The sufficient condition for defining social class is that such a group be hierarchically related to other groups according to a broadly accepted scale or system of evaluation. By these conditions, occupations could define social classes because of the relative homogeneity in occupations within classes and the hierarchical ranking of occupational groupings with respect to each other. Similarly, income could constitute an empirical indicator of social class for the same reasons. On the other hand, a grouping of people by their interest in particular sports might satisfy the necessary condition for the definition of social class (shared characteristic) but not the sufficient condition (hierarchical ranking). Thus, an empirical indicator measuring a preference for particular sports could not be taken as a measure of class position.

It will be recalled that in the last chapter we examined the idea of validity. It was concluded that the traditional view of validity has little to recommend it except in the limiting case where we can consider invalid those empirical indicators producing artificial values. The idea that any empirical indicator may be created that meets both the necessary and sufficient conditions of the definition of a theoretical unit suggests that the problem of validity may be further simplified. As we shall presently see, many theoretical units have the potential of being measured by a large number of empirical indicators. In the face of this, and providing each empirical indicator satisfies the necessary and sufficient conditions defining the unit, it seems pointless to be concerned about the traditional issue of validity. A more pressing problem is to determine the strategies of hypothesis construction so that limited research time and resources may be employed to maximum effect in testing a model.

Number of Hypotheses

Every proposition has the potential of being converted to a large number of hypotheses. For example, in a single proposition containing two theoretical units, if one unit may be measured by the two different empirical indicators, then there is the possibility of two hypotheses testing a single proposition. Should each of the two units be measured respectively by two empirical indicators, then the number of hypotheses increases to four, and if each may be measured by three empirical indicators, the number of possible hypotheses reaches nine.

The general rule is that a new hypothesis is established each time a different empirical indicator is employed for any one of the units designated in a proposition. This rule establishes the fact that the number of hypotheses is rapidly expanded as skill and imagination are utilized in developing empirical indicators.

It should also be recognized that some of the units of a model may not have empirical indicators available to measure values on them. It is then possible to state propositions employing such units, but because of the lack of availability of an empirical indicator, it is not possible to subject these propositions to an empirical test. This, of course, raises the interesting problem of whether or not it is useful to develop theoretical models of which portions are not empirically testable. There is no logic that insists that only those models whose propositions are all testable should be employed in science. Indeed, this restriction, representing the extreme position of operationists, has proved needless. All theoretical models need to be testable by converting at least *some* of their propositions to hypotheses. It is not a requirement, however, that *all* propositions of a model be testable. Indeed, the employment of units in theory building for which there is not a present empirical indicator may be an important stimulus to the development of such empirical indicators. For example, in some of his later work, Albert Einstein declared that it could be fifty years before adequate empirical indicators would be available to make a proper test of his theories. This did not deter him from developing them, and his imaginative concerns undoubtedly will stimulate experimental scientists to develop the necessary empirical indicators.

The question of number of hypotheses, ranging from zero to large numbers, poses a question of research efficiency to a discipline. The issue is whether or not trivial experiments and empirical studies will be conducted in order to exhaust the testing of the many hypotheses derivable from a single proposition of a model. Many scientists are relatively reluctant to do research because of the time and energy required and the often routine character of the operations involved. Given, then, the possibility of doing trivial research and the considerable investment necessary to accomplish any single piece of research, these constitute two strong pressures toward achieving some degree of efficiency in research operations. One obvious way of doing this is to standardize and agree to employ a single empirical indicator standing for a commonly employed unit. Such standardization eliminates the impulse to invent new empirical units and thereby limits the number of hypotheses that may be tested by employing the standard empirical indicator for a given theoretical unit. A recent volume by Miller, for example, attempted to catalog some standard empirical indicators for sociology.[1]

The obvious advantages of standardizing empirical indicators makes this an attractive method of reducing the number of hypotheses needing testing. It should also be recognized, of course, that standardization on a given empirical indicator for a single theoretical unit will make it difficult to invent other empirical indicators for the same unit because consensus among researchers will be difficult to overcome.

Strategies of Hypothesis Construction

In the chapter dealing with propositions, I suggested that focusing on strategic propositions was one way of reducing the number of tests made of a theoretical model. If tests of strategic propositions did not produce positive results, then there was no point in worrying about the other testable propositions. It remains, however, a fact that even the critical propositions may in turn be testable in the form of a number of hypotheses, insofar as alternate empirical indicators may be substituted for each unit in the proposition. There is, therefore, a need for selecting a strategy in hypothesis construction that fits the particular goals of the scientist and maximizes his profit in performing empirical tests.

Extensive and Intensive Tests

The first approach would be to employ an extensive strategy. The extensive strategy tests each of the strategic propositions that may be operationalized in an hypothesis. Each of the strategic propositions of a model is a prediction about that part of the theoretical system where something especially notable is happening. A test of each such proposition will prove the most adequate test of the theory as a whole in the most economical fashion possible.

The alternative to an extensive test of a model is to concentrate attention intensively on one or several of its strategic propositions. For per-

[1]Delbert C. Miller, *Handbook of Research Design and Social Measurement,* 2nd ed. (New York: David McKay Co., 1970).

sonal or other reasons, the researcher may have a special interest in a limited number of the propositions of a model. He may undertake the empirical test by deriving a number of hypotheses testing each selected proposition. Thus, for example, in the analysis of social stratification, a great deal of attention has been directed at the strategic propositions focusing on differential styles of living. In American sociology, almost no empirical tests have been made of those strategic propositions of models of social stratification dealing with class consciousness. It may be argued that propositions dealing with class consciousness are certainly strategic to theories of social stratification and that the empirical test of such propositions is necessary to determine how well the models make sense of a class structure. In short, American sociologists have adopted a strategy of intensive empirical testing of social stratification models rather than extensive testing.

We may illustrate the intensive empirical test of a strategic proposition in Table 10-1. Suppose we take as one strategic proposition of a model of intergroup relations the following: "Prejudice expressed by a superordinate group toward a subordinate group varies directly with the social distance between the two groups." Some illustrative hypotheses then become "Business executives, who are occupationally more distant from unskilled workers than industrial foremen (as measured on the Edwards occupational classification), will be less likely than foremen to eat lunch in the same locale as unskilled workers," and "Industrial foremen and time-and-motion-study technicians in the same company will have about equal degrees of willingness to use the same toilet facilities as unskilled workers because such foremen and technicians are in approximately equal occupational positions (as measured on the Edwards occupational classification)."

It should be observed that these two hypotheses test the same proposi-

Table 10-1

GROUP EVALUATING	GROUP EVALUATED	EMPIRICAL INDICATOR OF PREJUDICE	EMPIRICAL INDICATOR OF SOCIAL DISTANCE
Business executives	Unskilled workers	Sharing activities	Occupational position
Industrial foremen	Unskilled workers	Sharing activities	Occupational position
Time and motion study technicians	Unskilled workers	Sharing activities	Occupational position

tion, although the statement of each would not make this readily evident. It is easier to recognize the linkage between the hypotheses and the single proposition if they are derived from the latter. It would be more difficult to recognize their source in a single proposition if each of the hypotheses were encountered separately and, as is usually the case, in separate studies.

Inductive Test

A third strategy of hypothesis testing involves an inductive approach to theory building. Employing this approach, one starts with an *ad hoc* hypothesis. Having failed to disprove the hypothesis in an empirical test, the next step is to generalize the hypothesis to a proposition. In the process of generalization, the homology between hypothesis and proposition must, of course, be preserved. Once the proposition is established, the task then turns to constructing a total model from which the proposition is derived as a prediction. The general process is characterized in the following quotation from Merton.

> Not infrequently it is said that the object of sociological theory is to arrive at statements of social uniformities. . . . There are two types of statements of sociological uniformities which differ significantly in their bearing on theory. The first of these is the empirical generalization: an isolated proposition summarizing observed uniformities of relationships between two or more variables. . . . The theoretical task, and the orientation of empirical research toward theory, first begins when the bearing of such uniformities on a set of interrelated propositions is tentatively established.[2]

This third strategy of starting with an *ad hoc* hypothesis represents a characteristic ''fiddling around'' that may be encountered in social research. For example, a researcher finds a measuring instrument, proceeds to use it, discovers some relationship between the values measured on several units, and then asks the question, ''Into what kind of theoretical model can I refer this observed relationship between these two units?'' Mindless fiddling around of this sort may turn out, therefore, to have scientific value, providing the researcher is willing to build back to the theoretical model from the empirical uniformity he accidentally uncovered. It is thus a potentially profitable undertaking to test *ad hoc* hypoth-

---

[2]Robert K. Merton, *Social Theory and Social Structure* (New York: Free Press, 1949), pp. 91–92.

eses regardless of why the researcher has failed to start with a model whose predictions are being tested.

The attack on theory building starting from an empirical conclusion may be just as fruitful, if pursued with reasonable logic, as a deductive system starting with theoretically defined units, laws of interaction, boundaries, and system states. Indeed, this third strategy of going from *ad hoc* hypotheses to theoretical models is likely to give a strong empirical orientation to a discipline that it may otherwise lack if it remains preoccupied with theoretical models. This, for example, was the principal contribution of the Chicago School of sociology in the era between the two World Wars. The classic literature produced by this group of sociologists includes such descriptive titles as *The Gang, The Gold Coast and the Slum, The Ghetto, The Woman Who Waits, The Unadjusted Girl,* and *The Polish Peasant in Europe and America.* All these studies give great emphasis to extensive description and the testing of *ad hoc* hypotheses. From them came theoretical models such as Thomas's "four wishes" as a model of motivation, deriving from his study of the unadjusted girl. It was not until the late thirties and after that Parsonian and Mertonian influences on theory building in sociology reversed the influence of the Chicago School. Their "new theory" was not originated from empirical roots as had been the theory of the Chicago School. The Parsonian-Mertonian approach was to start with a theoretical model, and it often stopped short of the point of formulating enough propositions for which there was the possibility of making empirical tests.

The three strategies of hypotheses testing outlined in this chapter are not mutually exclusive. It may be desirable to combine extensive with intensive testing of a model because certain strategic propositions are believed to have special saliency for the model and intensive testing is deemed desirable. Induction may be employed along with extensive or intensive testing especially when the theorist is interested in securing the widest possible range of data in the empirical domain being modeled and is therefore constrained to search broadly among published studies for data that bear upon his propositions, data that were originally gathered in testing *ad hoc* hypotheses. There is, in short, no one best strategy of hypothesis construction to guide the theorist-researcher.

CHAPTER ELEVEN

Research

... Einstein's prediction of the deflection of light by the sun derived from his theory of general relativity.... I wish to use this theory to show that if Einstein guessed, he had a very solid basis for his guessing in physical facts.... The act of scientific imagination consists in divining the importance of a fact which in this case was known from Newton's own time, but had failed to excite the curiosity of many generations of physicists.... The new theory is a gigantic synthesis of a long chain of empirical results, not a spontaneous brain wave.

—MAX BORN, *Experiment and Theory in Physics*

... the future of social psychology and sociology calls for three developments:

1. *Formulation of theories, at least of some limited generality, which can be operationally stated such that verification is possible, and from which predictions can be made successfully to new specific instances.*
2. *Such theories demand that the objects of study be isolated and accurately described, preferably by measurement.*
3. *Once the variables are identified, the test of adequacy of the theory, in comparison with alternative theories, must be rigorous, preferably evidenced by controlled experiment, and preferably replicated.*

—SAMUEL A. STOUFFER, *Measurement and Prediction*

IT IS THE PURPOSE of this chapter to step back from the more detailed treatment of theory building and examine how theory and research interact. It is possible, for example, to distinguish between theoretical research, meaning theory building, and empirical research, meaning theory testing. This is a convenient way to sort out the paper-and-pencil scientists from the test-tube scientists, but it hardly serves to distinguish one scientist from another in terms of what he does, rather than what he does it with. This discussion is intended to relate theory and research as parts of a single system rather than as separate systems.

The chapter opens with a general statement emphasizing the continuous interaction between theory and research. There follows a distinction between descriptive research and hypothesis testing and a fervent plea that descriptive research be given its proper and permanent place among the respected activities of scientists. A brief excursion along a secondary path leads to an examination of the contrast between theory and theology. Three subsequent sections of the chapter examine the research stances to be taken toward a theoretical model, toward theory building, and toward hypothesis testing. A final section examines the issue of interdisciplinary research that has been so constantly in the attention of behavioral scientists.

Theory and Research

A theory is a model of some segment of the observable world. Such a model describes the face appearance of the phenomenon in such terms as structures, textures, forms, and operations. In order that such a model be considered dynamic, it also describes how the phenomenon works, how it functions. All scientific models, then, are the imaginative recreation of some segment of the observable world by a theorist interested in comprehending the forms and functions of selected segments of the world around him. It is clear, then, that scientific models are holistic in that they put together both structure and function into closed systems whose characteristics are the consequence of the elements composing the system and the laws by which the elements interact among themselves.

One major function of empirical research is to test the propositions of theoretical models. A model as a closed system is capable of predicting all the states of that system, as well as the values of the units composing it, that are the consequence of interaction among the components of the system. But if the model accurately portrays the observable world for which it stands, then the states of the theoretical system and the predicted values of the units should have correspondences in the states of the observable world that it portrays. It is a major task of empirical research to determine if such correspondence can be demonstrated or, alternatively, to show that the observable conditions of the world differ from those predicted by the theory. The stance of the researcher with respect to proof or disproof of a theory, and my preference for the latter, will be examined in more detail later in this chapter.

A theoretical model provides for the researcher one or more predictions that may be tested by marshaling data. The researcher provides the theorist with constant tests of the correspondence between his models and the portions of the world they purport to portray. Neither is complete without the other. Nor are the distinctive operations of theory building and researching necessarily segregated among separate classes of individuals. Most scientists know a theoretical model when they meet it, and are usually excited into making tests of some of its predictions through research, if the model captures their fancy. It is also true that any scientific discipline has its armchair paper-and-pencil theorists and its corps of hardware-statistics-laboratory researchers, each group of which has tended to specialize respectively in theory building and empirical investigation. That such a division of labor exists scarcely warrants the conclusion that either can ignore the other with impunity.

We start, then, with the explicit conclusion that theory and research are separable as distinctive operations but inseparable as necessary complementary components of scientific endeavor.

It is meaningless for empirical researchers to accuse theorists of being armchair philosophers. This gratuitously assumes that the theorist is not interested in testing the degree with which his theoretical models provide understanding of the observable world. Just because a theorist does not himself make the empirical tests of his models does not permit him to be condemned on the assumption that he does not want such tests made. All that is demanded of the theorist is (1) that he be willing that his theory be tested and (2) that he be willing to employ scientifically acceptable criteria in evaluating the results of the empirical tests.

The ultimate criterion of the theorist as an indispensable partner of the scientific endeavor is that he be sensitive to empirical tests and willing to modify his theoretical models as the empirical tests disprove the propositional predictions of his theory. The obvious affective investment of a scientist in a theoretical brainchild often prevents him from recasting or rejecting his theory, once it is launched in the world. This always rebounds to the discredit of the scientist. He may, through the weight of his reputation and status among his professional colleagues, prolong the illusion that he is right, even if the evidence does not confirm this. In the end, however, the scientific discipline will move ahead to more adequate theoretical models. The imperative of closure, of seeing that a model and what it purports to stand for in the observable world share some correspondences, takes hold in spite of any individual or organized opposition to prevent the closure.

The other side of the coin of bickering between theorists and researchers is the accusation that "raw empiricism" is akin to nit picking, pebble counting, or vacuum cleaning. Empiricism can never get so "raw" that it fails to make some contribution to the scientific endeavor, except in the rare instance when there is a total descriptive replication of some aspect of observable reality. Even such replication has the value of giving added certitude to the original description.

It serves no scientific purpose, although it may have some psychic value to the accuser, to precede the description *empirical researcher* with the sneering *raw*. The test of the worth of an empiricist, pure or polluted, is that he use reliable methods of observation. This fundamentally means that the criterion of reproducibility must be met; that is, that similarly inclined observers, using the same means, can reproduce the same results within acceptable ranges of observational errors. If the empiricist simply limits himself to reporting reliable observations of that portion of the observable world he chooses for his focus, he is making a worthwhile contribution to the scientific endeavor.

Descriptive Research and Hypothesis Testing

One of the common confusions to be found among researchers is that between doing research in order to build a theory and using research to test a theory. The first we call *descriptive research*. The second we call *hypothesis testing.*

You will recall that the first quotation opening this chapter directs attention to the role that facts played in Einstein's development of his general theory. As Max Born points out, the new theory developed by Einstein "is a gigantic synthesis of a long chain of empirical results." It was out of a sum of descriptive facts that Einstein built his theory, and in his case some of the facts were known, but ignored in theory building, as far back as Newton's time. In a comparable fashion, Stouffer emphasizes the need "that the objects of study be isolated and accurately described."

In this very sophisticated age, it is difficult to convince some working scientists, and especially those in the behavioral sciences, that they ought to spend a portion of their valuable time on descriptive research. Perhaps the temper of the times is epitomized in the statement of the Social Science Research Council announcing its faculty research grants for 1967–1968. A significant limitation on the kinds of proposals meriting awards is revealed in the following criterion: "Proposals for research aimed at synthesis and interpretation, and those that may yield contributions of theoretical or methodological significance for social science are given preference over those limited to description, narration, or the accumulation of data.''[1] With scarce funds available for faculty research grants, it is not surprising that explicit preference is given to theory testing rather than to the description that might result in providing the components for theory building. This may be an excellent distinction on the basis of which the limited funds may be allocated for productive results. It should not, however, be taken as a necessary indication of the advanced state of social-science knowledge and the disutility of descriptive research.

I cannot emphasize too strongly that there is a fundamental place for accurate description in any science. Description, as I have already indicated in the previous chapters, provides the input for developing units of a theory, its laws of interaction, the system states, and the boundaries of the model. Without adequate description, we would not have models that connect with the world that man perceives and about which he theorizes. This statement, of course, suggests that description is to be distinguished from definition. An adequate definition is fully descriptive of that which it denotes. What is indicated by the definition, however, may have no counterpart in the experiential world of man. Such a defined unit may very well be included in a theory. It is a scientific theory, however, only if some of the units employed in its construction have empirical counterparts on which values may be measured. If all the units of a theory are defined but not linked to the real world, then we are dealing with a belief system, not a scientific theory.

A moment's reflection on some of the landmark contributions to the social sciences makes clear that among them will be found essentially descriptive studies. Such a list would include Myrdal's *An American Dilemma,* Thomas and Znaniecki's *The Polish Peasant in Europe and America,* Stouffer and his associates' *The American Soldier,* Sherif's work on the autokinetic effect, Asch's research on social pressures in small groups, and Bales's categorization of interactions within small groups. Without these and a host of similar studies, we would lack the stuff out of which to develop theory in the behavioral sciences.

If the point requires any further emphasis, it need only be added that no theory was good enough to tell us the nature of the moon's surface. An elaborate, purely descriptive experiment in landing a vehicle on the moon and having its instruments ''feel'' the surface materials had also to be carried out to provide information on which to base a theory of how man

---

[1] Social Science Research Council, ''Announcement: Fellowships and Grants to be offered in 1967–68'' (New York: Social Science Research Council, 1967), p. 11.

could get there and survive. Natural scientists have always valued description, and it is hard to believe that behavioral scientists will be able to do without a similar appreciation for good description. As Merton has pointed out:

> Only by the seventeenth century, it seems, did "the dialogue" between quantified concepts and actual measurement begin to move toward a phase of maturity, although this appears not to have become thoroughgoing until the latter part of the eighteenth century. In that period chemistry, unlike physics, used its measurements, chiefly of properties of substances and their reactions, to arrive at more precise classifications. This use of measurement is found in other fields, such as medicine and the social sciences, at various phases in their history.[2]

Merton here clearly indicates how descriptive research entered into the classification of the chemical elements in what eventuated in the periodic table of chemical elements. I would not agree with his implication that this kind of descriptive research is limited only to certain phases in the history of a science. It is, I think, demonstrable that descriptive research runs concurrently with hypothesis testing at all times in the history of a science, the balance shifting between these two orientations depending on the richness of the theory of a field.

It is no doubt sufficient to say that all scientists believe that research should test hypotheses. We have already indicated that the test of an hypothesis is the point at which a theory and the empirical domain it models are made to confront each other. We have tried to give careful attention to the fact that to initiate a piece of research in order to test a single, isolated hypothesis is to operate with an *ad hoc* relationship until the underlying model can be set forth from which the hypothesis is derivable as a prediction.

The major emphasis of this section has been to urge the respectability and importance of descriptive research. This seems like a necessary caution, given the low esteem with which descriptive research is currently held in the social sciences.

Perpetual Theory Building

Scientific models serve man's purposes. It is man who creates these models of his sensory world, and it is man who uses these models as the

[2]Robert K. Merton, "The History of Quantification in the Sciences: Report on a Conference," *Items,* Social Science Research Council, 14:3 (March 1960).

means for comprehending that world. A scientific model summarizes what man can apprehend through his senses or infer from these sensory cues. But these sensory cues are not themselves meaningful until organized by the mind of man. Hence the scientific model operates over the range of received sensory cues to organize them for purposes of human comprehension.

Research technology is the means by which man as a scientist extends the domain over which sensory cues are perceptible. In the social sciences, projective tests permit a probing of the psychic life of a person in ways not previously attained by depth-interview or free-association techniques. Similarly, the development of scaling techniques in attitude measurement now permits the observer to apprehend objectively the cluster of associations in expressed attitudes. All forms of correlational and associational analysis provide means for the observer to manipulate recorded observations, which in many instances could not be done directly in experimental situations. Research technology is essentially unbounded by any fixed limits of possible refinement. When we reach the point of the finest discriminations of human perception, we develop mechanical, electronic, or other sensing apparatuses that are capable of translating their subliminal cues into those gross enough to fall within the range of human perception.

Constructive imagination increases man's comprehension of his observable world. If we picture thinking as the combination of bits of information, then the combinations and permutations of such bits provide, for all practical purposes, an unlimited number of possible models that can be the product of man's mind. This would be approximately true if the fund of information bits was finite and fixed, for the unexplored combinations and permutations far exceed the number as yet produced by man's thought. The fund of information bits is not, however, finite and fixed. Each new advance in research technology provides accretions of information bits. Each model of man's world likewise adds to the sum total of information bits. Consequently, the opportunity to construct new models of the world as man sees it is never exhausted.

A minor consequence of the inexhaustible possibility of building models of the world from man's vantage point is the explicit encouragement that this provides for each budding scientist to feel that he too can make a contribution, that man's past intellectual effort has not exhausted the creative possibilities available.

The major effect of the possibility of an infinite number of models of man's world is that the individual scientist is faced with making choices among a vast array of possible models whose predictions he wishes to test or whose content he wishes to build. This suggests at once a fundamental difference between the scientific goal of discovering "God's laws of the world" or "the harmony of the spheres," on the one hand, and the scientific goal of ordering the sensible world according to man's needs and desires, on the other.

The search for the immutable laws of God assumes the existence of ultimate true models whose discovery is the object of man's inquiry. There must be a final answer in the absolute laws of the universe that man humbly seeks. This view is a fundamental impertinence of man, for it leads him to assume that he can ultimately think like God and understand His laws for the universe.

On the other hand, with a man-centered world, the models of observable reality constructed are for the purpose of satisfying man's needs, however he defines them. So long as these needs may change, the models of experience that provide comprehension of how the needs can be satisfied will also change. This humanistic position assumes no finality for any particular way of characterizing the behaviors of the observable universe. Indeed, the position specifically holds that there are no ultimate laws and that scientific models are relative to the purposes to which they are put and the power of analytical comprehension they provide. This is comparable to holding that Einsteinian mechanics have not supplanted Newtonian mechanics, though they differ markedly in the ways in which they model aspects of the universe. If we need to build internal-combustion machines, we use the laws of Newtonian mechanics and they work fine. If we need to comprehend stellar mechanics, then the Einsteinian model may provide more understanding than the Newtonian one.

I choose the position that the explicit goal of science is to model the sensory world of man in terms of his perceptual skills and for the purposes he defines as his needs for practical knowledge or simply for comprehension to satisfy his current curiosities. This stance explicitly makes of science a never-ending process of data gathering and of reprocessing old data, of theory building in areas of curiosity where models had not previously existed, and of reconstructing old theories that no longer encompass in their predictions the data they purport to model.

Theory and Theology

In structure, theory and theology are identical. Both are complete, holistic pictures of the sensory or imaginative world as seen by man.

There is a fundamental similarity in the rules of logic by which the models of theory and those of theology are constructed. The crucial difference between a theory and a theology lies in the certitude of each kind of model. A theological model, say of man's relation to a God-figure, is presented as fixed, invariant, absolute, and true. The very certitude that underlies its existence precludes the need for subjecting the theological model to tests. Indeed, the attempt to test a theological model is properly labeled blasphemous, for it represents an implicit or explicit rejection of faith in the verity of the model. Thus, the certitude of a theological model rests on the consensual faith of those who accept it. This is right and proper for those areas of human life where faith is the dominant motive for action, including the act of believing.

A theory, on the other hand, (and we are not here limiting the term only to scientific theory) is clothed in uncertainty. This uncertainty is the product of the orientation of those who act according to the predictions of the theory, and is not inherent in the nature of theory itself. That is, when those who act in accordance with a theory are not wholly taken by surprise when the theory does not work in practice, the theory is properly distinguishable from a theology.

When a theology does not work in practice, the fundamental orientation of the actor leads him to search for causes in his own acts of omission or commission (i.e., sins) or the intervention of malevolent agents (i.e., devils). The theology is not called into question, but built-in reasons for its failure to model the reality of the actor's situation are called into play to explain the lack of correspondence of theological prediction with behavioral reality. When a theory does not work and the surprise is not total at its failure, on the other hand, then the experiencing individual is in a stance to raise questions about possible modifications of the theory itself in order that its predictions will accord more adequately with experienced reality.

Theory is constantly approached as tentative and subject to immediate revision of the face of the first deviant case that does not conform to the predictions of the model. Theology is approached as grounded in absolute faith, with the nonfitting cases being viewed as the product of indigenous forces and undesirable consequences predicted as retributions visited on the unfaithful or on sinners against the behavioral demands of the theology.

Before we become too enthusiastic, however, that theory building represents the fruition of man's capacity to think, we must distinguish between two quite different grounds for changing a theoretical model. Acceptance of a theoretical model may be the product of a consensus among the members of a relevant public (like a profession or a subject-matter discipline) or of some change in this consensus, for whatever reason. This consensus need not be grounded in any demonstration that a previously existing theory has been wrong in modeling the observable world. Thus, Freud's emphasis on the unconscious as a component of man's psyche did not rest on a demonstration of its existence. On the other hand, empirical data may be the basis for changing the nature of a model. Harvey's "discovery" of the circulation of blood importantly changed the existing descriptive model of human physiology. Pasteur's researches in the etiology of diseases forced on a bitterly reluctant medical and scientific world the need for modifying existing models of the etiology of organic diseases. In both instances, the empirical data were so compelling that existing theoretical models had to be junked, however distasteful this change in consensus about the model was to those who had to modify their views.

It is only with the development of modern science, roughly since the beginning of the eighteenth century, that systematic empirical tests have been made of theoretical models. Prior to that time, the changes in models resulted from changes in consensus among the interested publics that could have been grounded in new data, new fashions on thought, or the liberalization of secular or eclesiastic constraints on freedom of thought. Indeed, it is historically accurate to say that the Reformation and Enlightenment were characterized by a plurality of theological models, choice among which opened up to contemporary thinkers the startling opportunity to consider alternative models of the universe. Thus, pluralism in theological models made for pluralism in theoretical models of the sensory world of man. In this early period of man's systematic model building, the pluralism of theoretical models depended on consensus for support. Indeed, the culture lost significant contributions to theoretical knowledge because of the failure of a consensus to sustain theoretical models developed before their time.

The shift from consensus to empirical testing of theoretical models as the basis for their acceptance depended almost completely on the development of research technologies that permitted a significant extension of man's sensory observations.

Research Stance Toward a Theoretical Model

There are two possible research stances toward a theoretical model.

1. The researcher may set as his task the *proof* of the adequacy of his theoretical model.

2. The researcher may set as his task to *im*prove the starting theoretical model.

If the empirical task is to prove a theoretical model, then certain covert influences operate on the researcher in his actual investigations. The most important is that he is given license to find means for throwing away data or rejecting experimental results that do not conform to the hypothetical predictions of his theoretical model. The only limitation here is that there be some reasonable grounds for discarding the nonconforming data or results. Discarding data or excluding results is a tricky business, regardless of how apparently legitimate or reasonable are the grounds for so doing.

If the empirical task is to *im*prove a theoretical model, then influences in the opposite direction operate on the researcher in his actual investigations. The most important is that he focus attention particularly on the deviant cases and nonconforming results that do not accord with the predictions made by the hypotheses of his theoretical model. It is from the evidence contained in the deviant cases that the insights come on the basis of which the extant theory is improved by reformulating it to generate predictions that will encompass all the data, including those initially considered deviant.

The research stance that the investigator takes is crucial for the way in which he will treat his data. This research stance is also critical for the ease with which the research pays off in new theoretical models.

It should be clear by now that the position taken in this volume is that the test of a theoretical model is directed at its potential improvement. There are two fundamental reasons why this research stance is adopted. (1) From this standpoint all data that are marshaled in an investigation are likely to be retained as relevant to the test of the theoretical model. (2) The intellectually interesting feature of a model is its unexpected outcomes or its disproof, not its proof. Let us examine these two points individually.

In the very process of doing scientific research, especially in the behavioral sciences, there occur accidents in data collection. These accidents involve observations not initially planned in the design of the study, ranges of values measured on particular units that exceed the anticipated ranges expected to be found in the sample population, as well as relationships among units that were not perceived in the original model. These unanticipated consequences of the research operation may be treated as experimental error and rules out of consideration because they do not conform to the original plan of research. There is some belief among scientists that skill in designing a piece of research includes the ability to limit, if not eliminate, experimental error in the execution of the research. This orientation has a sound base in the belief that a controlled experiment is one that controls the influence of variables known to have an impact in order that the relationship between the experimental variables may be better understood and examined. This purification of the experimental situation in order to limit attention to the relationship among a restricted number of variables or units is obviously desirable and wholly necessary in testing out specific hypotheses of a theoretical model. The same reasoning, however, does not apply to the occurrence of accidental data that may intrude into the experimental results. These data may contain an important body of information highly relevant to the test of the theoretical model, and discarding such data may, in fact, inhibit the effectiveness of such tests.

When an experimental situation is controlled, the nature of the control is based on some knowledge of the units or variables that may intrude upon the results. Thus, a controlled experiment is grounded in positive information about when and how the variables controlled may relate to values on the experimental variables.

Accidental data result precisely because some unit or variable not anticipated by the researcher has intruded its influence on the results of the experiment or study. The class of controlled units or controlled variables is known in advance and anticipated as having an influence. The class of accidental variables is unknown to the theorist-researcher and not anticipated. Put another way, the controlled variables and their relationships to the experimental variables were known in advance from the knowledge of the model being tested. Accidental results were not, of course, known in advance.[3]

---

[3]You will note that I have used the terms *controlled variables* or *controlled units,* on the one hand, and the term *accidental results,* on the other hand. In the experimental control of observations, it is units that are eliminated from the experimental situation. This may be done experimentally by eliminating the possible appearance of values on these units in the actual experiment. It may also be done statistically by grouping the data so that comparisons are made within a homogeneous class on the values of other units (e.g., age of children may be held constant and the rate at which they learn arithmetic versus English may be studied). The accidental results may include more than evidence of the operational unit in the empirical situation. The accidental results may also give us values on these units and the relationships between the values on the unanticipated units and those which were incorporated in the model being tested. Accordingly, accidental results include the discovery of unanticipated units lawfully related to those incorporated in the model, ranges of values on these and the units utilized in the initial theory, boundary or system state characteristics not anticipated, and the laws of interaction. Thus . . . I have used the term *accidental results* to cover a heterogeneous category of possible discoveries that may be made in a body of research data.

A second reason for believing that the researcher ought to be oriented toward improving a theoretical model is that a well-developed theoretical model leaves nothing more to be learned. This statement means simply that if all the propositions of a model are worked out, the theorist has nothing more to learn from his model. The job of theory building is complete, and there remains only the task of either testing the theory to see that it accurately models reality or leaving this task for someone else. With an orientation to improve a model, the theorist-researcher may tinker with the model in order to determine whether, with minor changes, it will generate different propositions. One of the theorist's prime sources for ideas about tinkering with a model is the empirical world that is supposed to be described by the model. Thus, attention on improving a model makes the theorist constantly on the alert for those disconfirming ideas or data that constitute a signal for redoing the theory.

Research Stance Toward Theory Building

It should be abundantly clear from what has been said in this volume that the central issue in theory building is to know the materials out of which a scientific theory is built and the manner in which its components are articulated with each other. I have repeatedly insisted that this is essentially a descriptive knowledge of the theoretical model and that the more profound the descriptive knowledge, the better the theory is likely to be. By *better* I mean, of course, that the theory more accurately mirrors the empirical domain it attempts to describe. It is perhaps desirable to appeal to authority on this point, as the fundamental notion that all good models are based upon an empirical knowledge of the world being modeled is so simple and obvious that it is likely to be ignored, if not derided, among sophisticated social scientists. I quote the following from Henri Poincaré.

> What I have attempted to explain in the foregoing pages is how the scientist is to set about making a selection of the innumerable facts that are offered to his curiosity. . . .
> There is a hierarchy of facts. Some are without any positive bearing, and teach us nothing but themselves. . . .
> There are, on the other hand, facts that give a large return, each of which teaches us a new law. And since he is obliged to make a selection, it is to these latter facts that the scientist must devote himself. . . .
> The facts that give a large return are those that we consider simple,

whether they are so in reality, because they are only influenced by a small number of well-defined circumstances, or whether they take on an appearance of simplicity, because the multiplicity of circumstances upon which they depend obey the laws of chance, and so arrive at a mutual compensation.[4]

It is perhaps not to farfetched to suggest that every good theorist is an inveterate collector of facts, with an especially well-developed sensitivity to their interrelationships. I have been impressed by a textual contrast in the discourse that takes place between natural scientists, on the one hand, and social scientists, on the other hand. It is striking to note that natural scientists talk to each other largely in terms of evidence. Furthermore, when one asks for the history of a model or a theory, the physical scientist's reply is almost universally given in terms of a point of origin, at which data were first collected, and the subsequent sequence of experiments accumulating further data relevant to the theory as it grew and became modified. Natural scientists use as a major subject of discourse the experimental data that their theories model. When a theory is modified, this is almost invariably done by presenting experimental data for which the theory does not make sense. The discourse among social scientists has an essentially different content. There is a considerably higher level of ignorance about the empirical world and the data base that theory attempts to model. Disagreements and controversies with respect to a field of inquiry are likely to focus upon the characteristics of the contrasting theoretical models and the disputes often center on their logical coherence or the value preference for one over another. This orientation is especially notable in sociology, anthropology, and political science. A natural-science orientation is more nearly approximated in psychology and economics.

Another way to characterize the contrast between a natural-science and a social-science orientation to theory building is the following. In the natural sciences, there is a primary emphasis upon accumulating experimental evidence over long periods of time. The knowledge base in natural sciences is fundamentally a body of experimental and descriptive fact. The natural scientists fund facts and then demand that their theoretical models make sense out of the accumulating body of data. Much of the vast financial expenditures in natural-science research in the contemporary period is required for the development of research tools, the better to apprehend the physical world. The natural scientist is an inveterate fact

---

[4]Henri Poincaré, *Science and Method* (New York: Dover Publications, 1952).

gatherer, exceptionally skilled at developing more and more accurate and subtle means for accumulating experimental facts.

By way of contrast, social scientists have tended to accumulate theories and theoretical models. The social scientist funds theory and not data. It is not unusual for courses in the area of theory in a social-science discipline to be a recital of what each notable historical figure in the field believed or said. The student typically learns a history of ideas about the empirical world that falls within the range of his particular social-science discipline. But he may be singularly ignorant of the descriptive and factual character of that domain. The behavioral scientist tends to accumulate belief systems and call this the *theory* of his field.

It is not surprising, therefore, that the great scientific revolutions have occurred in the natural sciences and not in the social sciences. With the vast increases in the sophistication of research technologies, natural scientists have been overwhelmed with new and important facts to which they must address new and significantly modified theories. The empirical world is always far more complex than man's models of it. The rate of change in theory about the empirical world will be directly related to the quantity of information man has about it. In the past several decades, for example, the theories of physics have been thrown into a state of major disarray because the factual foundations of that discipline have expanded so rapidly that the old theoretical models can no longer make sense of the data.

In the social sciences, our relative indifference to facts has left us with a comfortable and very narrow range of alternative theoretical models with which to deal. The social scientist's imagination, when it feeds only upon its logical capacity to combine and recombine a fixed set of elements, can create only a limited range of alternative theories. It is not surprising, therefore, that in the social sciences there are remarkably slow developments of major innovations in theory. Furthermore, there are frequent reinventions of the same theoretical models that were current in an earlier period.

The burden of this section of the chapter is that theory building must be empirically rooted. The behavioral sciences are trying to make sense out of the world in which man behaves. The curse of introspection has been that it has seduced many behavioral scientists into believing that they can imaginatively recreate the experiential world of the subjects of their study. It is not considered necessary accurately to describe this world of experience because the analyst can imaginatively create or recreate it.

I am therefore urging that the research stance toward theory building among behavioral scientists be that of constant alertness to the descriptive knowledge of the domain about which they wish to theorize. It is facts against which the adequacy of the theory is always tested. It is also facts out of which the theory is developed in the first place. The inductions from the facts to the units, laws, boundaries, and system states of a theoretical model have already been suggested in the preceding chapters. The deductions from the model lead to the propositions and hypotheses that predict characteristics of the model for which empirical counterparts are sought to test the model. The back-and-forth flow of induction and deduction make these coordinate and not competing processes of theory building and testing. This is what the working scientist knows and does. It is perhaps unfortunate that sometimes the philosopher of science or the self-proclaimed ''pure theorist'' ignores the essential continuity and inseparability of induction and deduction in theory building and insists on preferring one or the other, or even condemns one thought process as though it were inadmissible.[5]

Research Stance Toward Hypothesis Testing

We have already concluded that a proposition is a truth statement about a theoretical model and that an hypothesis is the operational analog of such a truth statement. We also recognize that the truth of the statement rests upon its logical congruence with the conditions of the model about which the statement is made. Thus the test of truth is a logical and not an empirical one when we make a propositional statement about a model. The competence required to determine truth in this context is that of logical thinking and not empirical skill.

The empirical problem arises when the theorist asks, ''Does my theory model its designated empirical domain?'' In answer to that question, the theorist must now either become a researcher or ask his researcher colleague to marshal data that will provide a test of the truth of hypothetical predictions made from the model. At this point, there is an abrupt shift from a logical test of truth to an empirical test of truth. The empirical test determines whether the model does, in fact, adequately represent its empirical domain.

[5]Cf. Karl R. Popper, *The Logic of Scientific Discovery* (London: Hutchinson & Co., 1959), pp. 27ff.

The theorist at this point should be very eager to have the empirical test made. His assistance to the researcher is largely in terms of determining what are the strategic propositions of the model and, therefore, what are the strategic hypotheses that warrant highest priority for testing. The theorist may be of immeasurable help to the researcher by locating the strategic propositions and clearly differentiating them from the nonstrategic ones.

Beyond the location of strategic propositions and their homologous hypotheses, however, there is an additional choice that rests with the theorist and researcher. This is the choice of whether the purpose of the empirical test is to prove or to improve the theoretical model. (I have already touched briefly on this matter in the section on research stance toward a theoretical model.) If the purpose is to prove the adequacy of the theoretical model, then important limitations are placed upon the research operations. If, on the other hand, the purpose is to improve the theoretical model, then some of these limitations may be set aside.

The limitations of the proof orientation are the following.

1. Data are likely to be collected for values on only those units incorporated in the theoretical model. This usually means that, either experimentally or by discarding data, attention in the empirical research is focused solely upon values measured on units incorporated in the theory.

2. In very much the same fashion, either experimentally or by discarding data, values on any given unit incorporated in the study beyond the predicted range may also be excluded from attention. In this manner, important data on the units that have been incorporated in the theoretical model are ignored because the model does not predict values in the empirical range of values.

We may conclude now that the orientation of seeking to prove the empirical truth of a theoretical model is wholly legitimate and important in establishing the initial linkage between a theoretical model and its empirical domain. Furthermore, it is psychologically important that the theorist have some certitude that his theoretical model does indeed link up with the empirical world.

At the same time, it should be recognized that the knowledge added by an empirical test to prove the accuracy of a model is limited only to the fact, namely, that the model does link in some useful way with an empirical domain. The knowledge of the phenomenon being modeled is contained in the theory, not in the empirical world. Furthermore, so long as subsequent tests continue to prove the theory, the theory remains unchanged.

The alternative approach of improving a theory is one that does not contain the limitations of the proof orientation. Consequently, it is likely to give rise to a constant reevaluation and reformulation of the theoretical models of a discipline as the empirical knowledge requires such modifications. The essential operations involved in a research approach to theory oriented toward improving it is to give particular attention and prominence to deviant cases and nonfitting data that feed back immediately into the theory-building process by resulting in theory modifications. None of the advantages of the theory-proving orientation is lost. But, in addition, the opportunities exist for theory modification and, therefore, for growth and improvement in the theoretical structure of a discipline. It seems sensible to conclude that the more viable orientation, but not necessarily the only right one, is to seek improvement of a theory when an empirical test is made, rather than proof of it.

Interdisciplinary Research

There is a good *methodological* reason why social-science theory has not added up in the same productive manner that theory has grown in the natural sciences. In brief, the tendency for several scholars to focus on the same analytical problem has a stultifying consequence, the conditions of which are elaborated in the next several sections. This methodological constraint is especially noteworthy in interdisciplinary endeavors.

It is my purpose to demonstrate that we may improve the quality of interdisciplinary cooperation. The suggestion is advanced that scholars working in interdisciplinary cooperation give up the attempt to deal with a common analytical problem. As an alternative research and theory-building strategy, the method of *contiguous problem analysis* is put forward.

A useful point for starting is to ask whether scientists coming from several intellectual disciplines, and therefore with different frames of reference, will willy-nilly develop different and competing models in attacking the same analytical problem. The answer so far seems very clearly to be no. When students from several disciplines deal with the same analytical problem, there is considerable identity in the models they employ. This similarity in the systematic theories developed around a shared problem is achieved in one of two ways: (1) by the point of view of a single discipline dominating the structure and content of the model developed, or (2) by the reduction of a model to the lowest common denominator of shared variables and methodologies of the participating disciplines.

The dilemma that is therefore posed is a straightforward one. Does interdisciplinariness, when focused upon a shared analytical problem, lead to a homogenized theoretical model that contains few, if any, of the distinctive contributions expected from the cooperating disciplines? Another way to pose this dilemma is to ask whether or not concentrating men and resources from several disciplines upon a common analytical problem does not force them to "sing out of the same prayer book" in order that a minimum of cooperation may be achieved. I want to underscore this dilemma by restating it once more. Does a shared model of social organization utilized by several cooperating disciplines get built out of either the dominant analytical tools of a single discipline or out of the lowest common denominator of the analytical tools of the several disciplines?

My answer to this dilemma is direct and pessimistic. I will conclude that interdisciplinariness, when focused upon a common analytical problem, will produce no better results than if a single discipline had zeroed in on the same problem with its substantial professional talents. Indeed, the result may be substantially worse if several disciplines cooperate at the level of their lowest common denominator of discourse and mutual understanding. I therefore hold out very little hope for interdisciplinary research where the analytical problem is common to all members of the research team.

Before the conclusion is reached that I have only a negative message, let me hasten to add that interdisciplinary research as I will define it—as a series of coordinate analytical problems simultaneously attacked by scientists from several behavioral disciplines—has a high probability of being very productive of systematic theories of social organization. The critical point is that the cooperating behavioral scientists each choose their special analytical problems and together work over a coordinate body of data. Another way to put this conclusion is to suggest that science makes progress by competition and not by consensus, a position Karl Popper[6] has made popular.

A systematic theory or model must define the units employed in it and the laws by which they interact with each other within a defined boundary. When this is done with respect to a single analytical problem, the

---

[6]Popper, *op. cit.*

units tend to be the same, as do the laws by which they are presumed to interact and the boundaries within which the lawful relationship holds, regardless of the disciplines from which the theory builders come.

It follows that we get competing systematic theory primarily when we shift the analytical problem and therefore have to change the components out of which we build the models. I will conclude that it is the shift in problem focus, however minor, that is the engine by which we make progress in the development of systematic theory of social organization. I will further argue that the separate disciplines are most distinctive from each other by virtue of their special discipline-bound analytical problems. This generates competing models that have high value in forcing empirical testing and critical evaluation in judging the relative merits of several theories. The most important consequence of all is the shift in analytical focus permits behavioral-science models to add up in a manner not possible to achieve by any other means.

Contiguous-Problem Approach

Interdisciplinary research is best pursued by attacking contiguous analytical problems. This approach involves defining analytical problems that lie close together and yet retain a significant individual identity. Several students, regardless of discipline, may attack these problems simultaneously. If they clearly understand that the boundary of each problem is contiguous with others, they may readily perceive the additivity of the results that each will obtain from his theorizing and the subsequent research test of the theories. The major result is that one may predict in advance the connectedness of one individual theory with another by noting that the boundary of its domain is contiguous with the boundary of the domain of the other theory addressing a slightly different analytical problem.

The operating problem in doing contiguous-problem research is to be clear that the theory boundaries are indeed contiguous. Once this is established, then the linkage among areas of theory and their interrelationships become quite clear. Furthermore, it then becomes possible to establish a temporal ordering of analytical problems to be attacked, insofar as the theoretical solution to one problem suggests means for grappling with a contiguous problem. Let me illustrate this by suggesting that a theory of pedagogy and a theory of learning are obviously contiguous analytical problems. They have, through much of the history of education, remained singularly noncontiguous in the view of many pedagogues. When learning theorists begin to get curious about the contiguous problem of teaching, there developed revolutionary notions about pedagogy. Programmed instruction derives from a learning theory, and contemporary experimentation with early-infancy learning will undoubtedly have important consdquences for the development of teaching theory in the preschool as well as the school years.

Let us now turn to a more detailed look at the contiguous-problem approach. It involves three requirements: (1) that at least two models or theories be under consideration simultaneously; (2) that the theorist-researchers be aware that two or more models are under test; and (3) that the domains of the separate models be viewed as touching each other so that there are at least some common boundaries or even areas of overlapping domains. When these three conditions are met, there is a high probability that the cooperating scientists will achieve some additivity in their results.

If what has already been said is understood, then the reason for the first condition is obvious. For there to be cooperation that is intellectually viable, it is necessary to have two or more different things that are joined in the cooperative effort. Failing that, if two or more researchers join forces to test a single model, they merely engage in a technical division of labor in the research operations. They may divide up the parts of the research operations among themselves for purposes of efficiency, but this is only a technical and not an intellectual basis of cooperation.

It may also seem obvious that the cooperating scientists be aware that two or more models are under investigation. What is obvious may not always be perceived, however. The pressures to appear to be employing the same model may actually lead to an artificial claim that what is different, in fact, is asserted to be part of the same intellectual package. An excellent example of this is the volume *Toward a General Theory of Action*[7] in which several authors, notably the psychologist Tolman, are dealing with contiguous (if not independent) problems under the guise of joining in production of a general theory. The casual reader might infer that the general theory has been realized.

Shared Boundaries

The most difficult criterion to meet in contiguous-problem analysis is to insure that the analytical problems share a common boundary or overlap. This can be determined in at least four ways.

[7]Talcott Parsons and Edward A. Shils (eds.), *Toward a General Theory of Action* (Cambridge, Mass.: Harvard University Press, 1950).

1. The most obvious method is one in which the same units and the laws by which they interact are employed in several analyses. The only difference among the several analyses is that they separately focus on different states of the same system. What is contiguous here are the system states, and each may be separately studied by employing a common model. Thus, the sacred and secular are different system states of a society, and each may be analyzed by employing the same units or variables.

2. A second method for testing contiguity is to employ only some common units. The contiguity is established when the same unit is seen as simultaneously or serially interacting with others so that the several domains of interaction either touch or overlap. For example, parental reports of how children are handled and children's own perceptions of such handling are contiguous analytical problems, having the child as a unit common to several domains.[8]

3. A third method for determining contiguity is through formal definitions of model boundaries. When the boundaries of a model are defined, it may turn out that they are contiguous. Thus, for example, the study of human response to extreme sensory deprivation has a domain boundary that is formally defined as the nature of response under conditions of minimal stimulus, and this boundary is contiguous to each domain in which a particular sensory stimulus operates.

4. A fourth method is to have overlapping but nonidentical domains for several competing models. For example, the idea that lower-class juvenile delinquency is the product of valuing middle-class goals and styles of life without the means for their attainment[9] must compete with an attempt to model this behavior as a group status-seeking phenomenon.[10] The variables or units employed in the competing models and the laws by which they interact are not the same, but the behaviors being predicted, juvenile delinquency, are shared between the two models.

I have suggested enough to indicate that the contiguous-problem analysis approach is readily identified in operational terms. More can be said on the subject but not within the limits of this chapter.[11]

[8]See, for example, Robert Dubin and Elisabeth Ruch Dubin, "Children's Social Perceptions," *Child Development,* 36:809–838 (1965).

[9]Albert K. Cohen, *Delinquent Boys* (New York: Free Press, 1955).

[10]Louis Yablonsky, "The Delinquent Gang as a Near Group," *Social Problems,* 7:108–117 (1959).

[11]See Robert Dubin, "Contiguous Problem Analysis: An Approach to Systematic Theories About Social Organization," Chap. 4, pp. 65–76 in M. Sherif and C. W. Sherif (eds.), *Interdisciplinary Relations in the Social Sciences* (Chicago: Aldine, 1969).

It should be added that contiguous-problem analysis does not require interdisciplinary sources of its practitioners. Indeed, an important source of *intra*discipline advance is the ability to add pieces of knowledge together because they are the product of contiguous-problem analysis. But it is especially important to note that this method is essential to interdisciplinary cooperation. If this method is not employed, then the disciplines remain genuinely separated and incapable of achieving coordination. The alternate result is to homogenize several disciplines with a loss of their distinctive contributions.

Another point of emphasis is that simultaneity is not a requisite of contiguous-problem analysis. Contiguous problems may be analyzed at quite different time periods with constructive results. Interdisciplinary cooperation is not time-bound and may, indeed, span long time periods and involve cooperation among scholars who never meet or engage in direct discourse. Thus, Lasswell[12] and Freud or Parsons[13] and Freud have worked on contiguous problems without contact and widely separated in time.

Finally, it should be clear that contiguous-problem analysis is not limited to model testing. It also applies to descriptive research. One of the important but lowly valued aspects of behavioral science is good description. Indeed, we make progress slowly because we value description so lowly. Nevertheless, good description proceeds in parts, and the additivity of the described parts depends on their contiguity. The blind men feeling the elephant have no means for determining each man's area of search and cannot thereby gain a sense of the whole. The jigsaw puzzle is the appropriate analogy for contiguous-problem analysis at the descriptive level. The whole picture is revealed when the parts are exactly fitted to each other at their borders.

[12]Harold Lasswell, *Psychopathology and Politics* (Chicago: University of Chicago Press, 1931).

[13]Talcott Parsons et al., *Working Papers in the Theory of Action* (New York: Free Press, 1954).

CHAPTER TWELVE

Systems Analysis

Compared to the analytical procedure of classical science, with resolution into component elements and one-way or linear causality as basic categories, the investigation of organized wholes of many variables requires new categories of interaction, transaction, organization, [and] teleology.

—L. VON BERTALANFFY, *General Systems Theory*

THE PURPOSE OF THIS CHAPTER is threefold: (1) to show the relationship between systems analysis and the methodology set forth in this volume; (2) to distinguish the idea of teleology from the notion of causality when used in systems analysis; and (3) to present examples of systems theory and analysis to illustrate how the basic idea of models, as presented here, provides the means for developing theories of systems.

What Is a System?

There are a number of ways to define and characterize a system. For example: ''A system is a set of objects together with the relationships between the objects and between their attributes.''[1] From a psychological perspective, this definition has been given: ''Systems are bounded regions in space-time, involving energy interchange among their parts, which are associated in functional relationships, and [of their parts] with their environment. . . .''[2] An eminent sociologist who has made systems analysis central to his many theoretical contributions has presented the

[1]A. D. Hall and R. E. Fagen, ''Definition of a System,'' *Yearbook,* Society for General Systems Research, 1:18–28 (1956), p. 18.
[2]J. G. Miller, ''Toward a General Theory for the Behavioral Sciences,'' *American Psychologist,* 10:513–531 (1955), p. 514.

following definition: " 'System' is the concept that refers both to a complex of interdependencies between parts, components, and processes that involve discernable regularities of relationship, and to a similar type of interdependency between such a complex and its surrounding environment."[3] Still another view of system is provided by the following:

> In common usage the word refers to widely separate concepts. Engineers are concerned with systems as functionally related aggregates of technological devices. Physiologists single out functionally related portions of living organisms (circulatory, digestive, nervous systems). Social scientists speak of economic and political systems; philosophers about systems of thought. . . .
>
> I accept the definition of a system as (1) something consisting of a set (finite or infinite) of entities (2) among which a set of relations is specified, so that (3) deductions are possible from some relations to others or from the relations among the entities to the behavior or history of the system.[4]

For our purposes it is sufficient to consider a system to be any assemblage of elements that interact repeatedly and in the same manner when the identical elements are in contact with each other.

This definition has three components. (1) A system is composed of defined elements that remain the same throughout the life of the system. (2) The elements describe the system because their systematic interactions with each other (laws of interaction) make it possible to characterize the states of the system. (3) In order for each of the elements of the system to be able to interact with at least one other element, the interactions take place within some defined boundary.

With this way of characterizing a system, analysis of the system can focus on the whole system rather than on its parts. The analytical consequence is that one can reach conclusions about the system that could not be reached from a knowledge of its parts. As Bertalanffy has stated:

> The meaning of the somewhat mystical expression "the whole is more than the sum of parts" is simply that constitutive characteristics are not explainable from the characteristics of isolated parts. The characteristics of the complex, therefore, compared to those of the elements, appears as "new" or "emergent." If, however, we know the total of parts

[3]T. Parsons, "Social Systems," *International Encyclopedia of the Social Sciences* (New York: Macmillan and Free Press, 1968), 15:458.

[4]A. Rapoport, "Systems Analysis: General Systems Theory," *International Encyclopedia of the Social Sciences* (New York: Macmillan and Free Press, 1968), 15:453.

contained in a system and the relations between them, the behavior of the system may be derived from the behavior of the parts.[5]

Few persons would deny that, in an intuitive sense, the whole is always more than (or different from) the sum of its parts. However, it was not until the formalization of systems analysis that the uniqueness of the characteristics of systems was made explicit. This formalization is essentially a twentieth-century development.

Antecedents of Systems Ideas

The fundamental idea of a *system* has, of course, always been part of analytical thinking. The Trojan Horse before the gates of Troy was a diabolically clever military system for infiltrating city fortifications. In the aqueduct (and Roman building construction generally), the Romans combined materials of special strength, special structural shapes, and structural functions to provide an architectural system of remarkable durability and utility. The Wright brothers made a fortuitous combination of motive power and wing design to produce the prototype of that familiar system we call the airplane.

It has been asserted that the development of scientific models proceeded with the recognition that they could be couched in a systems format. For example, the issue has been well stated in relation to the utilization of a systems approach in the social sciences.

> This brings us to the interesting question posed in modern systems theory: to what extent can the hard system-theoretic approach be extended to other than physical systems?
>
> The main difficulty is that, once we pass to systems other than the simple ones studied in the physical sciences and engineering, we are not sure what variables best describe the state of such a system. In all likelihood they are not physical variables like masses, electrical potentials, concentrations, etc. If we do single out certain variables which we think are important, we do not know the laws of interaction that govern their rates of change, since these variables do not as a rule obey the known, simple laws of physics. Nevertheless, certain portions of the nonphysical world are being investigated from the mathematical system-theoretic point of view.

[5]Ludwig von Bertalanffy, *General Systems Theory* (New York: George Braziller, 1968), p. 55.

The clearest example is an economic system. Economics is the oldest of the "hardened" social sciences for the very good reason that economists have singled out certain easily quantifiable concepts. Therefore, mathematical models of interaction among "economic variables" can be constructed as hypotheses. The variables of an economic system are prices, quantities of goods produced, man-hours of work required to produce them, capital investments, interest rates, tax rates, volume of international trade, gold reserves, amount of money in circulation, etc. All of these variables are clearly inter-related in some way, but just how they are inter-related is not explicitly known. Nor is it easy to discover "the laws of inter-action," assuming they exist. . . .

Spotty as the successes of theoretical economics has been, the systems point of view has undoubtedly helped it to mature. It may well follow in the footsteps of meteorology, increasing the scope of its accuracy as more and more relevant variables can be incorporated into models of large scale economic events. At any rate, concern with some global properties of economic systems is now commonplace. . . .[6]

And so throughout history and even in prehistory, the idea of systems was a fundamental feature of human thought and action. It is all the more surprising, therefore, that formal development of systems theory was delayed until the twentieth century.

It is not our purpose here to engage in a sociology-of-knowledge explanation of the lateness in developing systems theory. Perhaps two more or less concurrent social and technological conditions should be cited as influential.

The high social and economic cost of war technologies, as well as production technologies, increasingly forced a strong emphasis on decision making with respect to the development of technologies and their alternative utilizations. Since decision making is essentially a mental operation, very self-conscious attention was directed at formulating the rules by which the mental operations of *comparing* outcomes of systems in operation could be readily achieved. In order to solve this general problem, the rules of systems analysis were developed.[7]

---

[6]A. Rapoport, "Modern Systems Theory—An Outlook for Coping with Change," *General Systems,* 15:15–25 (1970), quoted from p. 19.

[7]See, for example, one of the first texts to attempt such rule ordering of systems: P. Morris and G. Kimball, *Methods of Operations Research* (Cambridge: MIT Technology Press, 1951). This was followed a decade later by another innovating text: A. D. Hall, *Methodology for Systems Engineering* (New York: Van Nostrand, 1962). In special fields applied texts appeared. For example, in the design of man-environment systems see Kenyon B. DeGreene, *Sociotechnical Systems* (Englewood Cliffs, N.J.: Prentice-Hall, 1973). The specific military roots of systems analysis are set forth in numerous documents

It should be recognized that decision making involved in high-cost decisions generally preceded the actual investment. This was crucial for the development of systems analysis for it explicitly rejected as irrelevant the classic procedure of science—the experiment. One simply did not experiment with high-cost alternatives. It was necessary to have some preferred choice before any investment would be made.

The second major influence on the history of systems analysis was a technological development, the computer. The computer-in-use was a post–World War II development. The computer rapidly developed capabilities for handling many variables with many different values for each variable. The variables (*units* in our terminology) could be treated as interacting in a multivariate structure so that it was no longer necessary to restrict analysis to bivariate problems. The systems theory and the technology for handling multivariate systems problems were joined in a most powerful intellectual development. The beauty of this combination was made clear when *simulation* of systems-in-operation on the computer became standard procedure for searching out a preferred decision involving high-cost investments.

There was still another development in science that converged in time with the solution to the costly decision problems. In biology and in the social sciences, a growing recognition developed that analytically the two-variable analysis was inadequate for providing comprehension of biological or social systems. In the 1930s Rashevsky, a physicist, developed mathematical models of cells, and later extended his work *to include* systems of social behavior.[8] Professor Sommerhof was instrumental in bringing a systems orientation to biology.[9]

In the social sciences the most notable advances in systems analysis were made in economics with the development of econometric models of

---

published by the Rand Corporation. Illustrative of the Rand contributions in the early period are Charles Hitch, "An Appreciation of Systems Analysis" (1955) and Malcolm W. Hoag, "An Introduction to Systems Analysis" (1956), both of which are reprinted at pages 19–52 in Stanford L. Optner (ed.), *Systems Analysis* (Harmondsworth, England: Penguin Books, 1973).

[8]Rashevsky's pioneering work was done while he was a professor at the University of Chicago where he influenced students like Professor Anatol Rapoport and colleagues such as Professor James G. Miller, both of whom were leaders in the Society for General Systems Research. See Nicolai Rashevsky, "Outline of a Mathematical Theory of Human Relations," *Philosophy of Science,* 2:413–430 (1935); "Further Contributions to the Mathematical Theory of Human Relations," *Psychometrika,* 1:21–31 (1936); "Studies in Mathematical Theory of Human Relations," *Psychometrika,* 4:221–239 (1939); and "Studies in Mathematical Theory of Human Relations, II," *Psychometrika,* 4:283–299 (1939).

[9]See G. Sommerhof, *Analytical Biology* (New York: Oxford University Press, 1950).

entire economic systems.[10] These models are notable, irrespective of their success in predicting future events, because of their influence in making a systems-analytic outlook the typical mode of thought in that academic discipline.

In psychology, developments in physiological psychology, where biology and psychology intersect, early on led to a systems orientation in which the problem of "reductionism" was central. The issue, of course, was whether psychological phenomena, such as perception (of sight, sound, smell, taste), could be modeled as the outcome of a biological system in operation. Both reductionist and nonreductionist answers depend on utilizing a multivariate or systems approach. More recent advances in social psychology have leaned very heavily on a systems approach pioneered by Kurt Lewin and his elaboration of "field theory."[11] The study of attitudes, values, motivation and their linkages with behavior has basically been multivariate in the models employed.[12] Furthermore, the time dimension is an integral part of the models as in answering the questions: "Do attitudes influence behavior?" or "Do goals guide motivation and thus influence behavior?" Multivariate,

[10]It is now quite common to identify a particular model with the school at which it was developed, as with The Wharton School or UCLA models. Professor Forrester has been a leader in developing regional and later world-wide models of resources and their consumption. See Jay W. Forrester, *World Dynamics* (Cambridge: Wright-Allen, 1971), and also his *Industrial Dynamics* (Boston: Little, Brown, 1970).

[11]Lewin's early book, *Principles of Topological Psychology* (New York: McGraw-Hill, 1936), is almost never cited although its title *and* content foreshadowded his work on field theory as summarized in the collection of his papers entitled *Field Theory in Social Science,* edited by D. Cartwright (London: Tavistock, 1963).

[12]See, for example, Thurstone's development of factor analysis as a form of multivariate analysis to define the dimensionality, and therefore the units, that compose a system (L. L. Thurstone, *The Vectors of Mind* [Chicago: University of Chicago Press, 1935]). Spearman had much earlier developed a two-factor theory of intelligence which utilized a systems mode of analysis (C. Spearman, "The Theory of Two Factors," *Psychological Review,* 21:101–115 [1914]). Guttman, a sociologist, developed "small-space analysis" (L. Guttman, "A General Nonmetric Technique for Finding the Smallest Space for a Configuration of Points," *Psychometrika,* 33:469–505 [1968]) and also "facet analysis," two very advanced methods for handling multivariate problems and building theoretical models of systems (L. Guttman, "An Outline of Some New Methodology for Social Research," *Public Opinion Quarterly,* 18:395–404 [Winter 1954–55]; and also his "Introduction to Facet Design and Analysis," *Proceedings of the Fifteenth International Congress of Psychology, Brussels, 1957* [Amsterdam: North-Holland Publishing Co., 1959], pp. 130–132). A variety of applications of multivariate techniques to social-science problems will be found in R. N. Shepard, A. K. Romney, and S. B. Nerlove (eds.), *Multidimensional Scaling: Theory and Applications in the Behavioral Sciences* (New York: Seminar Press, 1972); and in an earlier volume: R. B. Cattell (ed.), *Handbook of Multivariate Experimental Psychology* (Chicago: Rand McNally, 1966).

time-ordered relationships are the hallmark of a systems approach. It is notable, for example, that the methodological preoccupation with multivariate analysis owes more to economists and psychologists than it does to scientists in any other social science discipline.

It is interesting that the decisional problems to which systems analysis was applied were generally problems of subsystems. Thus, the noncongruence between processing time for handling a single transaction or operation and the rate of arrival of the individual or item to be handled gave rise to *queuing theory;* the balancing of surpluses against shortages led to the development of *inventory theory;* the interactions between individuals or groups under conditions of uncertainty of outcome where the particular outcome could be influenced by the actor's choices led to the development of *game theory.* All of this can be summarized under the general heading of operations research (OR). In general, OR technologies employ systems concepts to provide operational decisions, usually for parts of a total organization or a large social system.

Roughly paralleling the development of operations-research technologies were the major advances in cybernetics, which got its name and major impetus from Norbert Wiener.[13] The theory of cybernetics depends on a systems outlook in which an organism, a machine, or a social system is viewed as being goal-directed and moving toward the goal with a transfer of information from the environment to the system (and from one part of the system to another) in order to control, through feedback to the system, its functioning in the environment. Ashby[14] carried forward the contributions of Wiener. There has been a vigorous flourishing of cybernetic applications in machine design particularly, with the computer, an intricate but exceedingly accurate and rapid system of data processing, as the crowning achievement.

Open Systems

One of the major contributions to general systems theory was the idea of open systems which Bertalanffy claimed to have originated. Built into this idea is the notion that no system can be analyzed without taking

---

[13]Norbert Wiener, *Cybernetics or Control and Communication in the Animal and the Machine* (New York: Wiley, 1948).

[14]See: W. Ross Ashby, *An Introduction to Cybernetics* (London: Chapman & Hall, 1956), and also his *Design for a Brain,* 2nd ed. (New York: Wiley, 1960).

into account its interactions with its environment consisting of other systems.[15] From the point of view of Bertalanffy, this proposition freed analytical thinking by focusing attention on the interrelatedness and interactions that characterize the multiple systems of nature. Obviously fruitful developments have followed from this idea, especially in biological sciences, where the chains of biological relatedness have come to be described as ecosystems.

Two analytical problems of theory building follow from the open systems idea. (1) The so-called hierarchy problem centers on describing and analyzing the order that is to be found in the interconnections among systems themselves. (2) If systems are conceptualized as being open so that interactions can take place with environment, what is the nature of the boundaries across which this linkage takes place?

With respect to the hierarchy problem, it will be recalled that in our treatment of units of a theory (Chapter 4), summative units were found to be useful as a way of characterizing "wholes" where this proves to be necessary when the interactions among "wholes" are being examined. But it was also suggested that summative units do not enter into theoretical models that are testable empirically for the simple reason that an empirical indicator taken to stand for the "whole" can never be an adequate measure of it. Thus, in conceptual schemes of "frames of reference" summative units are almost always employed. This is a very positive contribution to thinking, but not directly a contribution to the development of testable scientific models. For example, in analyzing ecosystems, the interactions of plants as food for animals, whose wastes are nutrients for plants, reveal a remarkable chain of interdependence among the several biological systems (there are, of course other interdependencies with additional systems, such as the sun as a source of energy, etc.). We can understand such interdependencies in a general way, but if we propose to do research on the subject, we then choose specific empirical indicators to stand for one or more of the systems interacting. Thus, particular plants are examined to determine the specific food values they contribute to herbivores, whose droppings return certain nutrients to the soil where they become available as fertilizer agents for the plants. The research operation is concerned no longer with plants and animals but rather with a specific plant (or even only that part of it that has food value for the animal) and a particular animal for whom the plant is "food." So the plant enters into the interaction only in that portion of its "wholeness" that is measured to be an element of food for the animal.

[15]L. von Bertalanffy, *op. cit.*

The fundamental reason why a "whole" does not interact in its totality with another "whole" lies in the impossibility of specifying the laws governing such interactions. We have the choice of accepting the fact that the theoretical model specifies only the interaction of a portion of one "whole" with another or believing that the number and complexity of the laws of interaction necessary to encompass the total interactions among "wholes" are beyond any rational formulation. In the former case we can build a theory precisely because we have given up the summative unit in favor of an attribute of the "whole" in order to build the model. In the latter case we retreat to religion or humanistic psychology as the ultimate refuge for problems beyond rational formulation.

What, then, happens to the hierarchy aspect of the "hierarchy problem"? Is it possible to think of systems in interaction as having an hierarchical relationship? Is the animal at a higher level (or more important) than the plant with which it is linked in an eco-chain? I believe that the answer to this question is entirely a matter of personal preference of the scientist. There may be criteria that determine such preferences. For example, if two systems are in interaction but their survival is not symetrically dependent, then the system that can survive without interaction with the other *may* be assigned the higher level or more important status on the basis of its survival characteristic. Or, more importance *may* be assigned to a particular system, in complex interactions among many systems, which has the most such interactions with other systems. Now it will be noted that these bases for preference in assigning hierarchical positions are perfectly objective and fully specified and, therefore, give a sense of face validity to the derived hierarchy. But it will also be noted that such criteria are related only to the *consequences* of interaction when the systems are in active interaction. Thus, whatever hierarchy is derived does not relate directly to the systems' dynamic relationships. Hence, hierarchies are not ways of characterizing features of systems in interaction.

Turning now to the second problem that analytically derives from the open-systems concept, how do we treat boundaries of open systems? If a system is considered to be open and therefore interacting with other systems that constitute its environment, it seems to follow that the boundary of the first system must also be open or permeable. Operationally, what can we mean by an open boundary? We mean that there is a unit lying outside the presently conceived boundary of the system that has a lawful relationship with, and therefore the potentiality of interacting with, a unit inside that boundary. The moment we discover what the law of interaction is, we are in a position to incorporate the "outside" unit into the model. If we do that then the formerly open boundary is closed, but with the significant consequence that there is now bounded a larger system than formerly. This point has already been made in Chapter 6.

Another and most intriguing feature of theory building is derivative from the boundary problem. That has to do with what may be called the movable theoretical model. Suppose that at the same time a new unit is incorporated into an open system to close its boundary around a new domain, the theorist is also inclined to drop out of the model one or more units that were previously incorporated in it. There may be a number of reasons for doing this, including trying to meet a criterion of parsimony, or taking into account a previously ignored unit that is believed to be more important than some utilized in the theory. The effect of substituting one or more ''new'' units for those already incorporated in the model is to produce a new theoretical model. Thus, by utilizing the open-systems notion, the theory builder is able readily to create new models.

The open-systems idea of Bertalanffy has been important as a stimulus to theoreticians to create new theoretical models, a significant contribution. It is also clear that any particular model is formulated as a closed system so that in the process of building a theoretical model the system is constructed with a closed boundary. The idea of open system has not achieved what was initially hoped for the notion: that it would provide a concept useful in analytically understanding the relations among systems themselves. I believe this problem is a frontier one in the philosophy of science and remains to be solved.[16]

Purpose and Goal

In the analysis of social behavior and social systems the idea of purpose and goal is often central. Considering individual behavior, for example, most theories of motivation focus on the forces that move the individual toward a goal or impede goal-directed movement. Social systems ranging in size from a two-person group to an entire society are considered to be goal-oriented, and a great deal of analytical attention is

---

[16]The problem has been variously formulated, for example, in the behavioral sciences in terms of subsystems, or endogenous-exogenous variables, or what has come to be called structural analysis.

focused on describing such goals and the group actions designed to attain them.[17]

How to take account of goals in analyzing social behavior is a problem in the construction of models of social action. One of the grand solutions to this scientific problem has been to utilize a teleological formulation. All systems being analyzed are considered to have goals toward which the activities within the system, and the interactions with the system's environment, are directed. Thus, business organizations and other formally constituted groups are said to have survival as an organization as one goal. The family as a social institution has been modeled as achieving the goal of perpetuating the species; armies, in the very nature of their operations, have the goal of winning battles and wars; and person-to-person social interaction has attributed to it the achievement of the goal of the individual's self-concept—the "looking-glass self."

This kind of usage of the notion of "goal" is usually blurred by the possibility that "goal" will be translated into "function." Thus, the business organization may be said to have the function of insuring its own survival (instead of survival being its goal); and the family system may have the function (instead of the goal) of perpetuating the species. This "function" takes on the usual meaning of "goal." This becomes apparent when, in the given case, the phrase "have the function of" is translated as "fulfill the function of." Thus, the family fulfills the function of perpetuating the species when children are born into it. Or, the business firm fulfills its function of surviving by driving competitors out of the marketplace.

---

[17]The paradigm utilized by Parsons is a good example. See Talcott Parsons, *The Social System* (New York: Free Press, 1951). Operations Research (OR) problems are always formulated with the goal or outcome as the anchor for the designated operations that will effectively permit a system to attain the designated goal(s). Game theory, and the strategies employed, such as mini-max strategy, is entirely concerned with the relationships between playing the game (interactions employed) and the goals sought by the players. Game theory is devoted to the analysis of the relations between defined ends and the rational means for their attainment in situations of conflict, and only in application does game theory become "useful." For example: "Game theory, it cannot be emphasized too strongly, is not a theory of behavior in conflict situations, as is often assumed by the non-specialist. Game theory is rather a branch of pure mathematics, where all paradoxes can be resolved by recourse to precise definitions, which sometimes uncover distinctions that had not been apparent. Whatever connections can be established between game theory and a theory of behavior, whether prescriptive or descriptive, must involve correspondence rules between game-theoretic models of conflict and their real-life components. It may or may not be possible to establish such connections." Anatol Rapoport, "Preface," *General Systems*, XX:ix (1975).

Two characteristics distinguish the idea of ''goal'' from the idea of ''fulfills the function of'': (1) the state in which the system is found, and (2) the time period meant in relation to the action of the system. Normally, when the idea of ''goal'' is the focus of attention the system is viewed as being in a resting state with its goal being some future state of the system at some indefinite future time (the goal of a business organization is to survive to some future and unspecified time). When the idea of ''fulfills the function of'' is the focus of attention, the system is viewed as being in an active state with the outcome of that state condition being the function of the system's behaviors (driving a competitor out of business makes it evident that survival is a function of business organizations).

While we can distinguish between ''goal'' and ''fulfills the function of'' on these two characteristics, the distinction does not become a difference. The two ideas are utilized as alternative ways to describe a system in relation to its environment. The ''goal'' formulation says that in relation to its environment, a system operates to achieve a specified future system state. The ''fulfills the function of'' formulation says that in relation to its environment, a system has reached a system state, the outcome of which is what the system was intended to accomplish. Functionalism, for all its tortured elaboration at the hands of distinguished social scientists, has never been able to overcome this teleological formulation.[18]

[18]The two early giants in functional analysis of social behavior were B. Malinowski (see his *A Scientific Theory of Culture, and Other Essays* [Chapel Hill: University of North Carolina Press, 1944]) and A. R. Radcliffe-Brown (see his *Structure and Function in Primitive Society* [London: Cohen & West, 1952]), both anthropologists with wide influence on social sciences generally. The sociologist Robert K. Merton contributed significantly to the development of functional analysis in his various essays, especially ''Manifest and Latent Functions'' (see his *Social Theory and Social Structure* [New York: Free Press, rev. ed., 1957], which contains this essay). The philosopher Ernest Nagel utilized Merton's formulations as a basis for a further analysis of functionalism (see his *Logic Without Metaphysics* [New York: Free Press, 1957] pp. 247–283). C. G. Hempel, also a philosopher, presented a fundamental analysis of functionalism in a lengthy essay entitled ''The Logic of Functional Analysis.'' In this essay he concluded: ''Furthermore—and this is the crucial point in our context—for most of the self-regulatory phenomena that come within the purview of functional analysis, the attribution of purposes is an illegitimate transfer of the concept of purpose from its domain of significant applicability to a much wider domain, where it is devoid of objective empirical support. In the context of purposive behavior of individuals or groups, there are various methods of testing whether the assumed motives or purposes are indeed present in a given situation; interviewing the agent in question might be one rather direct way, and there are various alternative 'operational' procedures of a more indirect character. Hence, explanatory hypotheses in terms of purposes are here capable of reasonably objective test. But such empirical criteria for purposes and motives are lacking in other cases of self-regulating

In our analytical framework we can now see that the usual treatment of purpose and goal in analyzing human systems arises in an attempt to relate a system to its environment. The relationship is considered to be the interaction of the system *as a whole* with its environment that lies outside its boundary. But we have seen in Chapter 4 that when a system as a whole is the focus of attention, then the system is defined as a summative unit and is *not* amenable to incorporation in a theoretical model. We conclude that the typical use of purpose and goal as characteristics of systems may have heuristic utility, but no scientific value in building testable models. (Recall that summative units have utility in providing a frame of reference for a field in spite of the fact that they do not have utility in framing scientific models.)

Are we now to discard the idea of "purpose" or "goal" in the construction of theory? The answer is no. But it is necessary to have a much more precise and limited notion of what is meant by purpose and goal.

It is illuminating to consider that the solution to this problem is one achieved by early pioneers in systems analysis. Clear recognition was gained when the usual link between causality and purpose was challenged. Purpose and goal typically are thought to play the role of "causing" a system to operate to achieve them. The system (or its agents) is pulled by the knowledge of its goal to reach it. But goal and purpose can be given a much more limited meaning that completely divorces them from causality. In the process, they can be made useful units in the construction of theoretical models.

Let us start with an important quotation from pioneers in cybernetics.

> Teleology has been interpreted in the past to imply purpose and the vague concept of a "final cause" has often been added. . . . It may be pointed out, however, that purposefulness, as defined here, is quite discredited chiefly because it was defined to imply a cause subsequent in time to a given effect. When this aspect of teleology was dismissed, however, the associated recognition of the importance of purpose was also unfortunately discarded. Since we consider purposefulness a concept necessary for the understanding of certain modes of behavior we suggest that a teleological study is useful if it avoids problems of causality and concerns itself merely with an investigation of purpose. We have restricted the connotation of teleological behavior by applying this designation only to purposeful reactions which are controlled by the error of the reaction—i.e., by the difference between the state of the behaving object at any time and the final state interpreted as the purpose. Teleological behavior thus becomes

---

systems, and the attribution of purposes to them has therefore no scientific meaning" (pp. 299–300 in Hempel's chapter published in L. Gross [ed.], *Symposium on Sociological Theory* [Evanston, Ill.: Row, Peterson & Co., 1959]).

synonymous with behavior controlled by negative feed-back, and gains therefore in precision by a sufficiently restricted connotation. . . . The concept of teleology shares one thing with the concept of causality: a time axis.[19]

Dropping the idea of causality from the notion of teleology is a necessary but not the sufficient condition on the basis of which we can retain the usefulness of purpose and goal. Note that the authors suggest that two important conditions also be satisfied: (1) that some terminal state of the system be designated as the purpose of the system; (2) that the system be linked with its environment through feedback mechanisms. Let us consider each of these conditions.

We can now formulate purpose or goal as some defined state of the system under analysis. System states are characteristic features of a theoretical model, as we saw in Chapter 7. These system states are readily specified from a knowledge of the units composing the theoretical system, and their laws of interaction. What the analyst chooses as the terminal state in order to designate it as the ''purpose'' of the system can be clearly and exactly specified. Furthermore, this choice of terminal state is acknowledged by the analyst as being an arbitrary choice, for a succeeding state, or a prior one, may be chosen by another analyst as an alternative way of defining the system's purpose. The argument about purpose ascribed to the system now becomes one of comparing and expressing preferences for one or another system state, all of which are explicitly and fully described.

The linkage between the system under consideration and its environment is made through feedback mechanisms. A feedback mechanism is a direct and lawful relationship among two or more units. Indeed, the idea of feedback is grounded in the notion that the linkage among units that are the sensors and respondents in the feedback system is explicit and operates in a lawful manner. Putting this now into our analytical framework, it

[19]A. Rosenblueth, N. Wiener, and J. Bigelow, ''Behavior, Purpose and Teleology,'' *Philosophy of Science,* 10:18–24 (1943). This statement of the distinction between teleology and causality centers on the notion of feedback. Contrast that view with Bertalanffy's notion of ''equifinality,'' which also depends on the idea of feedback, but does not establish the relationship with as great clarity as do Rosenblueth, et al. [cf.: L. von Bertalanffy, ''The Theory of Open Systems in Physics and Biology,'' *Science,* 111:23–28 (1950)]. The causality issue never seems to get settled for the focus on systems and the role of feedback in them has led some writers to have recourse to the notion of ''mutual causality'' as one way to slip back to the comfortable notion that any dynamic phenomenon is ''caused.'' See, for example, M. Maruyama, ''Mutual Causality in General Systems,'' in J. H. Milsum (ed.), *Positive Feedback: A General Systems Approach to Positive/Negative Feedback and Mutual Causality* (Oxford: Pergamon Press, 1968).

becomes clear that when there are feedback linkages with units that lie outside the initial defined boundary of the system, the acceptance of the idea of feedback now succeeds in including the "outside" linked units within the boundaries of a newly defined system. This idea is more fully set forth in Chapters 5 and 6.

The effect of using this "new" idea of purpose, as developed from systems thinking, is to provide one means for developing new theoretical systems. Always the effect of doing this is to close the boundary of the new system around units that were initially thought to lie outside the boundary of the system from which the new one is derived.

Complexity and Systems Analysis

The view of the world that modern analysts employ makes complexity a leading feature of the description of the empirical world as well as one central criterion for modeling that empirical world. Complexity has three different dimensions.

Complexity in a scientific model may result when: (a) there is a large number of units of analysis introduced into the model; (b) there is exceptional form in one or more of the laws of interaction of the model; (c) there is a large number of system states that are specified for the model. Of course, any combinations of these conditions would produce complexity in the model.

Adding one more unit of analysis to a scientific model has clear implications for making the model more complex. As a very minimum, the additional unit will demand that at least one more law of interaction also be added to the model since it is only through the law of interaction that the new unit can be linked with one or more of the original units included in the model. But it may also turn out that the new unit is linked by different laws of interaction to more than one of the original units, with the result that more than one law of interaction may have to be added to the model to accommodate the added unit. No doubt, this simple source of complexity in scientific models is what gives urgency to the search for parsimony in building such models.

Turning our attention to the form of laws of interaction as a source of complexity, it is evident that laws of differential association among units provide a complicating form to models. When two units are related to each other differentially over the range of their correlated values, their interaction is complicated compared to what it would be if the relationship were a uniform one between them. For example, a linear law of interaction between two units is much less complex than a curvilinear one. In the linear relationship any unit change in the value of one unit is associated with the same defined change in the value of the other unit, over the entire range of their lawful interaction. In a curvilinear relationship, a change in the value of one unit may be associated with a variable amount of change in the value of the other and may even result in a decrease or increase in the value of the other unit, depending on the shape of the curve of lawful relationship (as, for example, in a parabolic relationship).

The third source of scientific model complexity lies in the number of system states that is specified for the system. As this number increases, the problem of specifying the oscillation among system states, as well as the persistence of any single state, becomes more complicated. The theoretical model is burdened with having to have specified within it the conditions for oscillation from a given system state to all others. For each system state added to the model, the rule of permutations gives the number of possible system state changes that may occur over the entire life of the system. Thus, in a three-state system there are six ways in which the system may change from one state to another; but if the system has four possible states, then there are twelve ways in which the system may move from one state to another.[20] In addition, of course, if the model also specifies the persistence of system states, this is an additional requirement to be met for each new system state added. Clearly, the specification of each additional system state for the theoretical model is another way to make the model more complex.

The advantage of using the analytical framework of this volume in designing theoretical systems is again revealed in our ability to specify exactly the sources of complexity in the design. Furthermore, the theorist is also given a basis for knowing when the theoretical model is incomplete. The complete theoretical system must be specified to that level of complexity that accords with the number of units, the character of the laws of interaction, and the number of system states designed into the system.

If the empirical world is viewed as complex, and our theoretical models of it are intended to reflect that complexity, then theorists need to

---

[20]The formula for permutations is:

$$_nP_r = \frac{n!}{(n-r)!},$$

where n is the set of things that are taken r at a time. Since the system can only move from one state to one other, in either direction, r is always 2 for the case of moving from one system state to another, and n is the number of system states.

be self-conscious of the manner in which their models are made more complex. This can be done in the manner set forth here.

Systems Analysis in the Behavioral Sciences

For purposes of illustrating the variety of ways system models have been employed in the behavioral sciences we will present a very abbreviated and not very representative sampling of the field. The intent here is to indicate that this kind of theory building has been going on for some time and to conclude that the manner in which such theories have been constructed follows the procedures outlined in this volume.

This very brief treatment of the examples of systems application is deliberately limited. We have excluded all consideration of computer programming, which is the most common example of systems thinking. A computer program turns the computer into a limited and special system run according to the explicit instructions contained in the program. Most readers of this volume will have enough knowledge of programming to recognize that each individual program is designed to meet the criteria for a model set forth in this volume.

We have also excluded from consideration a wide range of applications of systems analysis as applied to the problems generally encountered in operations research (OR). Here also the nature of the problems dealt with and the means for their solution should be well known to the reader who will recognize that the OR models conform to the criteria for models described in this book. The focus of attention in this section is to present some examples of social science analysis that have employed a systems approach. The intent is to reveal how the systems approach utilizes the building blocks of theory as set forth here, rather than to provide advocacy for the systems approach itself. Such advocacy has been admirably handled elsewhere.[21]

[21]See, for example, William Buckley, *Sociology and Modern Systems Theory* (Englewood Cliffs, N.J.: Prentice-Hall, 1967), and also the volume he edited, *Modern Systems Research for the Behavioral Scientist* (Chicago: Aldine, 1968). A later volume presents still other applications of systems analysis: G. J. Klir (ed.), *Trends in General Systems Theory* (New York: Wiley-Interscience, 1972). *General Systems,* the Yearbook of the Society for General Systems Research, has been published since 1956 and contains many examples of systems analysis, as does the *International Journal of General Systems,* published since 1974. See also the *Journal of Systems Engineering,* which commenced publication in 1969. General treatments of particular subjects will be found in H. H. Goode and R. E. Machol, *Systems Engineering: An Introduction to the Design of Large*

When the behavioral sciences became "scientific" the standard intellectual tool was the analysis of two variable problems. Correlational analysis was the principal statistical procedure and "holding constant" by partial correlation techniques or through random sampling methods were honorable means for reducing multivariate situations so that they could be handled as two variable problems. But the real world of social behavior remained too full of units that were lawfully related to the selected variables. The two-variable analysis simply did not provide the understanding that an adequate science should produce. In sociology, for example, we were predicting that improved housing would alleviate the curse of the slums (without perceiving that the housing projects would in turn be made into slums when slum culture was settled in); we were suggesting that desegregation of schools by busing would provide better schooling for blacks (not even speculating about the consequences for black education as a result of the flight of whites from the central city); we were piously predicting that the "revolution" would spread from the counterculture cadres of the campuses to the body politic (without giving even a careless thought to the resiliency of the body politic and its Establishment, not to mention the short attention span of the "hippies"); and we even zeroed in on the individual criminal as the center of the "crime problem" (with little thought to the big-business features of crime embodied in the "mob").

The very urgency of the social problems faced in complex societies demanded action which hopefully could be based on scientific knowledge. As Bertalanffy has suggested:

Modern technology and society have become so complex that traditional ways and means are not sufficient any more but approaches of a holistic or systems... nature become necessary. This is true in many ways. Systems of many levels ask for scientific control: ecosystems the disturbance of which results in pressing problems like pollution; ... the grave problems appearing in socio-economic systems, in international relations, politics and deterrence. Irrespective of the questions of how far scientific understanding... is possible, and to what extent scientific control is feasible or even desirable, there can be no dispute that these are

Scale Systems (New York: McGraw-Hill, 1957); A. D. Hall, A Methodology for Systems Engineering (Princeton: Van Nostrand, 1962); O. Lange, Wholes and Parts: A General Theory of Systems Behavior (Oxford: Pergamon, 1965); W. Gosling, The Design of Engineering Systems (London: Heywood, 1962); K. E. F. Watt (ed.), Systems Analysis in Ecology (New York: Academic Press, 1966); R. Thom, Structural Stability and Morphogenesis: An Outline of a General Theory of Models (New York: Addison-Wesley, 1974); and G. E. Nichols, "Four Systems Analysis Tools," Journal of Systems Management, 27:6–11 (April 1976).

essentially "systems" problems, that is, problems of interrelationships of a great number of variables.[22]

We can illustrate the fundamental shift in approach that is the product of a systems orientation by contrasting the classical concern with business cycles and modern forecasting by economists. In an important way the two analytical problems are joined, since most forecasting is designed to predict the state of the economy in the future while the analysis of business cycles is usually historically oriented. Concerns with the business cycles initially centered on finding single economic or other variables whose variation in values "caused" swings in the business cycle. Thus, Mitchell in 1927 described the approach to business cycles as follows:

> Among the factors to which the leading role in causing business cycles has been assigned by competent inquirers within the past decade are the weather, the uncertainty which beclouds all plans that stretch into the future, the emotional aberrations to which business decisions are subject, the innovations characteristic of modern society, the "progressive" character of our age, the magnitude of savings, the construction of industrial equipment, "generalized over-production," the operation of banks, the flow of money incomes, and the conduct of business for profits.[23]

By way of contrast, the modern forecasting models that developed after World War II were multivariate analyses, with each unit of the theory linked lawfully with at least one other. The relationships are expressed in mathematical terms, although the models themselves can be set forth diagrammatically.[24] Still utilized as a very simple way of forecasting future economic states is the *Index of Leading Economic Indicators*, prepared by the Department of Commerce, which uses the present value of each economic variable employed to predict the future value of the

[22]L. von Bertalanffy, *General Systems Theory* (New York: Braziller, 1968), p. xx.

[23]W. C. Mitchell, *Business Cycles: The Problem and Its Setting* (New York: National Bureau of Economic Research, 1927), p. 12.

[24]The models for the United States were developed early in the 1950s. The Wharton School model is discussed in M. Evans, *Macroeconomic Activity: Forecasting and Control* (New York: Harper & Row, 1969). The Brookings Institution model is presented in J. S. Duesenberry, G. Fromm, L. R. Klein, and E. Kuh, *The Brookings Econometric Model of the United States* (Chicago: Rand McNally, 1965). The Federal Reserve Board–MIT model is described in F. de Leeuw and E. M. Gramlich, "The Channels of Monetary Policy: A Further Report of the Federal Research–MIT Model," *Journal of Finance,* 24:265–290 (1969). These are simply illustrative of a number of models developed, many of which are still used. An early example of a general treatment of modeling for the purposes of socioeconomic analysis is Guy Orcutt et al., *Micro-Analysis of Socio-Economic Systems* (New York: Harper, 1961).

general business cycle.[25] This mode of forecasting is essentially an ex-trapolation of past empirical relationships and does *not* represent the use of a theoretical model, but is a continuation of a classical two-variable approach where the "sum" of the individual economic indicators be-comes one unit, and the state of the economic system is considered to be the other unit.

Among notable behavioral scientists who have employed a systems-analytic approach will be found Pareto,[26] Sorokin,[27] Ashby,[28] Merton,[29] and Parsons.[30] Parsons exemplifies a grand systems analysis. He charac-terized a social system by the universal problems needing solution for the system to persist. For Parsons these were the operational problems of (1) adapting to the sudden or extreme changes in values among the units composing the social system, (2) formulating and moving toward goals of the system, (3) keeping the system integrated, and (4) managing tensions and conflicts arising within the system. On analysis, it turned out that these system problems were ways of defining system states that were characterized by the predominance of a particular system problem. Clearly, more than two system problems may be the simultaneous focus of attention so that more than four system states were postulated by Parsons for social systems. Much of Parsonian analysis was devoted to the description and analysis of single system states, and the conditions under which a social system moved from one system state to another. (This last point is one for which he is not given enough credit since his emphasis on describing single system states has led to the accusation that he ignores social change. This accusation is simply inaccurate.) A thorough reading of Parsons's works makes clear that he does specify his units and the laws of interaction among them.[31] Furthermore, at a general level he carefully defined the boundaries separating the social, cultural, and personality systems.

A particularly enthusiastic and self-conscious attempt has been made

---

[25]These are called "leading" indicators because their past values at time t are highly correlated with the state of the business cycle at some later time, $t + k$.

[26]V. Pareto, *Sociological Writings* (New York: Praeger, 1966).

[27]P. Sorokin, *Social and Cultural Dynamics,* 4 vols. (New York: American Book Co., 1937–41). See also his *Sociocultural Causality, Space and Time* (Durham, N.C.: Duke University Press, 1943).

[28]W. R. Ashby, *Design for a Brain,* 2nd ed. (New York: Wiley, 1960), and also his *Introduction to Cybernetics* (London: Chapman & Hall, 1956).

[29]R. K. Merton, *Social Theory and Social Structure* (New York: Free Press, 1949).

[30]T. Parsons, *The Social System* (New York: Free Press, 1951); *Social Structure and Personality* (New York: Free Press, 1970); and his *Politics and Social Structure (New York: Free Press, 1969)*.

to use a system formulation for the understanding of all living systems.[32] An interesting approach to understanding idealistic behavior built a model of human systems that seek four system ideal goals of plenty, truth, good, and beauty for whose pursuit appropriate functions are assigned to various units of a society.[33] Organizations have been studied as systems, as has the management of organizations.[34] A well-done study of two competing systems models for occupational mobility contrasts manpower flows within an organization with job vacancy chains. The author defined the units employed in each model, clearly set forth the laws of interaction and the boundaries, and then developed empirical indicators to test the two models from data drawn from a single organization.[35]

A variety of different modeling techniques, related to systems analysis, will be found in a recent volume that focuses on decision making in relation to the formation of public policy.[36] Another good example of the use of systems analysis in dealing with macrosocial phenomena is a multinational study of conflict within nations. In this study nine separate kinds of events (assasinations, general strikes, purges, riots, etc.) were analyzed for a number of nations. The study was an attempt inductively to develop a theoretical model by reducing the number of empirical indicators to a number small enough to represent the units defining the system state of "domestic conflict." The study was primarily methodological in its illustration of the manner in which factor analysis may be employed to discover the units that may be used for theory building (see Chapter 4

[31]An interesting example of the exploration of a theory to discover its propositions is represented in the analysis of Parsons's model of the social act. See R. Dubin, "Parsons' Actor: Continuities in Social Theory," *American Sociological Review,* 25:457–466 (August 1960).

[32]J. G. Miller, "Living Systems: Basic Concepts," *Behavioral Science,* 10:193–237 (1965).

[33]R. L. Ackoff and F. E. Emery, "On Ideal-Seeking Systems," *General Systems,* 17:17–24 (1972). See also their *On Purposeful Systems* (Chicago: Aldine, 1971).

[34]J. H. Collins and R. Whittaker, "An Example of a Systems Approach to the Study of an Organization," *Journal of Systems Engineering,* 2:49–64 (Summer 1971), and M. Hamburg et al., "A Systems Approach to Library Management," *Journal of Systems Engineering,* 4:117–130 (January 1976). Indeed, the idea of systems analysis has become almost a fad in the field of business management and this is revealed in the popular habit of putting "systems" in the title of textbooks in that field, as, for example, A. J. Melcher, *Structure and Process of Organizations: A Systems Approach* (Englewood Cliffs, N.J.: Prentice-Hall, 1976).

[35]S. Stewman, "Two Markov Models of Open System Occupational Mobility: Underlying Conceptualizations and Empirical Tests," *American Sociological Review,* 40:298–321 (1975).

[36]M. Greenberger, M. A. Crenson, and B. C. Crissley, *Models in the Policy Process* (New York: Russell, Sage, 1976).

above).[37] The senior author of the previously cited study has also analyzed urban riots from a systems standpoint.[38]

The individual as well as interpersonal relations have been approached through systems analysis. A wide-ranging attempt to formulate analytical problems of psychiatry is represented in a work of collected papers setting forth systems views of psychodynamics and therapy.[39] A novel attempt to cast a complex social interaction in systems-analytic terms was the highly original formulation of the Soviet scholar Lefebvre, now an émigré from the USSR. He modeled a two-person interaction with special reference to the subjective aspects of the interaction.[40]

Studies that have placed particular emphasis on the development of laws of interaction include the psychiatric concern with the interactions of the cognitive and emotional aspects of personality,[41] and the interesting idea that information can be stored by continuous transmission and that that is one way to model the transmission of culture in preliterature as well as modern societies.[42] In the analysis of social problems it has been suggested that problems such as drug addiction, alcoholism, and violent crime occur within closed systems. The laws of interaction within such closed systems permit effective remedy at a low cost through treatment of symptoms. Thus, methadone will substitute for heroin, and heroin addicts' antisocial behavior will be modified without eliminating addiction itself.[43] Forecasting of future system states has been related to present

[37]J. M. Firestone and D. McCormick, "An Exploration in Systems Analysis of Domestic Conflict," *General Systems,* 17:79–119 (1972).

[38]J. M. Firestone, "On the Underlying Causes of Urban Riots," *General Systems,* 19:117–134 (1974).

[39]W. Gray, F. J. Duhl, and N. D. Rizzo (eds.), *General Systems Theory and Psychiatry* (Boston: Little, Brown, 1969).

[40]See V. A. Lefebvre, "A Formal Method of Investigating Reflective Processes," *General Systems,* 17:181–188 (1972), and also his "Iconic Calculus: Symbols with Feeling in Mathematical Structure," *General Systems,* 20:71–93 (1975). In general definition of the problems that Lefebvre attacks there are parallels to the seminal work of G. H. Mead [*Mind, Self, and Society* (Chicago: University of Chicago Press, 1934) and *The Philosophy of the Act* (Chicago: The University of Chicago Press, 1938)] and the work of one of his important followers, E. Goffman [*Presentation of Self in Everyday Life* (Garden City, N.Y.: Doubleday, 1959) as well as his later works, notably his collection of essays entitled *Interaction Ritual* (Garden City, N.Y.: Anchor Books, 1967)].

[41]W. Gray, "Emotional Cognitive Structure Theory and the Development of a General Systems Psychotherapy," *General Systems,* 20:95–102 (1975).

[42]E. Krippendorff, "Principles of Information Storage and Retrieval in Society," *General Systems,* 20:15–35 (1975).

[43]A. Etzioni and R. Remp, *Technological Shortcuts to Social Change* (New York: Russell Sage, 1973).

behavior through feedback laws of interaction that make a prophecy self-fulfilling or self-altering according to an interesting analysis of these phenomena.[44]

In the simulation of an urban community, Forrester established a complex systems model and proceeded to examine its internal dynamics to determine how urban problems were generated. He made central to his model the explication of the laws of interaction he employed. As he stated:

> The first step in modeling is to generate a model that creates the problem. Only if we understand the processes leading to the difficulty can we restructure the system so that the internal processes lead in a different direction. If the model is to create the difficulties, it must contain all the *interacting relationships* [emphasis added] necessary to lead the system into trouble. The troubles are not imposed on the system from outside the structure being modeled. The model will be a closed model which is not dependent for its inherent characteristic behavior on any variables transmitted across its boundary from the external world.[45]

It will be noted that here Forrester also gives strong emphasis to the fact that the model needs to be bounded. The attention to boundaries is so central that a full chapter has been given to the subject in this volume (Chapter 6). Forrester has put the issue succinctly: "To develop a complete concept of a system, the boundary must be established within which the system's interactions take place that give the system its characteristic behavior."[46] Another fine exposition of the critical character of boundaries in understanding system behavior is the treatment of ecosystems when applied problems, such as that of maintenance of water quality in a reservoir, are addressed.[47]

Turning attention to the consideration of system states, studies in a number of areas have focused on the analysis of system states. For example, an early review of the self-structuring of small groups pointed out that such groups move toward a simple structure from any present structure of a more complicated character, where the measure of "complication" was the number of links utilized by the members of the group in interacting with each other. The author suggested that the state of minimal

---

[44]R. L. Henshel and L. W. Kennedy, "Self-Altering Prophecies: Consequences for the Feasibility of Social Prediction," *General Systems,* 18:119–126 (1973).

[45]J. W. Forrester, *Urban Dynamics* (Cambridge, Mass.: MIT Press, 1969), p. 113.
[46]*Ibid.,* p. 12.

[47]K. W. Thornton, "Systems Thinking in Applied Ecological Research," *General Systems,* 20:59–62 (1975).

linkage among small-group members was the most stable state for such a system.[48] Subsequent theories of group structure have suggested that a group passes through progressive system states, never returning to any previous state,[49] or that a small group may pass through recurrent system states.[50] In the area of political behavior, the political environment of a social system was characterized as composed of learning groups that employ different strategies in receiving information about the body politic and then responding. The author speculated about the possibility of building a systems approach that will account for the shift of a group from one strategy to another—an emphasis on shifts among possible system states.[51]

This has been a cursory review of some recent examples of systems analysis in the behavior sciences. Much more literature exists and is readily accessible. The point of this review is (1) to suggest the wide range of applications already made of systems thinking, and (2) to provide some examples of how the elements of a theoretical model (units, laws of interaction, boundaries, and system states) are treated in systems thinking.

The utilization of a systems approach has not been without its critics. The most sweeping attacks have declared the approach to be devoid of utility. A recent polemic against systems analysis claims that it is incapable of modeling the inherent complexity, discontinuity, and nonlinearity of social life.[52] But these very aspects of social systems that Berlinski claimed cannot be modeled are dealt with in interesting fashion in the explication of "fuzzy systems."[53] At a more restricted level, a social scientist criticized the attempts of engineers to model social systems because engineers tend to make a mechanical application of systems-analytic technologies without having a genuine understanding of, and knowledge about, the social phenomena that they are trying to model.[54] But this contention finds the counter

[48]R. Dubin, "Stability of Human Organizations," Chapter 8 in M. Haire (ed.), *Modern Organization Theory* (New York: Wiley, 1959), pp. 218–253.

[49]T. Dolgoff, "Small Groups and Organizations: Time, Task, and Sentient Boundaries," *General Systems,* 20:135–141 (1975).

[50]C. F. Bion, *Experiences in Groups* (New York: Basic Books, 1959).

[51]M. Horn, "Learning Strategies for Public Learning: A Cybernetic Approach," *General Systems,* 21:125–129 (1976).

[52]D. Berlinski, *On Systems Analysis* (Cambridge, Mass.: MIT Press, 1976).

[53]R. Jain, "Outline of an Approach for the Analysis of Fuzzy Systems," *International Journal of Control,* 23:627–640 (1976).

[54]I. R. Hoos, "Engineers as Analysts of Social Systems: A Critical Enquiry," *Journal of Systems Engineering,* 4:81–88 (January 1976).

point being made by pioneers of operations research who declared that substantive ignorance of a phenomena being analyzed could be an asset by permitting unbiased approaches to the analysis that those familiar with the phenomenon might be incapable of realizing.[55] Both the extreme and limited criticism help to clarify the object of attack and, in general, contribute to improved understanding.

Wholeness and the Analytical Characteristics of Wholes

We are now able to summarize the reasons why the "whole is greater than the sum of its parts." Furthermore, we are now in the position of understanding why it is a greater contribution to knowledge to know the whole picture, as well as the partial picture of paired relationships among the parts, than to have only the latter knowledge.

First of all it is a misconception to make central the idea of a "system" that it encompasses many units and not just two. That, of course, is what is involved, giving rise to the notion that systems analysis is multivariate analysis. But partial and multiple correlation analyses are multivariate, yet are not systems analyses. So, multivariateness is a necessary but not a sufficient condition of a systems approach.

We can provide an approach to the "wholeness" issue by responding to the query: "What is there about a system that we want to know?" This can be broken down into four basic questions.

1. How many states of the system are there? (And, of course, what are the features of each system state?)

2. What are the trajectories of the system as it moves from one of its states to another? (To what other system states is it possible for the systems to move given a particular present state? Under what conditions does each change from one to another system state occur? Is the system state change reversible or irreversible?)

3. What are the conditions for the destruction of the system (lethality) or its transformation into another system?

4. What is the value, or range of values, taken on by any given unit of the system, given a specific system state?

[55]P. Morris and G. Kimball, *Methods of Operations Research* (Cambridge, Mass.: MIT Technology Press, 1951), "The operations research worker need not be an expert in the operation involved (indeed, too great familiarity with its details may handicap him). . . ." (p. 4).

These four questions and their subsidiary ones are all self-evident. They have been dealt with at various points in this book (see especially Chapter 7). The purpose of reintroducing the questions at this point is to give a down-to-earth meaning to the idea of wholeness.

There are two features of these four kinds of knowledge we seek about systems. It is to these features of the four general questions that the following discussion is addressed. The characteristics of the questions are:

A. They all involve the system as a whole. They are not focused on the individual units of the system, or the values that any unit can attain. Even the fourth question, which is centered on a single unit of the system, refers its value, or range of values to the state of the system, thereby taking the entire system into account.

B. The knowledge about the whole system that results from answering the four questions is a different body of knowledge than that obtained about individual units that are included in the system. The systematic knowledge complements and supplements knowledge about individual units, and may even be dependent upon the prior existence of the latter body of knowledge.

Turning to point (A), it should be clear that a systems analysis is about a system, and not about its parts. The analysis is *sui generis* systematic. This, for example, is the fundamental notion that Durkheim had when he insisted that social behavior and social systems are to be understood through a knowledge about social facts and their interrelationships. He concluded that his system-analytic problem, namely, that of the nature and basis of social solidarity, had to be understood through a knowledge of system characteristics and could not be based on a knowledge of individual psyches.[56] Durkheim's position is much more than a diatribe against reductionism (see Chapters 3 and 5 above). He insisted that to understand a social system, and particularly the conditions of social solidarity within it, the system as a whole must be the point of explanatory reference.

What is learned about a system cannot be deducted from a knowledge of the parts that compose the system. The reason is evident. System units, as they interact within the boundaries of the system, *together* have properties that cannot be known solely from knowledge of the individual units. This is why an industrial process or manufacturing facility needs to

[56]E. Durkheim, *The Rules of Sociological Method* (New York: Free Press, 1938), *loc. cit.*

be "run in" during a start-up period to determine how its components will interact as a system; why simulations are attempted in order to imitate a real-time system in operation to discover its systemic characteristics; and why experiments with interactions of drugs and biological systems (animals or human beings) precede the approval of chemicals and drugs for relief of human maladies.

Turning to point (B) above, the questions asked and the conclusions reached about a system are based upon a special body of knowledge about the units composing the system. This is the knowledge about what happens to each unit as the system functions. Each unit contributes in some way to the functioning of the system. Each unit also interacts with other units of the system and the interactions themselves are what produce the characteristics of the system that are the focus of attention. For example, as has been pointed out in Chapter 7, the persistent values of all units during a period of time are the basis for defining a system state. Changes from these values to another set of values signal that the *system as a whole* has changed state. The propositions (see Chapter 8) we make about theoretical systems include a set of propositions regarding the four analytical questions posed about systems. These propositions become testable when we are capable of inventing empirical indicators (set forth in Chapter 9) of the values that can be measured on each unit composing the system.

We conclude then that knowledge about individual units is indispensable to building knowledge about a system in which the units are included. But what will happen inside the system when it is functioning can be understood only when system characteristics are examined. The whole indeed becomes more than the sum of its parts because *interaction* among the parts can be understood only through laws of interaction that are not purely deducible from a knowledge of the attributes of the parts (units) alone.

We can now recast the central features of systems analysis as including: (a) the analysis of multiple units, (b) with focus on their laws of interaction, (c) producing characteristics ("attributes" as in Chapter 3) of the system, that (d) are different from the characteristics of the individual units composing the system. This says more than that systems analysis is equivalent to multivariate analysis. We have additionally concluded that it is the interactional features of systems that lead to the need for specifying the characteristics of systems independently of the characteristics of the units composing the systems.

Clearly, it is not being asserted that knowledge about system characteristics substitutes for knowledge about unit characteristics. These are two different kinds of knowledge. They complement each other. Knowledge about units employed in theories is the descriptive base on which rests the ability to build meaningful scientific theories (as has been argued in Chapters 4 and 11).

The Closing Circle

This book opened with a chapter setting forth the "big picture" of theory building, accompanied by an illustration designed to clarify the setting. We have ended by linking theory building and systems analysis for the purpose of showing that the ideas set forth in this volume are closely associated with a modern development in scientific thought. In between the initial and closing chapters it is hoped that something useful has been said. The real test, of course, is your ability, dear reader, to build your own theories.

POSTLUDE: THE THEORY GAME

For it is necessary to insist upon this extraordinary but undeniable fact: experimental science has progressed thanks in great part to the work of men astonishingly mediocre, and even less than mediocre.... The reason of this lies in what is at the same time the great advantage and the gravest peril of the new science ... namely, mechanization.... For the purpose of innumerable investigations it is possible to divide science into small sections, to enclose oneself in one of these, and to leave out of consideration all the rest. The solidity and exactitude of methods allow of this temporary but quite real disarticulation of knowledge. The work is done under one of these methods as with a machine, and in order to obtain quite abundant results, it is not even necessary to have rigorous notions of their meaning and foundations.

—Jose Ortega y Gasset, *The Revolt of the Masses*

GOOD SATIRE, written in an informed and sympathetic manner, pointedly spikes the pretentiousness of self-declared experts. The following piece deals with those who know and practice the *form* of theory-research but either ignore or do not know its substance. This volume has dealt with the substance of theory building. It is therefore useful to close with some telling admonitions of what *not* to do. Marvin Dunnette is a knowledgeable expert in the behavioral sciences. I hope that the reader's amusement will not diminish awareness of the import of the underlying serious message.

FADS, FASHIONS, AND FOLDEROL IN PSYCHOLOGY*

Marvin D. Dunnette
Department of Psychology
University of Minnesota

This seemed to be a great idea six months ago when the Division 14 program was being arranged. When I chose the title, it seemed *very* clever, and I looked forward to venting my spleen a bit and to saying sage things about what's wrong with psychology and how its ills might be cured.

It wasn't long, however, before I felt misgivings about the whole enterprise and doubted whether I could meet the Challenge to put up or to shut up that my own foolhardiness had cast upon me. . . .

So—seizing upon one of my own pet types of methodological folderol—I decided to run a survey! I contacted older or wiser heads,[1] to inquire what, if anything, was currently bothering them. . . .

With their suggestions, however, I was faced suddenly with a plethora of fads, fashions, and folderol and the need to make some systematic sense of them. . . .

But, even armed with my list, about all I could say is that there are many things going on in psychology that reasonably responsible people were willing to label faddish folderol. . . . What was needed was a better taxonomy for listing psychology's ills than the rather artificial trichotomy established by my title.

Just when I was facing this impasse, I received the best selling book by Eric Berne titled *Games People Play*. I was stimulated by this magnificent book to give thought to the games psychologists play. . . .

In this new-found role as clinical taxonomist, I was able to discern six games probably played by all of us from time to time, to greater or lesser degree, as the spirit moves us. . . .

---

*This article is a shortened version of an invited address delivered at the 73rd annual convention of the American Psychological Association, Chicago, Illinois, Sept. 1965, excerpted from *American Psychologist*, 21:343–352 (April 1966). Copyright 1966 by the American Psychological Association. Reprinted by permission of APA and the author.

[1] I should like to thank these helpful colleagues for their readiness to come to my aid, but please understand that I do so only because of a strong sense of gratitude and with no thought of dragging them out to the end of the limb with me. They are: David P. Campbell, John P. Campbell, Alphonse Chapanis, Edwin E. Ghiselli, Mason Haire, James Jenkins, Quinn McNemar, Paul Meehl, William A. Owens, Jr., Bernard Rimland, Auke Tellegen, Raines Wallace, and Karl Weick.

The Pets We Keep

Subtitled "What was good enough for Daddy is good enough for me," this game is characterized by an early and premature commitment to some Great Theory or Great Method. One major effect is to distort research problems so that they fit the theory or the method. The theory, method, or both can be viewed as pets inherited by fledgling psychologists ... protecting them from all possible harm due to the ... attacks from other psychologists who, in turn, are keeping their own menageries.

At a general level, the premature commitment to a theory is usually accompanied by the set to *prove* rather than to modify the theory. . . .

A pessimist might, in fact, find it difficult to identify any psychological theories which do *not* currently enjoy this form of affectionate nurturing. In industrial psychology, the most obvious current example of such nurturance is the so-called Two Factor Theory of Job Motivation. . . .

The problem in psychology is made more severe, however, by the inexplicitness (Feigl, 1962) and, as Ritchie (undated) has called it, the "incurable vagueness" with which most theories are stated—but then, it should be clear that vagueness in theory construction may simply be part of the game, insuring higher likelihood of a pet theory's long life.

Methodologically, our favored *pets* include factor analysis, complex analysis of variance designs, the concept of statistical significance, and multiple regression analyses. It is common for psychologists to apply so-called sophisticated methods of analysis to data hardly warranting such careful attention. I shall not try to enumerate the nature of the painstaking activities included in the game of statistical pet keeping. I refer those of you who are interested to excellent papers by McNemar (1951) and by Guilford (1960). The net effect, however, is that attention to relevant and important scientific questions is diminished in favor of working through the subtle nuances of methodological manipulation. As my colleague, David Campbell (1965) remarked, "We seem to believe that TRUTH will be discovered somehow through using more and more esoteric techniques of data manipulation rather than by looking for it in the real world. . . ."

The Names We Love

An alternate title for this game is "What's new under the sun?" ... coining new words and labels either to fit old concepts or to cast new facts outside the ken of a theory in need of protection.

Just one from among many possible examples is the great emphasis in

recent years on Social Desirability—a new label for a phenomenon in
test-taking behavior dealt with extensively by Meehl and Hathaway
(1946), Jurgensen, and others many years previously, but which did not
create much interest because they failed at the time to coin a label sufficiently attractive to ''grab'' other psychologists.

As Maier (1960) has so aptly pointed out, one major effect of the
Name Game is to sustain theories even if the facts seem to refute them. If
facts appear that cannot be ignored, relabeling them or renaming them
gives them their own special compartment so that they cease to infringe
upon the privacy of the theory.

Perhaps the most serious effect of this game is the tendency to apply
new names in psychological research widely and uncritically before sufficient work has been done to specify the degree of generality or specificity
of the ''trait'' being dealt with. Examples of this are numerous—anxiety,
test-taking anxiety, rigidity, social desirability, creativity, acquiescence,
social intelligence, and so on—*ad infinitum*.

The Fun We Have

A suitable title for this game would be—quite simply—''Tennis anyone?'' But the game has many variants, including ''My model is nicer
than your model!'' ''Computers I have slept with'' or the best game of
all—''A difference doesn't need to *make* a difference if it's a *real* difference.''

As should be clear, the underlying theme of the game—''Tennis,
anyone''—is the compulsion to forget the problem . . . because of the fun
we may be enjoying with our apparatus, our computers, our models or the
simple act of testing statistical null hypotheses. Often, in our zest for this
particular game . . . we may even literally forget to look at the data!

In my opinion, the most serious yet most common symptom of this
game is the ''glow'' that so many of us get from saying that a result is
''statistically significant.'' The song and dance of null hypothesis testing
goes on and on—apparently endlessly. In my opinion, this one practice is
as much responsible as anything for what Sommer (1959) has called the
''little studies'' and the ''little papers'' of psychology.

As so many others have pointed out (Rozeboom, 1960; Grant, 1962;
Binder, 1963; Meehl, 1963; Nunnally, 1960; Hays, 1964), the major
difficulty with psychology's use of the statistical null hypothesis is that
the structure of scientific conclusions derived thereby is based on a foundation of triviality. When even moderately small numbers of subjects are

used (say 75–100) nearly all comparisons between means will yield so-called "significant" differences. I believe most psychologists will agree, in their more sober and less fun-loving moments, that small differences and inconsequential correlations do not provide a sufficient yield either for accurately predicting other persons' behavior or for understanding theoretically the functional relations between behavior and other variables. . . .

It may seem that my criticism of this particular game is unduly severe. Perhaps the differences reported in our journals are not really all that small. In order to examine this question, I asked one of my research assistants, Milton Hakel, to sample recent issues of four APA Journals—the *Journal of Applied Psychology, Journal of Abnormal and Social Psychology, Journal of Personality and Social Psychology,* and *Journal of Experimental Psychology.* He selected randomly from among studies employing either t-tests or complex analysis of variance designs, and converted the t or F values to correlation ratios (*eta*) in order to estimate the strength of association between independent and dependent variables.

The distribution of the 112 correlation ratios ranged from .05 to .92 with a median value of .42. Five percent of the studies showed values below .20; over one-sixth were below .25; and nearly one-third failed to reach .30. The only encouragement I derive from these data stems from my identification with industrial psychology. At a time when many in industrial psychology are worried because predictive validities rarely exceed .50, it is at least reassuring—though still disconcerting—to note that our brethren in social and experimental psychology are doing little better.

It is particularly informative to note the conclusions made by the authors of the articles sampled by Hakel. Authors of the study yielding the *eta* of .05, concluded "that rating-scale format is a determiner of the judgment of raters in this sample" (Madden and Bourdon, 1964). In an investigation yielding an *eta* of .14, the authors concluded "that highly creative subjects give the greatest number of associations and maintain a relatively higher speed of association throughout a 2 minute period" (Mednick, Mednick, and Jung, 1964).

Surprisingly, these rather definite conclusions differ little in tone from those based on studies yielding much stronger relationships. For example, a study yielding an *eta* of .77 is summarized with "Highly anxious subjects tended to give sets of word associates higher in intersubject variability than nonanxious subjects" (Brody, 1964). In like manner, the conclusion stated for a study yielding an *eta* of .63 was simply "It was found that reinforcement affected subjects' verbalizations" (Ganzer and Sarason, 1964).

It seems abundantly clear that our little survey provides convincing and frightening evidence that playing the game of null hypothesis testing has led a sizable number of psychologists to lose sight of the importance of the strength of relationships underlying their conclusions. I could not agree more fully with Nunnally (1960), who has said:

> ... it would be a pity to see it [psychology] settle for the meager efforts... encouraged by the use of the hypothesis testing models. ... We should not feel proud when we see the psychologist smile and say 'the correlation is significant beyond the .01 level.' Perhaps that is the most that he can say, but he has no reason to smile.

The Delusions We Suffer

This is probably the most dangerous game of all. At the core, it consists of maintaining delusional systems to support our claims that the things we are doing *really* constitute good science. The game develops out of a pattern of self-deceit which becomes more ingrained and less tractable with each new delusion. Thus, an appropriate subtitle is "This above all, To thine own self be *false!*"

The forms of these delusions are so numerous and so widespread in psychology that time permits only brief mention of a few.

One common variant of the game can be called, "Boy, did I ever make them sit up and take notice!" The argument is often made and seemingly almost always accepted that if a new theory or method stimulates others to do research, it *must* be good. Although I greatly dislike analogic arguments, I am compelled to suggest that such reasoning is very similar to stating that accidental fire must be good simply because it keeps so many firemen busy. Unfortunately, an inestimable amount of psychological research energy has been dissipated in fighting brush fires spawned by faddish theories—which careful research might better have refuted at their inception. ...

Many investigators fall victims to a second delusion, because they discover early in their careers that gathering data from real people emitting real behaviors in the day-to-day world proves often to be difficult, unwieldy and just plain unrewarding. Often they retreat to the relative security of experimental or psychometric laboratories where new laboratory or test behaviors may be concocted to be observed, measured and subjected to an endless array of internal analyses. These may lead eventually to elaborate theories of behavioral taxonomies, entirely consistent within themselves but lacking the acid test of contact with reality.

McNemar (1964) in last year's presidential address reminded us once again of the abysmally poor record of factor analytically derived tests for reflecting or predicting day-to-day behavior. . . .

A third unfortunate delusion rationalizes certain practices on the grounds that they are intrinsically good for humanity and that they need not, therefore, meet the usual standards demanded by scientific verification. In this regard, Astin (1961) has done an effective job of analyzing the functional autonomy of psychotherapy and offers a number of reasons why it continues to survive in spite of a lack of evidence about its effectiveness. Essentially, the reasons are predicated on the delusion that psychotherapy "must be good" and therefore need not be put to the test. . . .

Finally, yet another pair of delusions, representing polar opposites of one another, were discussed by Cronbach (1957) in his 1957 APA presidential address. One extreme, shown chiefly by the experimentalists, treats individual differences as merely bothersome variation—to be reduced by adequate controls or treated as error variance in the search for General Laws. Such assumptions cannot help but lead to an oversimplified image of man, for the simplification is introduced at the very beginning. . . .

The other extreme, actually extending considerably beyond the correlational psychology discussed by Cronbach, is just as delusory. . . . Differences between individuals are regarded as so pervasive that it is assumed *no* laws can be stated. The likely outcome of a strong commitment to this point of view must ultimately be an admission that the methods of science cannot be applied to the study of human behavior. Yet, this outcome is not often openly recognized or honestly accepted by those believing in the ultimate uniqueness of each individual. Instead, they speak of "new approaches," less "mechanistic emphases," and a more "humanistic endeavor". . . .

Cronbach, nearly a decade ago, sounded an urgent call for his fellow psychologists to cast aside the delusions represented by these two extremes. Unfortunately, today we seem no closer to achieving this end than we were then.

The Secrets We Keep

We might better label this game "Dear God, please don't tell anyone." As the name implies, it incorporates all the things we do to accomplish the aim of looking better in public than we really are.

The most common variant is, of course, the tendency to bury negative results. I only recently became aware of the massive size of this great graveyard for dead studies when a colleague expressed gratification that only a third of his studies "turned out"—as he put it.

Recently, a second variant of this secrecy game was discovered, quite inadvertently, by Wolins (1962) when he wrote thirty-seven authors to ask for the raw data on which they had based recent journal articles. Wolins found that of thirty-two who replied, twenty-one reported their data to be either misplaced, lost, or inadvertently destroyed. Finally, after some negotiation, Wolins was able to complete seven re-analyses on the data supplied from five authors. Of the seven, he found gross errors in three—errors so great as to clearly change the outcome of the results already reported. Thus, if we are to accept these results from Wolins' sampling, we might expect that as many as one-third of the studies in our journals contain gross miscalculations. In fact, this variant of the secrecy game might well be labeled "I wonder where the yellow (data) went." In commenting on Wolins' finding, Friedlander (1964), impressed by the strong commitments psychologists hold for their theories, tests and methods, suggests that "Hope springs eternal—and is evidently expressed through subjective arithmetic"—a possibility which is probably too close to the truth to be taken lightly.

Another extremely vexing and entirely unnecessary type of secrecy is clearly apparent to anyone who takes but a moment to page through one of our current data-oriented psychological journals. I chose a recent issue of the *Journal of Personality and Social Psychology*. It was very difficult to find such mundane statistics as means or standard deviations. Instead, the pages abounded with analysis of variance tables, charts, F-ratios and even t-tests in the absence of their corresponding means and SD's. The net effect of this is to make very difficult and often impossible any further analyses that a reader might want to undertake. The implication of this, it seems to me, is that many authors have actually failed to bother computing such statistics as means or SD's and that, further, they probably have not examined their data with sufficient care to appreciate in any degree what they may really portray.

Other examples of the secrecy game abound, but they can only be mentioned in passing. They include such practices as dropping subjects for the analyses—a practice discussed at some length in the critical review of a sampling of dissonance studies by Chapanis and Chapanis (1964), experimenter biasing factors, incomplete descriptions of methodology, failure to carry out or to report cross-validation studies, and the more general problem of failure to carry out or to report replication studies.

I believe you will agree that these tactics of secrecy can be nothing but severely damaging to any hopes of advancing psychology as a science. . . .

The Questions We Ask

There are many titles that might be appropriate for this last game that I shall discuss. One might be, ''Who's on first?''—or—better yet—''What game we are in''—or—a rather common version in these days of large Federal support for research—''While you're up, get me a grant.'' My major point here is quite simply that the other games we play, the pets we keep, our delusions, our secrets, and the Great Name Game interact to cause us to lose sight of the essence of the problems that need to be solved and the questions that need answers. The questions that get asked are dictated—all too often—by investigators' pet theories or methods, or by the need to gain ''visibility'' among one's colleagues. One of my respondents—a younger but undoubtedly wiser head than I—summed it up nicely. He said:

> Psychologists seem to be afraid to ask really important questions. The whole Zeitgeist seems to encourage research efforts that earn big grants, crank out publications frequently and regularly, self-perpetuate themselves, don't entail much difficulty in getting subjects, don't require the researchers to move from behind their desks or out of their laboratories except to accept speaking engagements, and serve to protect the scientist from all the forces that can knock him out of the secure ''visible'' circle. . . . (Campbell, J., 1965)

An even more serious and unfortunately probably more common form of the question-asking game is the game of ''Ha! Sure slipped that one past you, didn't I?'' Here, the investigator shrewdly fails to state the question he is trying to answer, gathers data to provide answers to simpler questions and then behaves as if his research has been relevant to other unstated but more important and more interesting problems. The vast majority of studies devoted to measuring employee attitudes have committed this error. It is no trick to develop questionnaires to gather systematically the opinions of workers about their jobs. It is quite something else, however, suddenly to begin talking about measures of employee *motivation* and to suggest that the employee responses have direct relevance to what they may actually do on the job. . . .

Thus, it seems to me that we all are far too eager to ask such questions as "What problems can be *easily* answered?" "What else can I do with my test?" "What problems or questions does my theory lead to?" "What aspects of behavior can I study with my computer or with my apparatus?" or "What problems can I find that I can fit this method to?"

Certainly, as psychologists—as scientists presumably interested in the subject matter of human behavior—we should be able to do better than this! . . .

The Remedy

In order to convince you of my good intentions and my hope for the future, I had better get on with some constructive suggestions. My suggested remedy . . . can be summarized in five imperative statements: (1) Give up constraining commitments to theories, methods, and apparatus; (2) Adopt methods of multiple working hypotheses! (3) Put more eclecticism into graduate education! (4) Press for new values and less pretense in the academic environments of our universities; and, finally, (5) Get to the editors of our psychological journals!

Let me elaborate briefly on each of these recommendations.

First, I advocate a more careful and studied choice of research questions. As should be apparent, I believe research energy should be directed toward questions that contain as few as possible of any prior unproven assumptions about the nature of man. We must be constantly alert to the narrowing of research perspectives due to prior theoretical or methodological commitments. . . .

I am not advocating the abandonment of deduction in psychology. . . . What I am advocating is the more systematic study of lawful relationships *before* interpretations are attempted. When explanation *is* attempted, the data should be sufficient to allow hypotheses to be stated with the clarity and precision to render them directly capable of disproof. As the philosopher Karl Popper has said, there is no such thing as proof in science; science advances only by disproofs.

This leads directly to my second recommendation which is to state and systematically test multiple hypotheses. A recent article by Platt (1964) and a much earlier one by Chamberlin (reprinted: 1965) both advocate this approach, which Platt has called Strong Inference. The approach entails devising multiple hypotheses to explain observed phenomena, devising crucial experiments each of which may exclude or disprove one or more of the hypotheses and continuing with the retained hypotheses to develop further subtests or sequential hypotheses to refine the possibilities that remain. This process does not seem new; in fact it is not. It simply entails developing ideas or leads, stating alternative possibilities, testing their plausibility, and proceeding to develop predictive and explanatory evidence concerning the phenomena under investigation . . . the research emphasis is one of "studying hypotheses" as opposed to "substantiating theories." The difference seems slight, but it is really quite important. But in psychology, the approach is little used for, as we have said, the commitments are often to *A* theory rather than to the process of *finding out.*

The method of multiple hypotheses takes on added power when combined with greater care in the analysis and reporting of research results. Instead of serving as the sole statistical test of hypotheses, the statistical null hypothesis should always be supplemented by estimates of strength of association. The psychologist owes it to himself to determine not only whether an association exists between two variables—an association which may often be so small as to be trivial—but also to determine the probable magnitude of the association. As Hays (1964) has suggested, if psychologists are content to adopt conventions (such as .05 or .01) for deciding on statistical significance, they should also adopt conventions concerning the strength of association which may be sufficiently large to regard as worthy of further investigation. Obviously, such conventions cannot be the same for all areas and for all research questions, but it should be clear that an emphasis on magnitude estimation will demand that researchers give much more careful thought than they now do to defining ahead of time the actual magnitudes that will be regarded as possessing either theoretical or practical consequences.

By now, it is apparent why my fifth recommendation has to do with our journals. It will require a new kind of survilllance from both the editors and their consultants. . . . When and if null hypothesis testing is accorded a lower position in the status hierarchy and comes to be supplemented by emphases on Strong Inference and magnitude estimation, I would predict that the bulk of published material will, for a time, greatly diminish. That which does appear, however, will be guaranteed to be of considerably greater consequence for furthering our understanding of behavior.

One of the possible loopholes in the method of Strong Inference, it should be clear, is the great difficulty of designing and carrying out crucial experiments. Recently Hafner and Presswood (1965) described how faulty experiments had led physicists astray for several decades as they sought to explain the phenomenon of beta decay. We must broaden our conception of multiple hypotheses to include as one quite plausible hypothesis the possibility of poorly conceived or poorly conducted experiments. This, of course, simply speaks to the need for more replication in psychology of crucial experiments, a practice which undoubtedly would become more widespread if psychologists possessed . . . stronger motivation to examine systematically whole sets of contending hypotheses and alternative explanations.

My third and fourth recommendations need not be elaborated extensively. Both are intended to foster less pretense in the conduct of psychological research by enabling those scholars who may be ill-fitted for the research enterprise to gain appropriate rewards in other endeavors. The change in the academic atmosphere would need to take the form of according more status to good teaching and to good administration. Perhaps this change would be most rapidly fostered if the scientific games I have described would be more readily recognized for what they are and appropriately de-valued in the schema of things within academia.

Obviously, greater eclecticism in graduate education is crucial to the successful outcome of my other suggestions. It is difficult to know how this can be implemented.

But, at least, the goals seem clear. We desire to teach the core of psychology's knowledge and methods, its subject matter and its questions, the statistical methods and their appropriate applications—but most of all, through selection or training or both, we should seek to turn out persons with intense curiosity about the vast array of psychological questions and problems occurring everywhere in the world around us—with a willingness to ask *open* questions unhampered by the prior constraints of a particular point of view or method. Let us hope that graduate education, in the years ahead, will become more eclectic and that even the Great Men in our field may adopt a sense of humility when transmitting knowledge to the fledglings of our science. . . .

References

Astin, A. W. The functional autonomy of psychotherapy. *Amer. Psychologist,* 1961, 16, 75–78.

Berne, E. *Games People Play.* New York: Grove Press, 1964.

Binder, A. Further considerations on testing the null hypothesis and the strategy and tactics of investigating theoretical models. *Psychol. Rev.,* 1963, 70, 107–115.

Brody, N. Anxiety and the variability of word associates. *J. Abnorm. Soc. Psychol.*, 1964, 68, 331–334.

Campbell, D. P. 1965, personal communication.

Campbell, J. P. 1965, personal communication.

Chamberlin, T. C. The method of multiple working hypotheses. *Science*, 1965, 148, 754–759.

Chapanis, Natalia and Chapanis, A. Cognitive dissonance: five years later. *Psychol. Bull.*, 1964, 61, 1–22.

Cronbach, L. J. The two disciplines of scientific psychology. *Amer. Psychologist*, 1957, 18, 671–684.

Feigl, H. Philosophical embarrassments of psychology. *Psychologische Beitrage*, 1962, VI, 340–364.

Friedlander, F. Type I and type II bias. *Amer. Psychologist*, 1964, 19, 198–199.

Ganzer, V. J. and Sanason, I. G. Interrelationships among hostility, experimental conditions, and verbal behavior. *J. Abnorm. Soc. Psychol.*, 1964, 68, 79–84.

Grant, D. A. Testing the null hypothesis and the strategy and tactics of investigating theoretical models. *Psychol. Rev.*, 1962, 69, 54–61.

Guilford, J. P. Psychological measurement a hundred and twenty-five years later. Unpublished manuscript, 1960, invited address given at APA convention, Sept. 7, 1960.

Hafner, E. M. and Presswood, Susan. Strong inference and weak interactions. *Science*, 1965, 149, 503–510.

Hays, W. L. *Statistics for psychologists*. New York: Holt, Rinehart & Winston, 1964.

McNemar, A. The factors in factoring behavior. *Psychometrika*, 1951, 16, 353–359.

McNemar, A. Lost our intelligence? Why? *Amer. Psychologist*, 1964, 19, 871–882.

Madden, J. M. and Bourdon, R. D. Effects of variations in rating scale format on judgment. *J. Appld. Psychol.*, 1964, 48, 147–151.

Maier, N. R. F. Maier's law. *Amer. Psychologist*, 1960, 15, 208–212.

Mednick, Martha, Mednick, S. A., and Jung, C. C. Continual association as a function of level of creativity and type of verbal stimulus. *J. Abnorm. Soc. Psychol.*, 1964, 69, 511–515.

Meehl, P. E. Remarks on corroboration of theories by significance tests on nonexperimental data. Unpublished memoranda, 1963, dated January 21 and February 18.

Meehl, P. E. and Hathaway, S. R. The K factor as a suppressor variable in the MMPI. *J. Appld. Psychol.*, 1946, 30, 525–564.

Nunnally, J. The place of statistics in psychology. *Ed. and Psychol. Measmt.*, 1960, 20, 641–650.

Platt, J. R. Strong inference. *Science,* 1964, 146, 347–352.

Ritchie, B. F. Incurable vagueness in psychological theory. Unpublished manuscript, no date.

Rozeboom, W. W. The fallacy of the null-hypotheses significance test. *Psychol. Bull.,* 1960, 57, 416–428.

Sommer, R. On writing little papers. *Amer. Psychologist,* 1959, 14, 235–237.

Wolins, L. Responsibility for raw data. *Amer. Psychologist,* 1962, 17, 657–658.

Working Bibliography

... a developed culture is a way of looking at the world through an aggregation of symbols, so that empirical facts take on significance and man feels that he is acting in a drama, in which the cruxes of decision sustain interest and maintain the tone of his being. For this reason a true culture cannot be content with a sentiment which is sentimental with regard to the world. There must be a source of clarification, of arrangement and hierarchy, which will provide grounds for the employment of the rational faculty.

—RICHARD M. WEAVER, *Ideas Have Consequences*

THE FOLLOWING bibliography is presented, without annotation, to indicate some of the sources influential in the development and clarification of the ideas presented in this volume. It is hardly an exhaustive listing, being limited by a distinct personal bias and excluding a vast periodical literature found in professional journals. Since "... there must be a source of clarification ..." it is to this list of works that I have turned to find the "... grounds for the employment of the rational faculty." (PB = paperback edition).

Albin, P. S. *The Analysis of Complex Socioeconomic Systems.* Lexington, Mass.: Lexington Books, 1975.

Ando, A., F. M. Fisher, and H. A. Simon. *Essays on the Structure of Social Science Models.* Cambridge, Mass.: MIT Press, 1963.

Bentley, A. F. *Inquiry into Inquiries.* Boston: Beacon, 1954.

Berger, J., et al. *Types of Formalization in Small Group Research.* Boston: Houghton Mifflin, 1962.

Bergmann, G. *Philosophy of Science.* Madison, Wisc.: University of Wisconsin Press, 1957.

Beveridge, W. I. B. *The Art of Scientific Investigation.* New York: Random House, 1957. (PB)

Blalock, H. M., Jr. *Causal Inferences in Nonexperimental Research.* Chapel Hill, N.C.: University of North Carolina Press, 1961. (PB)

———. *Theory Construction*. Englewood Cliffs, N.J.: Prentice-Hall, 1969. (PB)

———, ed., *Measurement in the Social Sciences*. Chicago: Aldine, 1974.

Boole, G. *An Investigation of the Laws of Thought*. New York: Dover, 1951.

Born, M. *Experiment and Theory in Physics*. New York: Dover, 1956. (PB)

Braybrooke, D. *Philosophical Problems of the Social Sciences*. New York: Macmillan, 1965. (PB)

Bridgman, P. W. *The Nature of Physical Theory*. New York: Dover, 1936. (PB)

———. *The Way Things Are*. New York: Viking, 1961. (PB)

Brown, R. *Explanation in Social Science*. Chicago: Aldine, 1963.

Bunge, M. *Causality*. Cambridge, Mass.: Harvard University Press, 1959.

———. *Metascientific Queries*. Springfield, Ill.: Charles C Thomas, 1959.

Burr, W. R. *Theory Construction in the Sociology of the Family*. New York: Wiley, 1973.

Burtt, E. A. *The Metaphysical Foundations of Modern Physical Science*. Garden City, N.Y.: Doubleday, 1954. (PB)

Butterfield, H. *The Origins of Modern Science: 1300–1800*. New York: Macmillan, 1960. (PB)

Campbell, N. *What is Science?* New York: Dover, 1952. (PB)

Cangelosi, V. E. *Compound Statements and Mathematical Logic*. Columbus, Ohio: Merrill, 1967. (PB)

Cassirer, E. *Substance and Function* and *Einstein's Theory of Relativity*. New York: Dover, 1953. (PB)

Chapin, F. S. *Experimental Designs in Sociological Research*. Rev. ed. New York: Harper & Row, 1955.

Charlesworth, J. C., ed. *Mathematics and the Social Sciences*. Philadelphia: American Academy of Political and Social Science, June 1963.

Churchman, C. W. and P. Ratoosh, eds. *Measurement: Definitions and Theories*. New York: Wiley, 1959.

Cicourel, A. V. *Method and Measurement in Sociology*. New York: Free Press, 1964.

Cohen, M. R. and E. Nagel. *An Introduction to Logic and Scientific Method*. New York: Harcourt, Brace & World, 1934.

Conant, J. B. *Modern Science and Modern Man*. Garden City, N.Y.: Doubleday, 1953. (PB)

Coombs, C. H. *Theory of Data*. New York: Wiley, 1964.

Cortes, F., A. Przeworski, and J. Sprague, eds. *Systems Analysis for Social Scientists*. New York: Wiley, 1974.

Crombie, A. C. *Medieval and Early Modern Science*. 2 vols. Garden City, N.Y.: Doubleday, 1959. (PB) d'Abro, A. *The Evolution of Scientific Thought*. New York: Dover, 1950.

Denbigh, K. G. *The Thermodynamics of the Steady State*. New York: Wiley, 1951.

de Santillana, G. *The Origins of Scientific Thought*. New York: Mentor, 1961. (PB)

Dewey, J. *Essays in Experimental Logic*. New York: Dover, 1916. (PB)

_____ and A. F. Bentley. *Knowing and the Known*. Boston: Beacon, 1949. (PB)

DiRenzo, G. J. *Concepts, Theory, and Explanation in the Behavioral Sciences*. New York: Random House, 1966.

Duhem, P. *The Aim and Structure of Physical Theory*. New York: Atheneum, 1962. (PB)

Durkheim, E. *The Rules of Sociological Method*. New York: Free Press, 1938.

Eddington, Sir A. *The Philosophy of Physical Science*. New York: Macmillan, 1939.

Feigl, H. and G. Maxwell, eds. *Scientific Explanation, Space, and Time*. Minnesota Studies in the Philosophy of Science, vol. 3. Minneapolis: University of Minnesota Press, 1962.

Forbes, R. J. and E. J. Dijksterhuis. *A History of Science and Technology*. 2 vols. Baltimore, Md.: Penguin Books, 1953. (PB)

Frank, P. *Philosophy of Science*. Englewood Cliffs, N.J.: Prentice-Hall, Inc., 1957.

_____. *The Validation of Scientific Theories*. Boston: Beacon, 1956.

Freudenthal, H. ed. *The Concept and the Role of the Model in Mathematics and Natural and Social Sciences*. Dordrecht, Holland: D. Reidel, 1961.

Gardiner, P. *The Nature of Historical Explanation*. Oxford: Oxford University Press, 1952.

Gardner, M., ed. *Great Essays in Science*. New York: Washington Square, 1957. (PB)

Gellner, E. *Cause and Meaning in the Social Sciences*. London: Routledge & Kegan Paul, 1973.

General Systems: Yearbook for the Society of General Systems Research (starts with vol. 1, 1956).

Gibbs, J. *Sociological Theory Construction*. Hinsdale, Ill.: Dryden, 1972. (PB)

Gibson, Q. B. *The Logic of Social Enquiry*. London: Routledge & Kegan Paul, 1960.

Glazer, B. G. and A. Strauss. *The Discovery of Grounded Theory*. Chicago: Aldine, 1967. (PB)

Gross, L., ed. *Sociological Theory: Inquiries and Paradigms*. New York: Harper & Row, 1967.

————, ed. *Symposium on Sociological Theory*. New York: Harper & Row, 1959.

Hanson, N. *Patterns of Discovery*. Cambridge, Mass.: Harvard University Press, 1958.

Harary, F. and R. Z. Norman. *Graph Theory as a Mathematical Model in Social Science*. Ann Arbor: University of Michigan Institute for Social Research, 1953.

Heise, D. R. *Causal Analysis*. Somerset, N.J.: Wiley-Interscience, 1975.

Hempel, C. G. "Fundamentals of Concept Formation in Empirical Science," *International Encyclopedia of Unified Science,* vol. 2, no. 7. Chicago: University of Chicago Press, 1952.

————. *Philosophy of Natural Science*. Englewood Cliffs, N.J.: Prentice-Hall, 1966.

Hildebrand, J. H. *Science in the Making*. New York: Columbia University Press, 1957. (PB)

Horst, P., ed. *The Prediction of Personal Adjustment*. New York: Social Science Research Council, 1941.

Jevons, W. S. *The Principles of Science*. New York: Dover, 1958. (PB)

Kantor, J. R. *The Logic of Modern Science*. Bloomington, Ind.: Principia Press, 1953.

Kaplan, A. *The Conduct of Inquiry*. San Francisco: Chandler, 1964.

Kaufmann, F. *Methodology of the Social Sciences*. New York: Oxford University Press, 1941.

Kemeny, J. G. *A Philosopher Looks at Science*. Princeton, N.J.: Van Nostrand, 1959.

Koestler, A. *The Act of Creation*. London: Pan, 1970.

Kuhn, T. S. *The Structure of Scientific Revolutions*. Chicago: University of Chicago Press, 1952. (PB)

Lave, C. A. and J. G. March. *An Introduction to Models in The Social Sciences*. New York: Harper & Row, 1975.

Lazarsfeld, P. F., ed. *Mathematical Thinking in the Social Sciences*. New York: Free Press, 1954.

———— and M. Rosenberg, eds. *The Language of Social Research*. New York: Free Press, 1955.

Lenzen, V. *Causality in Natural Science*. Springfield, Ill.: Charles C Thomas, 1959.

————. "Procedures of Empirical Science," *International Encyclopedia of Unified Science,* vol. 1, no. 5. Chicago: University of Chicago Press, 1938.

Lins, M. *Foundations of Social Determinism*. Rio de Janeiro: M. Lins, 1959.

Madden, E. H., ed. *The Structure of Scientific Thought*. Boston: Houghton Mifflin, 1960.

Maquet, J. J. *The Sociology of Knowledge*. Boston: Beacon, 1951.

McKinney, J. C. *Constructive Typology and Social Theory*. New York: Appleton-Century-Crofts, 1966.

Mehlberg, H. *The Reach of Science*. Toronto: University of Toronto Press, 1958.

Miles, I. *The Poverty of Prediction*. Lexington, Mass.: Lexington Books, 1975.

Miller, D. C. *Handbook of Research Design and Social Measurement*. New York: McKay, 1964. (PB)

Muller, H. J. *The Uses of the Past*. New York: Oxford University Press, 1952.

Mullins, N. C. *The Art of Theory Construction and Use*. New York: Harper & Row, 1971.

Nagel, E. *The Structure of Science*. New York: Harcourt, Brace & World, 1961.

_____, P. Suppes, and A. Tarski, eds. *Logic, Methodology and Philosophy of Science*. Stanford, Calif.: Stanford University Press, 1962.

Nettler, G. *Explanations*. New York: McGraw-Hill, 1970.

Newman, J. R., ed. *What is Science?* New York: Washington Square, 1955. (PB)

Obler, P. C. and H. A. Estrin, eds. *The New Scientist*. Garden City, N.Y.: Doubleday, 1962. (PB)

Pearson, K. *The Grammar of Science*. London: J. M. Dent, 1937.

Platt, J. R. *The Excitement of Science*. Boston: Houghton Mifflin, 1962. (PB)

Pledge, H. T. *Science Since 1500*. New York: Harper & Row, 1959. (PB)

Poincaré, H. *Science and Hypothesis*. New York: Dover, 1952. (PB)

_____. *Science and Method*. New York: Dover, 1952. (PB)

Popper, K. R. *The Logic of Scientific Discovery*. New York: Science Editions, 1961. (PB)

_____. *The Poverty of Historicism*. London: Routledge & Kegan Paul, 1957. (PB)

Przeworski, A. and H. Teune. *The Logic of Comparative Social Inquiry*. New York: Wiley, 1974.

Rapoport, A. *Operational Philosophy*. New York: Harper & Row, 1953.

Rapport, S. and H. Wright, eds. *Science: Method and Meaning*. New York: Washington Square, 1963. (PB)

Reichenbach, H. *Experience and Prediction*. Chicago: University of Chicago Press, 1938.

Rescher, N. *Scientific Explanation*. New York: Free Press, 1970.

Rex, J. *Key Problems of Sociological Theory*. London: Routledge & Kegan Paul, 1961.

Ritchie, A. D. *Scientific Method*. Paterson, N.J.: Littlefield, Adams, 1960.

Rose, A. M. *Theory and Method in the Social Sciences*. Minneapolis: University of Minnesota Press, 1954.

Rudner, R. S. *Philosophy of Social Science*. Englewood Cliffs, N.J.: Prentice-Hall, 1966. (PB)

Ryan, A. *The Philosophy of Social Explanation*. Oxford: Oxford University Press, 1973. (PB)

Sarton, G. *Ancient Science and Modern Civilization*. New York: Harper & Row, 1954. (PB)

Shils, E. A. and H. A. Finch, eds. *Max Weber on the Methodology of the Social Sciences*. New York: Free Press, 1949.

A Short History of Science: Origins and Results of the Scientific Revolution. Garden City, N.Y.: Doubleday, 1959. (PB)

Sidman, M. *Scientific Research*. New York: Basic Books, 1960.

Simon, H. A. *Models of Man*. New York: Wiley, 1957.

Solomon, H. *Mathematical Thinking in the Measurement of Behavior*. New York: Free Press, 1960.

Stinchcombe, A. L. *Constructing Social Theories*. New York: Harcourt, Brace & World, 1968. (PB)

Stouffer, S. A., L. Guttman, E. A. Suchman, P. F. Lazarsfeld, S. A. Star, and J. A. Clausen. *Measurement and Prediction: Studies in Social Psychology in World War II*. Vol. 4. Princeton, N.J.: Princeton University Press, 1960.

Tomlinson, R. *Sociological Concepts and Research*. New York: Random House, 1965. (PB)

Toulmin, S. E. *Philosophy of Science*. London: Hutchinson, 1953.

Tuolema, R. *Theoretical Concepts*. New York: Springer-Verlag, 1973.

Walker, M. *The Nature of Scientific Thought*. Englewood Cliffs, N.J.: Prentice-Hall, 1963. (PB)

Wallace, W. L. *The Logic of Science in Sociology*. Chicago: Aldine-Atherton, 1971.

Webb, E. J., D. T. Campbell, R. D. Schwartz, and L. Sechrest. *Unobtrusive Measures*. Chicago: Rand McNally, 1966. (PB)

Weyl, Hermann. *Philosophy of Mathematics and Natural Science*. New York: Atheneum, 1963. (PB)

Whitehead, A. N. *Science and the Modern World*. Cambridge: Cambridge University Press, 1928.

Wightman, W. P. D. *The Growth of Scientific Ideas*. New Haven, Conn.: Yale University Press, 1953.

Wilson, E. B., Jr. *An Introduction to Scientific Research*. New York: McGraw-Hill, 1952. (PB)

Winch, P. *The Idea of Social Science*. London: Routledge & Kegan Paul, 1958.

Wolf, A. *A History of Science, Technology, & Philosophy in the 18th Century*. 2 vols. New York: Harper & Row, 1961. (PB)

Woodger, J. H. "The Technique of Theory Construction." *International Encyclopedia of Unified Science,* vol. 2, no. 5. Chicago: University of Chicago Press, 1939.

Zetterberg, H. L. *On Theory and Verification in Sociology.* Rev. ed. Totowa, N.J.: Bedminster, 1963.

Index